Praise for the Bambi Vincent and Bob Arno's performances

"Genius."
—*Variety*

"World-class. . . . Has no peers."
—*Las Vegas Sun*

"A fascinating and relevant message."
—Ronald Letterman, president, Classic Custom Vacations

"An enormous success. Thanks to your unique videotape footage and well-honed instinct for spotting the criminals BEFORE they do their dirty work, we put together a vivid demonstration of what tourists are up against. . . . Thanks for your invaluable assistance."
—Glenn Ruppel, producer, ABC News, *20/20*

"Sincere thanks for such an excellent presentation. . . . The value of your seminar became evident when three members of a distract theft team were captured while committing a grand larceny at a famous Strip hotel. Surveillance investigators, applying your techniques, were able to detect and recognize the actions of the distract team prior to the theft."
—Las Vegas Metropolitan Police Department

"Personnel made several arrests that they attribute directly to the excellent training you provided. By sharing the expertise you have developed over the years. . . you enabled [us] to better protect the tourists who came . . . for the Super Bowl."
—David Bejarano, chief of police, San Diego

"Thank you for your lecture. . . . My colleagues talked about it days after. I hope that you will be back in Stockholm to teach us more about the techniques, skills, behavior, and psychology of pickpockets."
—Anders Fohgelberg, criminal detective, Stockholm Police Department

"Bravo! . . . Your performance was splendid and our multicultural audience loved your witty, intense dialogue, humor, and natural ability to entertain and impress. . . What a laugh, what an evening, what a touch!"
—Giorgio Maria Rosica, president, Italian Chamber of Commerce

"Thank you for your outstanding, starring appearance. . . . Your success was quite exceptional considering the tough, blasé, international audience of Italian, French, American, and English, plus the gracious presence of Prince Albert of Monaco."
—Allan Blackburn, entertainment consultant, Monte Carlo Palace

"The audiences love this guy. Standing ovations, howling, screaming, carrying on nightly. He's one of the greatest acts we've had at Resorts since I've owned the place."
—Merv Griffin, owner, Resorts International Hotel and Casino

Travel Advisory!
How to Avoid Thefts, Cons, and Street Scams While Traveling

Bambi Vincent and Bob Arno

Chicago and Los Angeles

07 06 05 04 03 5 4 3 2 1

Library of Congress Cataloging-in-Publication Data

Vincent, Bambi.
  Travel advisory : how to avoid thefts, cons, and street scams while
traveling / Bambi Vincent and Bob Arno.
      p. cm.
  ISBN 1-56625-198-2
  1. Travel--Safety measures. I. Arno, Bob. II. Title.

  G151.V565 2003
  362.88--dc21

                                    2003013121

Bonus Books
875 N. Michigan Ave.
Suite 1416
Chicago, IL 60611

Printed in the United States of America

Contents

Chapter 5
Rip-Offs: Introducing the Opportunist 71

Giving it away • Opportunist techniques: speed, seizure, stealth, motion, impedence, impact, assumption, pretense • Finesse • Tools • Travel safety products

Chapter 6
Public Transportation: Talk About Risky 127

Subways, buses, trams, and trains • Lure of credit cards as plunder • Seedy stations • Taxi hazards, taxi joys • Risks in real life

Chapter 7
Scams—by the Devious Strategist 161

Flower gift lift • Café set-up • Postcard pick • Pile-up pick • Pseudo cops • Pigeon poop practitioner • Gender exploiters • Shoulder surfers • Protect your sphere • Gentlemen thieves

Chapter 8
Con Artists and Their Games of No Chance 185

Bait-and-switch • Touts on the take • Pavement wagers: three-shell game, three-card monte • Pigeon drop • Nigerian scam

Chapter 9
Identity Theft: You've Got a Criminal Clone 211

Definitions and statistics • How thieves get private information • Making and using false ID documents: account takeover, fraudulent accounts, credit card fraud, criminal identity theft • Victim consequences • Personal information: availability, trafficking, sharing, abuse, theft, protection of • Responsibilities of businesses, credit issuers, and credit bureaus • Biometric technology • Self-help • Victim assistance • Contacts and resources

Criminal limits are inside a person. How else can I explain why I cannot shoplift? I can't steal a candy bar from a supermarket, but I can walk in and rob the place with a gun.

—Frank Black
Reformed burglar, twenty-one-year prison inmate

Acknowledgments

We are deeply grateful to those who have aided and abetted us.

Marcia and David Vincent, Sergeant Timothy Shalhoob, Detective Ralph Ray, Lieutenant Robert Sebby, Sergeant Randy Stoever, Officer Daniele Conse, Ispettore Pasquale Borgomeo, Ispettore D'Amore Vincenzo, Officer Xavier Marin, Detective Lothel Crawford, Officer Giorgio Pontetti, Inspector Ashok Desai, Vasily Zhiglov, Linda Foley, Vladimir Kitov, Terry Jones, Andrina Harrison, Ann and Chris Lundén, Jared Kniffen, Ana Mosterin, Rod the Hop, Simon Lovell, Atul and Smriti Shah, Paul Polansky, Lubomír Zubák, Marc Gerald.

We also thank the many victims who've shared their experiences with us, and the law enforcement officers around the world whom we haven't named.

Ultimate gratitude goes to Shari Appleman.

Preface

If Bob's and my first priority is putting pickpockets and con artists out of business, our second is to encourage international travel. Nothing would disappoint us more than to learn that we discouraged a potential traveler's journey. Travel opens the mind and broadens the perspective. It's the ultimate supplement to education. Plus, it's fun.

This book is the culmination of ten years of intensive research in the streets of the world. Our hunt has taken us through more than eighty countries on six continents, to countless islands, and through the grit and glamor of cities from Cairo to Copenhagen, from Mombasa to Mumbai. In the places people love to visit most, distract theft, con games, credit card scams, and identity theft are rampant.

Bob and I stalk a moving target. We haunt the public frontiers where tourist and street thief collide ever so lightly, ever so frequently. We don't go off searching among the dim, deserted corners of a city; we merely join in the tourist parade, visit the guidebook highlights, and lurk where the crowds are. There, hovering near the tourist buck, waiting for or making an opportunity, can be found the thieves, swindlers, and con artists. And, very close, anonymous as sightseers in a tour group, we stand, cameras aimed.

After we observe a thief in action, we usually try to interview him (or her, of course). Because Bob speaks many languages, because he has "grift sense," that indefinable faculty for the con, and because he can absolutely prove himself to be a colleague, the thieves talk. Some remain reticent, but most seem to enjoy our chats. Some refuse to speak on camera, others don't mind at all. Kharem, a thief we found at work several times over the course of a year, is one who spoke openly with us, demonstrated his techniques on video, and arrived promptly for a meeting scheduled a week in advance. When we finished our third interview with him, Kharem had a surprise suggestion for us.

"Now I will steal and you can film me. I want to be the star of your movie," he offered.

"That's impossible, Kharem. We work onstage, not on the street. We cannot be part of real stealing. We cannot be with you knowing that you'll steal."

"I think he smells a big payment," our interpreter, Ana, said in English to us.

"We can split three ways," Kharem said, dispelling that theory.

"It would be great footage. . . ." Bob mused. "But we can't. No way." I agreed.

"What if he gives it back?" Ana tried.

"I don't think he'd understand that concept."

"He's going to steal anyway," Ana said. "If not now, later. Whether you're watching or not." She was well aware of the crime statistics in her city.

"No. We'd be accessories. We're treading morally murky water as it is. We have to draw a line and this is definitely it."

I tried to imagine the scenario: Kharem would slip his fingers into the pocket of some hapless tourist and we'd surround him with cameras and complicity. Would we root for his success? Applaud afterward? A few days earlier, I *was* filming Kharem as he tried to steal from three different individuals. How was that any different? I hadn't realized it was Kharem, but I'd certainly recognized the pursuit of purloinery.

At our shows and lectures, audience members occasionally ask us if we stop pickpockets before they actually take something. Or they ask why we don't shout out and warn potential victims. We squirm while defending ourselves because we *do* feel bad about letting it happen—or possibly happen—when we might have saved someone the money and trouble involved with the loss of a wallet.

But over the years we've received thanks from thousands of people: those who are now aware and informed and travel with confidence, and those who have foiled thieves after having seen us. The footage that Bob and I collect is seen by hundreds of thousands of people, millions when you count television, and it is shown not as entertainment, but as a prophylactic.

We're not entirely comfortable speaking respectfully to known thieves, laughing with them, and pretending to be friends with them. Respect, though, is what we believe opened Kharem to us. When we ask ourselves why he spoke with us, why he demonstrated his criminal craft, why he revealed his outlaw guts, we come to only one conclusion. We believe he treasured our attention and respect. He reveled in it. He blossomed in it.

I can think of a sappier story if you want the mawkish plot of a liberal: lonely, impoverished, immigrant outcast who lacks documents, education, and job skills is reduced to robbing tourists for his very survival. No family, no friends, no future, no reason to care what happens. A sensitive, poetic fatalist. Until his tragic trajectory is diverted by an angel dropping out of the sky in the shape of a filmmaker.

You think?

Nonsense.

Neither did he talk for money.

"Criminals are born, not made. Delinquency is a physiological abnormality." So said Cesare Lombroso, Italian professor of forensic medicine and psychology, in 1875. After meticulous measurements as a sort of computerless biometrics, he described "the delinquent" as a "precise anthropological type" who could be recognized by his physical attributes. If only! From our descriptions and photos, you'll see that rogues range from infants to the elderly, from the shifty-eyed to the doe-eyed. But for their inappropriate behavior and possibly a telltale "prop," they're all but impossible to pick out of a crowd.

Their modus operandi vary tremendously, too, and have become the basis for my own classification of street thieves. Those in the largest category, the opportunists, require a fool for a "mark." That may sound a bit harsh, but opportunists are looking for an invitation to steal. Give them a bit of a challenge and you needn't be their victim. They're quick to distinguish the vigilant from the vulnerable.

Thieves in my next category, the strategists, are also easy to thwart. They create their own opportunities, and make participants of their victims. You, the savvy traveler, will simply refuse to participate.

Con artists make up my third category. To these, the victim willingly gives money for supposed value. But the victim here is driven by greed. He's looking for a windfall, a deal too good to be true, inexplicable treasure fallen from heaven. For this victim, greed trumps reason and leads to loss.

I do not mention muggers. These are terrorist thieves who use violence or the threat of violence. Some are armed, or pretend to be armed, equally frightening to the victim. They're crude, smash-and-grab desperados whose advantages are speed and isolation. We can only advise trying to avoid them by staying out of dark, isolated, and dangerous areas. Ask locals about no-go zones. We also recommend keeping easy "give-up" cash in your pocket and submitting to their demands, whatever they are. Never resist a mugger.

Bob and I contend that the crimes of street thieves, so often dubbed "petty," are not that at all. First, tally the sheer number of them, particularly in favorite tourist cities: hundreds of incidents *per day* are reported to police. How many go unreported? Our research indicates that numbers are two or three times greater. Secondly, consider the personal and practical impact on victims. The monetary loss, the complications of replacing documents, the fear of further repercussions such as replication of identity; all these add up to an experience that isn't soon forgotten. Add to that the indirect costs and hours required by law enforcement, not to mention diverting officers from more serious work, plus costs involved in prosecuting and jailing these so-called petty thieves.

Pickpockets and property theft are the travel industry's dirty little secret. Understandably, no one wants to talk about them. Not the travel magazines with advertisers to placate, not the boards of tourism with countries to promote, not travel agencies or packagers with clients to enthuse, or cruise lines with a carefree ambiance to emphasize. And why should they? *It's just a petty crime.*

Who is to reveal the status quo but a stage-stealing Swede and his fancy accessory?

Because it represents our passion, as well as an integral part of our career, we'll continue to skulk underground and pound the pavement. Sometimes though, on sweltering trains so crowded I'm pressed like a daisy in a dictionary, I'll question our endeavors and the gritty reality of mingling with outlaws. Then we'll catch a thief. We'll capture a slick steal on tape, which will later be used to illustrate our presentations to the public and help train police departments. We'll discover some new artifice, an old trick twisted to exploit the moment. And that will be our satisfaction.

As you'll learn in these chapters, serious reductions in these crimes will not be due to law enforcement—no disrespect to them. It will be through travelers' smarter stashing and raised awareness. Personal security is an art, not a science. Once you know the risks, you can adjust your awareness and the level of your security precautions. Thus prepared, you'll turn your travel concerns into travel confidence.

Not every stranger you meet will be a cheat, but every cheat will be a charming stranger.

—Simon Lovell

High and Dry on the Streets of Elsewhere

1

"Hey! Hey! *Hey!* Get your fucking hand out of my pocket! You try to steal my wallet again and I'll *kill* you!" The would-be victim slapped away the comforting hand of a middle-aged local. "No, you're with him! I'm gonna call the cops."

The victim, an American man, vocalized his outrage as the tram lurched and squealed along its track. His opponents melted into the crowd, impossible to discern from the legitimate passengers. Despite the team's intricate choreography and precise techniques, they'd seemed as innocent and invisible as a white rabbit in a cotton harvest: beyond suspicion, even as they surrounded their mark. No one would detect the four functionaries of this tactical unit: the dip, his two blockers, and his controller. Not derelict losers, they looked like businessmen, like students, like men with respectable jobs.

The dip carried a jacket. His thieving hand concealed beneath it, he fanned the tourist, a feather-like pat down designed to locate the leather, the wallet. The blockers then positioned the mark, turning him, impeding his progress, expertly taking advantage of the physical contact natural in any tight crowd. Leaning into him, they caused his distraction, subtly directing his attention away from the dip's delicate work. A few steps away, the controller watched for cops and overly alert bystanders. Of the four, he alone was shifty-eyed. When the victim exploded, it was the controller who stepped in to defuse the situation. If it hadn't been for a sudden sway of the tram, the team would have succeeded, as they do in 35 percent of their efforts.

Now, busted, they pushed through the standing crowd toward the doors at the other end of the tram. At the first stop, the thieves made their escape. Bob and I hopped off after them.

This scene, in endless permutations, is repeated thousands of times every day. The victim of choice is the tourist, who is rich beyond reason in the eyes of thieves, and thieves will employ methods as subtle as stealth and as brutal as mugging to effect the transfer of wealth. Theft from tourists is on the rise and, unfortunately, it's becoming increasingly violent, more and more organized, and harder than ever to fight.

At work on the tram: Luciano (center), partners (one with arm up, one above wrist), and their controller (ducking under raised arm). Victim's cap is visible, lower left.

If law enforcement can't turn the trend, perhaps Bob and I can. Grandiose vision? As a two-person army out to fight street crime, we wouldn't have a chance. We'd be laughable. But we're not out to stop the thieves. We're here to educate the public. We'll turn the tide of loss from the back end. We also spread our knowledge base of current trends in thievery among the law enforcement agencies that deal with tourist crime. But it's the ground level dissemination of information that has the greatest effect. We may be steering the horse by the tail, but we know it works.

Bob has spent a lifetime studying scammers, thieves, and con artists and their wicked ways. From Pakistan in the 1960s, where leper pickpockets used emotions—fear and revulsion—as a means to their ends, to short-changers in Vietnam, to destitute orphans in Peru, to modern-day rogues in the capital cities of Europe and America, he has explored their methods and motivations.

Unlike police, criminologists, psychologists, and other researchers, Bob communicates with street thieves in their language; he can talk the talk and walk the walk because he is a thief himself. Bob is a thief who steals on stage and always returns what he takes. He incorporates the techniques he learns from the thieves into his stage presentations. With the

Shocking Statistics

Every summer day, one hundred tourists will be pickpocketed near the Coliseum in Rome; another hundred will be hit near the Spanish Steps, and another hundred in and around the Vatican. These three hundred individuals will report their thefts to the local police stations. Approximately three hundred more victims will not file a report, for lack of time, late discovery, or other reasons. Florence reports similar numbers. So do London, Barcelona, Paris, Prague, and numerous other favorite tourist destinations. Multiplied by the number of days in the tourist season, dollars in currency lost, hours of vacation ruined, aggravation, humiliation, hassle, and havoc, you can see that pickpocketing is a small crime with huge repercussions.

Numbers are difficult to obtain, but as far as can be measured, they're going up: "Among violent crimes, robbery showed the greatest increase, 3.9 percent . . . and larceny–theft increased 1.4 percent" says the FBI's "Crime Trends, 2001 Preliminary Figures." While that's not a very impressive increase, anecdotal evidence indicates otherwise.

It's estimated that at least half of all pickpocketing incidents are never reported at all. Of those reported, most, according to a New York cop on the pickpocket detail who wishes to remain unnamed, fall into the "lost property" category. "They don't even realize they've been pickpocketed," he said. "They think they just lost it." That's why Sergeant Timothy Shalhoob of the Las Vegas Metropolitan Police Department feels that lost wallet reports are the real indicators of pickpocket frequency. The numbers always peak during special events and holidays.

Incidents reported as thefts are lumped under one of several legal descriptions. Larceny is the unlawful taking of property from the possession of a person, and includes pickpocketing, purse snatching, shoplifting, bike theft, and theft from cars. Robbery is the same, but involves the use or threat of force. The theft of a purse or wallet, therefore, may fall into either of these categories, and usually cannot be extracted for statistical purposes. Similarly, the figures collected under larceny or robbery include offenses this book does not specifically address—shoplifting, for example.

In Europe, where the theft of cell phones has skyrocketed, numbers help propel industry changes—the development of security devices in phones, for example. Eleven thousand cell phones were stolen in the Czech Republic in the first eight months of 2001. More than twenty thousand cell phones were stolen in the city of Paris in 2000.

In September, 2000, British Transport Police reported a 94.6 percent increase in pickpocketing on the London Tube, and pickpocketing on the streets rose by almost 30 percent in the same period. Spain experienced a 19.5 percent increase over the course of 2001, and street robbery was up 28 percent in England. In Paris, pickpocketing on the underground Metro jumped 40 percent in 2001.

Frightening new trends are developing. What used to be simple snatches are now turning into brutal grabs resulting in serious injury or death. Perhaps the stiff competition from a glut of pickpockets is turning some to violent methods. Strangulation from behind is one terrifying method. Another involves squirting flammable liquid on the back of a target's jacket and igniting it. The victim throws down her bag and struggles to get the flaming jacket off while the thief grabs the bag and flees. Even ordinary bag-snatches are becoming deadly, with victims being pulled to the ground, some cracking their heads on the pavement, or falling into traffic.

benefit of Bob's backdoor perspective, we will give you the thief's-eye version of thievery, connery, scamdom, and swindlehood; and, more important, how to avoid becoming an unwilling participant.

Back in Naples, Bob and I leapt off the tram and I squinted at the gang.

"Luciano!" I said to one of the culprits as the tram trundled off. I recognized him as a pickpocket we'd interviewed four years ago.

"No, no Luciano," he said, shaking his head. He backed away.

"*Sì*, Luciano Barattolo, I remember you." Luciano bent and fiddled with a window squeegee in a bucket of water abandoned on the median strip. He removed the dripping squeegee and touched it to the toe of each of his shoes. I got ready for a blast of filthy water; I was sure he was going to fling it at us.

Head still bent, he peeked up at me through the corner of his eye, dropped the squeegee, and bolted.

After more than a decade prowling city streets around the world, we'd become accustomed to finding known criminals freely plying their trade right out in the open. Here was Luciano, still out lifting wallets on trams despite police and public awareness of him. You would think he'd have been put away by now.

It's a contentious political issue: law enforcement budget versus taxes, penal code versus perpetrator's rights, unemployment, immigration. It's the same story in most of the world's major cities and, therefore, street thieves abound, free to prey on the weakest, richest resource: the tourist. From a busy prosecutor's perspective, or an overworked judge's, or even an underpaid beat cop's, pickpocketing is a pretty insignificant issue. Real bad guys are on the loose: murderers, kidnappers, rapists, drug pushers. How much of a police force should be diverted to snag the bottom feeders of the criminal hierarchy?

Most countries blame illegal immigrants from poorer nations nearby. "We can't get rid of them," said Inspector D'Amore Vincenzo, a frustrated policeman in Milan, Italy. "When they are caught without work cards, we give them fifteen days to leave the country. Then they are released and what happens? They just don't leave! And if they have no papers, no passports, the countries they come from will not accept the repatriation of these people."

The problem may seem small. One man loses his wallet, which contains his money, driver's license, and credit cards. So what? But it's not just one man. In Westminster—one small district of London—768 cases of pickpocketing were recorded in June, 2002. And that's only the *reported* incidents. How many victims did *not* file a report? And, by the way, the figure doesn't include the 142 bag-snatches recorded in the same district in the same period.

Luciano paused a couple of blocks away, having finally dredged up the memory of us from four years ago. He was forty-nine now, but still looked thirty. He raised his children on a career of pickpocketing, and now was spoiling five grandchildren. Over lunch, he told us how he and his partners used legal loopholes to stay in the game.

"If the police catch us with a tool, they are angry and beat us up. If we don't have a tool and they see us they just say, 'Leave, get out of here.'"

"What's a tool?"

"A razor blade, for example. Or some use long tweezers to slip into a back pocket." Luciano's eyes scanned the sidewalk café for listening ears. "A scissors is a good tool," he whispered. "A scissors is okay to carry.

Luciano Barattolo, a pickpocket who works on trams and buses.

With scissors I can cut a pocket and let the wallet fall into my hand."

Luciano makes it sound easy. He and his ilk hit on moving targets in tight spaces, then fade away into churning crowds. It's a universal style. Police throw up their hands. "We must *see* the hand in the pocket!" they cry. "We have only six in our squad for all the city." "Our officers don't know what to look for." "It's impossible!"

The pickpockets aren't about to stop.

"I started doing it to eat, to get food, because there were no jobs. Now it's all I know," Luciano told us. Others steal to support drug problems, or have no legal status to work, or simply believe in taking what they want.

One man loses his wallet. It's a small crime, a small loss, a small inconvenience. Or maybe it's a huge loss, devastating, with trickle-down repercussions.

One man steals a wallet. Usually, he steals three to six of them each day. And so may his peers, possibly hundreds in the same city. That's a lot of wallets, a lot of money, inconvenience, and tears. Small crime, enormous problem.

Awareness works wonders.

Bob and I are on a mission. From a proactive angle, we teach travelers what to beware of, how theft happens, and how to protect themselves. Our jurisdiction is the world: as we roam and research, we're informed by local law enforcement, innumerable victims, and the thieves themselves.

At the end of our second interview with Luciano, he had a query for us.

"Why do you ask these questions?"

"To help tourists avoid pickpockets."

"But," he deadpanned, "that will make my job harder."

Exactly.

An Ordinary Day in the Center of Rome

A somber crowd was gathered outside the police station. While Bob helped a Japanese tourist file a report inside, I interviewed the congregation of victims.

Mary from Akron was waiting with her daughter while her husband told his sad story upstairs. Her husband's wallet had been stolen on Bus 64. Mary still had her cash and credit cards, so she was rather jolly about the loss. The family was scheduled to go home the next day, anyway.

"We'd been warned about these nuisance kids," Mary admitted, "but my husband is just too kind. He knew they were close, but he wouldn't shoo them away. Poor Wilma, though, she never had a chance."

Wilma from Tampa had just arrived that morning. She and her husband had flown into Rome and taken the airport express train to the city. They'd been hit at the airport train station.

"This was no kid!" Wilma spat out angrily. "It was a man, a regular Italian man."

"Take it easy, honey," Mary patted Wilma on the back.

"He lifted my husband's suitcase onto the train for us, then came back down to get mine. Before I could even thank him, he was gone."

Wilma had fresh tears in her eyes. Mary rubbed and patted her arm.

"In that instant, he got the wallet from my husband's pocket *and* the purse from my tote bag. He got *all* our money, *all* our credit cards, our airline tickets home, and our passports." Wilma was crying now. "We have nothing," she whimpered, "not even the name of our hotel."

"Sure you do, sweetheart," Mary soothed her. "It's going to be all right. I gave her $100," Mary explained to me. "They had absolutely nothing."

These two women had just met, here at the police station half an hour ago. Now they were sisters of misfortune.

I turned to two young men who had been silently slumped against their backpacks, listening.

"They got him on the bus, too." the blond one said. He sounded like a Swede.

"Where were you?" I asked.

"In the back," the other said.

"I mean, where was the bus?"

"Oh. Bus 64, like her. At the Vatican."

"And you guys?" Another family had appeared.

"Outside the Coliseum."

We also assist law enforcement. No police department has the budget to travel and gather intelligence at street level, as we do. Trends travel, as do perpetrators. As Bob and I acquire video of street thieves and con artists from Lima to Lisbon, from Barcelona to Bombay, we put together teaching tapes and show them to law enforcement agencies worldwide. Having seen our previews, cops are better prepared when foreign M.O.s roll into town.

X-Ray Glasses

Barcelona, a fusion of passion and creativity, chaos and order, where art is in every detail, is a living laboratory of street crime. It's one of our favorite places in which to study this bizarre subculture, and it supports a great diversity of practitioners from the various branches of thievery. With patience and practice, the keen-eyed observer will be rewarded with abundant examples of pickpocketing, bag-snatching, and three-shell games.

La Rambla is the marvelous main street of Barcelona. The crowds swirl doing La Rambla things. There's so much to look at: the Dr. Seuss-like architecture of Antoni Gaudi, caricature artists at work, caged doves cooing, couples performing the tango, living statues, musicians, puppeteers, intoxicating flower shops, and tempting cafés offering tapas, paella, and sangria. One can't help but be caught up in it all.

On duty, Bob and I saunter and prowl, observant and suspicious. It's the height of summer and the crowds are thick as—well, thick as thieves. We're hypertuned to inappropriate behavior; suspects pop out of the crowd as if they have TV-news graphic circles drawn around them. One of us merely has to say "ten o'clock" and the other glances slightly left and knows exactly who, of the hundreds in view, is meant.

What are those pop-art pictures called, the wallpaper-like fields of swirly patterns that, when stared at long enough, finally push forward an object or scene? Stereograms, I think. Blink, and the object disappears into the repetition of the pattern. Likewise our suspects: with concentration, we force them to materialize out of sameness into a dimension all their own.

But in two ways they easily return to the background. First, we may lose them: they're too fast; they turn a corner; they duck into an alley we don't want to enter; or we turn our attention elsewhere. Second, their behavior is suddenly validated: for example, a fast moving pair of men looking left and right, darting ahead of clusters, purpose in their pace and us on their tail, eventually catch up to their wives. Perfectly innocent! In Venice, in Lima, in Barcelona, we wasted energy observing the bizarre behavior of deviants who turned out to be perverts. They just wanted to rub up against women, not pick their purses. Once, we tracked a pair of plainclothes police. Sure, we follow lots of dead ends—just as directors audition endless rejects.

A typical summer crowd on La Rambla watches street entertainment. Pickpockets often prey on the perimeter.

Even at a local level we're able to help police forces. Rarely—if ever—does standard police-issue equipment include hidden video cameras. Bob and I, who look *nothing* like law enforcement, are able to get in the faces of thieves in action, and often provide the best, if not the only, descriptions of local criminal pests. We provided photos to the Barcelona tourist police, for example, who had received numerous reports of a devilish thief who "wore shorts". Yep. That's all the victims could ever describe about him. The police were ecstatic when they received our shot of his mug.

We do much of our research in summer, in the height of tourist season. We put ourselves smack where the crowds are, just as the thieves do. We carry video cameras, just as the tourists do. Then it's a game of eyes.

The tourists gawk at the sights, common sense abandoned. The thief has his head bent, eyes downcast; he's scanning pockets and purses. Bob and I stare at the thief—but not too much. We don't want to blow our cover.

I remember when I used to hunt for wild mushrooms in the Santa Cruz Mountains. I'd find nothing the first hour or so. But after spotting the first one, even if it wasn't a candy cap or chanterelle or boletus, other mushrooms would practically pop into view. It was just a matter of focus and concentration. Likewise, looking for pickpockets. "Watch their eyes," our favorite New York subway cop, Lothel Crawford, used to tell us. The eyes—and the body language as well. With their ulterior motives, these interlopers belong to a crowd like an inchworm to a salad. A practiced eye will spot them.

And what is the crowd doing? Enjoying the sights, as they should be. But too many travelers forget their good judgment when they pack their pajamas. High on excitement, relaxed after a beer or an unaccustomed lunchtime glass of wine, disoriented with jet lag, going with the flow—too many fall victim to the dreaded Tourist Suspension of Common Sense. I call it Holiday Headspace. It's an easy-going, carefree attitude that gives us an unequivocal handicap in a city that is not our own.

Like most Americans, I was raised to be kind, friendly, and open to strangers. Cynicism is an unnatural state for a traveler who has come far to experience a new land and unfamiliar customs. We're prepared to accept our local hosts, however alien or exotic they seem to us. After all, it's *their* country. We *want* to like them. Yet, we don't know how to read these foreigners, even though they may seem just like us. We can't always interpret their body language, their facial expressions, or their gestures. We're at a distinct disadvantage as tourists and travelers, due to our nature as much as our innocence.

Of all the victims we've spoken with, a couple robbed in Athens puzzled me most. The woman's bag had been slit with a razor on the infamous green-line train between the Parthenon and Omonia Square, the city center. Noticing the gash, we pointed it out to her as we exited the train. The couple was visiting Greece from Scotland, they told us as they inventoried the contents of the bag, and it was the last day of their stay. Their few remaining traveler's checks were missing, but the woman's cash was safe in a zippered compartment. The biggest loss was her passport, which would cost dearly in time and aggravation. They would miss their flight home the next morning, and would have to pay for expensive, one-way, last-minute tickets, as well as an unplanned hotel night. The complications of a delayed return home were another factor, with work, childcare, and other obligations.

They suffered more inconvenience than financial loss, and perhaps that is why they didn't seem as upset as most other victims we meet. Maybe they were secretly pleased to get another day away from the boredom or difficulties of their home routine—whatever it was they were escaping from.

In any case, we were amazed to hear them cheerily admit that they had been pickpocketed before. Bob and I tend to assume that an intimate encounter with a street thief bestows a sort of earned awareness on the victim, and he or she is thereafter unlikely to be had again. The Scottish couple, however, seemed almost to laugh it off, resigned to the fact that they were destined to be victims.

They had no concept of what made them such appealing marks and no idea that they had practically advertised their vulnerability. They were fascinated to learn that some pickpockets look out for a certain *type* of target, and that, even as tourists, they had control over their desirability toward pickpockets.

"Dress down," Bob always tells his audiences. "Leave your jewelry at home. Don't give off signals." In other words, if you're going to be in an unpredictable environment, try not to look like an affluent tourist. "Have pace in your face," Bob says, meaning: know where you are and where you're going. Try not to appear lost and bewildered. Lost and bewildered equals vulnerable.

Bob and I began our field research on street thievery in 1993, when we quit our steady jobs in Las Vegas to combine freelancing with travel. As our work took us around the world, we got into the streets, among the tourists, in cities and at historical sites, watching who was watching the visitors. Our early successes gave us an enormous charge and encouragement to continue. We were hooked on tracking. But I don't think either one of us believed, in the beginning, that we'd succeed in identifying so many perpetrators.

Rome was our teething ground as pickpocket hunters. We began with modest ambitions. We'd hang out at the Coliseum in hopes of photographing child and teenage pickpockets, who had become easy for us to recognize. They'd always carry a section of newspaper or, better for its stiffness, a slab of corrugated cardboard, with which they'd shield their dipping hands. Although the Coliseum was sometimes crawling with *Carabinieri* with not a thief in sight, we soon built up a healthy portfolio of red-handed children on film and footage.

Collision Course

Yoshi Sugohara stood stoic and penniless in a phone booth, using our phone card. He called a number given him by the Rome police, where he could report all his stolen credit cards at once. A Japanese-speaking operator was put on the line for him. Next, he called the Japanese embassy.

Mr. Sugohara owned a small chain of sushi restaurants in Osaka, Japan. He was in Italy to design a sleek new amalgam of Japanese and Italian decor for the three new restaurants he was about to open. He had traveled to Milan for business, then Rome for pleasure. He had granted himself two extra days away from his family in which to see the splendors of the ancient city.

We first saw him in a little triangular park between the Coliseum and the Trajan Column, while everything was still all right. Bob and I stood behind a low fence on Via Cavour, steadying our video camera on a stone column. We were observing a pair of young girls on the far side of the park as they drank at a fountain and splashed their faces.

Maritza, we later learned from the police, was about sixteen years old. Her sister Ravenna was about thirteen. The two girls looked like ordinary children, except for a few subtle details. They weren't dressed with the inbred Italian flair for style and color. And they seemed directionless, loitering in a tourist area where children had little reason to roam.

The girls cooled themselves in the punishing August heat, then turned toward Via Alessandrina. Maritza carried a telltale newspaper.

Mr. Sugohara had just rested on a shady bench. Now he, too, headed for Via Alessandrina. He wore a bright white cap and held a telltale map.

With their props displayed, both players advertised their roles in the game. The girls recognized the Japanese man as a tourist, but a tourist couldn't possibly recognize the girls as thieves. The two parties were on a converging course.

Maritza and Ravenna swiftly caught up with Sugohara. They skittered around him as if he were Daddy just home from a business trip. Walking backward, Maritza extended her hand as if begging. She had laid the folded newspaper over her forearm and hand, so only her fingers were visible. Ravenna trotted along beside Sugohara.

One of the girls must have made physical contact immediately. In our viewfinder from across the park, Sugohara leapt right out of the frame. He ran a few steps backward, then turned and hurried off. It was a very brief encounter.

The girls skipped away ahead of Sugohara, quickly putting space between them. Bob and I, still on the far side of the park, picked up the camera and hurried to catch up. As we came around the corner, Sugohara was groping the front pocket of his pants, just realizing that his wallet was gone. He looked ahead at the two girls and ran after them.

Maritza and Ravenna did not run away. In fact, they stopped and turned to face their accuser. Sugohara, who didn't speak English or Italian, nevertheless made his charges quite clear. There was shouting and confusion. A group of British tourists got mixed into the mêlée. Their concern was for the girls.

"The child will not be injured!" one woman kept insisting.

"They're pickpockets," I explained while Bob filmed.

"I don't care what they are, the child is not to be hurt."

"That girl just stole the man's wallet, that's why he's angry."

"Jeez, Sally, they're pickpockets, can't you see?" someone in her group said with disgust.

(continued)

Sugohara was surprisingly aggressive: not what one might expect of a Japanese victim. The girls could have run away. Instead, they faced him, yelling back in their own language. Then, without warning, Maritza lifted her T-shirt over her head, revealing enormous breasts in a purple bra. She brought her shirt back down, and Ravenna followed suit, showing her bare little breasts.

Then both girls pulled down their pants and did a quick pirouette. Sugohara was dumbstruck. The girls then strutted off jauntily, having proved their innocence. They looked back again as they walked away, and pulled down their pants once more for good measure. Then they turned off the sidewalk onto a narrow path through the ruins of Augustus' Forum and into the labyrinth of old Rome.

Where had the wallet gone? The girls had clearly taken it. By their comprehension of the Japanese accusation, by their practiced reaction to it, one could presume that they'd been accused before.

To my mind, they're guilty without a trial. So where was the evidence? Was the victim so bamboozled by bare breasts that he never thought to look in their pants pockets? Could the children be that brazen? Or had they tossed the wallet down into the excavation site of Nerva's Forum to be retrieved later?

In any case, the girls scurried off, and Sugohara stood alone, high and dry.

"Would you like to go to police?" we asked him.

"You police?" said Sugohara. He appeared more sad than angry.

"No, we take you. We help." I hate pidgin. "*Suri*," we added, Japanese for pickpocket.

Sugohara looked mournfully at the Trajan Column as we hurried him to the central Rome police station. He mopped his brow and followed us obediently.

Mr. Sugohara accuses pickpocket Maritza of stealing his wallet. Maritza tries to prove she doesn't have it by pulling up her shirt, then down her pants. Nearby tourists are fascinated.

The following year, 1994, we were decked out like pros. We lugged a video camera monster, a JVC 3GY-X2U, which is twenty-four inches long and weighs twenty-five pounds without its case. I wore a battery belt of about thirty pounds, which threatened to slip off my hips if I didn't keep a hand on it. Bob carried the camera and a huge, heavy tripod. In addition, we needed my purse, a 35mm camera, and a bag of video accessories. Thus burdened, we traipsed around the ancient city, filming ruin after ruin, milling crowds, and potential danger zones (pickpocketly speaking).

We usually began with the intention of filming the elusive urchin pickpockets who always seemed to congregate around the Coliseum, often in large family groups. But, apparently, video cameras repelled them in a great radius. I wondered if the police knew about this great tool for clearing the area of crime.

Sometimes we'd get a few minutes of unexciting footage and I'd take a few stills. Eventually, our prey would escape into the subway or onto a bus. We'd decide to go to the Spanish Steps, another popular venue for a theft show. Then, perhaps in an alley or a side street, a couple of girls carrying cardboard and babies would pass us. We'd about-face and follow stealthily, keeping downwind as if they were big game animals that might sniff us out. We'd get plenty of footage and photos before they'd notice us, and even then we'd follow. Around and around the back streets of Rome, we'd tail them as they led. But we'd no longer try to hide, and they wouldn't dare try to steal.

Eventually we'd give up on the girls and go back to the exclusive shopping streets around the Spanish Steps. The area is always mobbed with tourists, and with police, too. If there was nothing happening, off we'd go to Trevi Fountain, another popular spot.

We were exhausted by the end of those days. If we hadn't found much to raise our spirits, I'd be dragging around like nothing more than a pack animal pining for its stable. Except for quick lunches and a few standing-up coffees, that's how we spent countless ten-hour days in Rome. True, it's cheaper than shopping!

One day, on our way toward Trevi Fountain from the Spanish Steps, we spied a gang of suspect children. A pregnant girl of about sixteen led the younger ones. Each carried a large square of cardboard, announcing their intentions. Incredibly brazen, they tried for the pockets or purses of tourists every few yards, but with little success. The children eventually noticed us and our huge TV news-style camera, but we continued to follow. They were confused by our interest in them. Why were we following? Why were we taking photos?

Baby Thieves

Rome Police Officer Celini remembered us from previous visits and greeted us warmly. Without asking, he assembled an incident report with carbon paper, in triplicate. I filled out most of the report for Sugohara, and he wrote in his name and address. He had only lost about $100 worth of lire and two credit cards.

We offered to show our video of the crime. Celini first fetched Police Chief Giuseppe D'Emilio. Bob positioned the four-inch monitor of our digital camera and pressed play. The two policemen and Mr. Sugohara put their heads together and peered at the screen as the girl-thieves splashed their faces in the fountain.

"*Sì*," Chief D'Emilio said tiredly. "We know them. They're sisters. Maritza and Ravenna." He and Celini straightened up and turned away from the video. Sugohara still watched with intense interest.

"They have both participated in pickpocketing since before they were born. Their pregnant mother worked the buses. Then, as infants, they were carried in a sling by their mother as she worked these same streets. And when their mother wasn't using them, one of their aunts would."

Using children?

Sugohara's face was close to the screen. He watched intently as the sisters caught up with him so purposefully, arranging their sheet of newspaper and positioning themselves on either side of him. He watched himself leap and skitter backward.

"The big one, Maritza, she has her own child now," the police chief continued. "She usually carries her baby all day. A relative must be using the child today."

Using the child?

Sugohara turned to us, his brow knitted. "Play again," he demanded.

Bob did as he was asked and Sugohara leaned in. The source of his frustration became apparent. The video showed the moment of contact, but from a distance. Still, that must have been when the wallet was stolen. Then the film showed Sugohara bolting backwards and the girls hurrying away from him and turning the corner. After that, the next full minute was a swinging sidewalk and Bob's right shoe. Sugohara had hoped to see what the sisters had done with his wallet. But as they hastened along Via Alessandrina, as Bob rushed to catch up with them, as they stowed or stashed or emptied and threw the wallet, the camera filmed only a sea-sickening flow of auto-focused sidewalk. Whatever the girls had done with the wallet was done off the record.

Sugohara watched the useless picture, depressed.

Chief D'Emilio went on. "The only time these kids aren't stealing is between the ages of seven and eleven, when their parents sometimes let them go to school. Just enough school to learn to read and write, and that's all.

"I've seen them work as young as two years old," the chief said with eternal amazement. "The father carries the child and gets into a crowd. He leans close to a man. The baby is trained to steal from a man's inside jacket pocket!" He threw up his hands and exhaled with exasperation. "No wonder we can't fight this. We have an average of fifty pickpocket reports filed every summer day at this station alone!"

Finally, they came right up to us and asked. But as they spoke no English, we just waved them away. *No polizia,* we said. They walked on, pausing to try for pockets here and there, and every once in a while tried to duck away from us. We remained close behind. Then, just as they tried for a man's pocket, a police car zoomed up, officers jumped out, and the kids were rounded up against a wall. The police questioned them angrily while the kids pointed accusingly at us. Bob kept filming. One officer grabbed the kids' cardboard squares and threw them into a corner. They let the kids go, shooed them away (as they were all too young to arrest), and drove off. We waited. Sure enough, the scoundrels came back for their cardboard and we all continued where we'd left off. They led, we followed and filmed. Eventually, they ditched us.

Over the years we minimized our equipment as we acquired smaller and smaller cameras of broadcast quality. With lighter equipment we became more maneuverable, better able to dash into subways, less reluctant to venture into deserted or potentially dangerous areas, and quicker on our feet. With hidden cameras and remote controls to operate them, we were later able to film con men like the bait-and-switch masters in Naples, and the pigeon poop duper in Barcelona. As we learned to recognize more sophisticated thieves, we were able to capture their deeds with more sophisticated devices.

We trekked through Florence as we did Rome. Wherever the tourists flock there, the urchins prey: all around the wedding cake-like Duomo, outside the Ufizi, on and near the Ponte Vecchio, and at the outdoor markets. Women with children even operate inside the dimly lit cathedrals, where tourists least expect them. The child-thieves can be shockingly aggressive, blocking a person's progress while working busily under their cardboard shields. They're so accustomed to visitors with video cameras, they repeatedly dug into our pockets while we shot them at point blank range.

At some point we began to carry a wallet stuffed with cut paper instead of money. That raggedy bait was stolen from our pockets by a hundred hands, with slow stealth, crude speed, cunning, or clumsiness. We almost always got it back just by asking. But we found the actual extraction of the wallet near impossible to film. The thieves got too close and covered their steals with a jacket, bag, or some other shield. We needed a creative solution.

After infinite ideas and frustrating failures, Bob had a brainstorm. He got an empty shoebox and filled it with sophisticated electronics. He fitted a pinhole lens onto one of his small cameras, and poked its miniature eye through the bottom of the shoebox. He made another hole for a tiny red diode, which signified the camera's record mode. Lastly, he connected a remote control to a short wire and let it protrude unobtrusively from the box, providing a means to start and stop the camera. With a brick-like

At the Fork in the Road, I Went Left
Bob Arno Recounts His Path to Pickpocketing

I can thank the Parsis for my passion for photojournalism.

Another man might have turned away, but when I saw a vulture picking the limbs of a dead child, I raised my camera. Perhaps that says more about me than I should reveal.

Instead of burning their dead and feeding the ashes to the River Ganges as Hindus do, Parsis lay the bodies of their dead on a grid suspended over a high tower. To attract vultures to the burial tower, corpses are smeared with rancid animal fat. The scavenger birds pick away the flesh and the cleaned bones then fall onto the earth, lime, and charcoal floor of the tower to decompose into the soil. How I came to witness this alien rite was through the same set of circumstances that so profoundly impacted my career.

At twenty I hadn't yet decided whether to become an entertainer or a photographer. My true passion was travel, and the more offbeat and distant the destination, the better. To fund my expeditions, I took engagements as a performer for four to six weeks in faraway countries, and at the end of the gigs I would trek into surrounding villages and countryside.

Performing in the Far East in the 1960s gave me a unique opportunity to visit cities that I otherwise would never have had a chance to visit for such extended periods. While my craving for photojournalistic excitement was supported by my show income, I made an effort to meet local authorities and make the right contacts, intending to pursue photojournalism with a bent toward the absurd.

Even way back then my show was unusual—pickpocketing had never been seen as entertainment. It was my ticket to the exotic destinations most people only dream of. And on my journeys, I witnessed, sometimes inadvertently, headline news. Neither ordinary tourists nor visiting journalists could have had such easy access to behind-the-scenes briefings. For I was tied to the U.S. military.

I had always had a strange desire to capture macabre images with a camera. It started as a hobby, then became a semi-profession during my first journey to Asia. In 1961, I toured Pakistan, India, Thailand, Malaysia, Laos, Vietnam, Hong Kong, and Japan as an inexperienced entertainer. I augmented my performance salary by taking freelance photography assignments in locations where Western photographers were still a bit of a rarity.

The world was hungry for unusual stories from Asia then. As a young and raw journalist with little comprehension of the underlying political issues of the area, I came face to face with the dramatic events of the day. Being in the right place at the right time was at the heart of my earliest photojournalistic adventures.

With the beginning of the war in Vietnam, U.S. forces were building steadily in the Far East. These were the darkest years of the Cold War and the fear was of China's involvement in the Indo-Chinese conflict. Everyone was concerned about the war escalating and spilling over into the Philippines, Thailand, and Korea. The large U.S. bases in the Philippines, Taiwan, Thailand, and Japan all needed entertainment for the troops.

Most of my performance engagements then were for these American soldiers. My comedy pickpocketing was new and different, and audience participation was always a hit. I had long contracts on the military bases, as well as in the civilian clubs—camouflaged girlie-joints, really—that attracted the soldiers. It was this environment that fueled my taste for absurd and offbeat news stories.

(continued)

Photographers in those early years of the conflict hung out together in the hotel bars of Saigon. That's how I met Larry Burrows, a British war journalist who worked for *Life* magazine and was one of the most-awarded photographers to come out of the Vietnam War. Burrows helped me gain contacts in Saigon, both with the American military command and with the opposing factors. Without leads and the contacts you wouldn't get "the story".

It was because of Larry Burrows that I was one of only five photographers in Saigon who were privy to the intelligence leak that a monk was about to commit suicide. An immolation was to occur in the early hours of June 11, 1963, at a compound outside Saigon in front of a few select journalists. The Buddhist leaders orchestrating the sacrifice schemed that the global reaction to the front-page photos of the monk setting himself on fire would create an anti-war movement. The goal was to speed up peace negotiations.

At three in the morning, we photographers were rushed from the hotel out to the compound. The unlucky monk who had been selected for the sacrifice had already been drugged into a semi-comatose state and sat on the ground. As soon as the media were ready with their cameras, other monks poured petrol over the "victim," and he was then set alight. We let our Nikon motordrives spin throughout the ordeal and the resulting pictures, mine included, created enormous impact and news coverage in all major newspapers around the world.

My first photo essay was from Pakistan, where I shot the story on the Parsis and their infamous Towers of Silence. Their disposal of the dead isn't so gruesome when you understand their belief in preserving the purity of fire, water, earth, and air. So as not to pollute these elements, they will not burn, bury, or sink their dead. Still, mine were morbid photos by an immature photographer. It wasn't the historical perspective of the burial rituals that sold the story, but the stark and grisly images of vultures ripping limbs from human corpses.

In similar stark-but-shallow style, I photographed Hindu cremations at the burning ghats in Benares on the Ganges River, morning bathing rituals in the Ganges in Calcutta, opium dens in northern Thailand, the Bridge at River Kwaii, faith healers in the Philippines, and leper colonies in India.

One particular photo project had a strong impact on my career path. The story was on beggars and pickpockets accosting foreign visitors in Karachi. This was my introduction to a cynical distraction method based on sympathy and compassion. The pickpockets were lepers, and they were exploiting pity for profit.

In the early 1960s, leprosy was still a serious threat to the populations of India and Pakistan. It was common to see sufferers in various stages of deterioration roaming the streets of Karachi, Calcutta, Bombay, and New Delhi. Banding together, they often surrounded Western visitors coming out of banks, hotels, and churches. The sight of an outstretched hand with missing or rotting fingers usually caused people to react with horror and drop some coins, if for no other reason than to get the infected limbs to go away. Compassion and revulsion metamorphosed into currency. The ploy was effective, diabolical, and unique to Pakistan and the Indian subcontinent.

My story showed a team of lepers who specialized in pickpocketing under the guise of begging. While one tugged at the left side of the mark and held out his diseased hand for *baksheesh,* his accomplice on the mark's right fanned, or softly felt for the wallet.

(continued)

When the victim looked left, aghast at the touch of such ravaged hands, his reaction would be a sudden jerk to the right to get away from the loathsome encounter. The partner on the right would lift his wallet in that moment of abrupt contact.

This was the most primitive of survival instincts, where rules of civility, shame, and respect didn't apply—just raw confrontation between the haves and the have-nots. I was only twenty-two years old when I first witnessed this subterfuge, and I was both stunned and fascinated. Stunned at the callousness of using a primeval emotion, fear, to accomplish distraction. Fascinated by the realization that there were people so desperate that they would go to any extent to find money to survive for the next couple of days. It was a rude awakening for a youth raised in the privileged shelter of socialist Sweden.

Watching this base encounter is what inspired my lifelong effort to document and unravel the mind games that nearly always accompany pickpocketing. I was intrigued by the fact that wit was as much a part of it as technique. This is what challenged me to explore the criminal mind. Pickpocketing is not an activity that one only practices now and then. It's a daily routine performed several times in a fairly short time span. It's an intense crime based on dexterity and, equally important, on psychological analysis of the opponent. A good pickpocket must be able to read many signals and make an instant decision on whether to go for the *poke* or wait for a better opportunity.

I was also intrigued, in those early years, by the cleverness of the setup. Although the theatrical theft of a wallet on stage is entirely different from lifting one in the street, the principles of distraction are the same. By studying the real thieves, I realized I could incorporate their techniques into my performance. I began a fanatical collection of stratagems, always on the lookout for the clever, devious, cunning, slick, duplicitous, ingenious, innovative, inventive, and creative new trick.

Thirty years after I first saw the lepers' technique—begging on one side of a victim, pickpocketing on the other—I noticed nearly identical methods being used by thieving gangs in southern Europe.

Another pivotal moment arrived for me in India when I realized that gangs of beggars and pickpockets usually worked under controlling leaders. Not protectors or father figures to homeless children, these leaders were brutal mutilators who intentionally crippled children in order to make them better beggars, allotted them territories, and demanded daily payments from them. My discovery of this grim reality was the spark that fired my quest to find, understand, and expose the manipulators' deception.

From Indian beggars to eastern European gypsy families to American inner-city street toughs to North African pickpockets to Colombian tricksters, I have always asked this question: how did you learn your trade? Was it passed down within the family? Was it learned in prison? Was destitution the motivator?

For more than forty years, a rumor has been whispered among police forces in America that an organized school for pickpockets exists. The School of the Seven Bells is said to graduate a certified pickpocket when he can steal from all the pockets of a man's suit while it hangs on a mannequin, without ringing little warning bells tied to the clothes. A pickpocket in Cartegena told us that the school is nestled high in the mountains of Colombia. An American cop told us of a variation in Chicago, in which razor blades buried in the suit pockets replace the bells. And yet I have never spoken to a

(continued)

policeman who has succeeded in getting any details from detained pickpockets about the school. Perhaps it is mere myth. My search continues.

One of the most common questions people ask me after they've seen my lecture or one of our documentaries on con games is how I got so interested in tracking criminals. The easy answer is that one thing led to another: stage pickpocketing to observing street thieves to adapting their tricks for the stage. But that denies the force of my own personality in steering my expedition through life. It's more difficult to define the eccentric quirk in my psyche that attracted me to deceit, deception, and double-dealing—but always on the right side of law and morality. I am fascinated by confidence games and have the great fortune to enjoy my interest as my career.

In my younger years, my trio of passions—travel, photography, and entertaining—seemed to be in conflict; I thought an inevitable choice would have to be made. Maybe I never grew up. I still travel the world nonstop and I still love it. I'm still deeply involved in photography, though it has mostly evolved into videography. And I am still a full-time entertainer working theaters and private corporate events around the world. I'm having a blast. How lucky can one man be?

battery and a tangle of wires completing the package, Bob's ominous box would never have made it through airport security.

I snapped a few rubber bands over the lid and Bob tucked the box neatly under his arm, lens pointing down toward his pocket. That's how the shoebox-cam was invented.

Thus rigged, we'd created a space not easily blocked by a thief, a void full of light, which preserved the camera's view of Bob's pocket. The shoebox-cam proved useful in many situations and became one of our favorite capturing devices along with the cell phone-cam, eyeglass-cam, and button-cam.

Caught-in-the-act criminals aren't always keen on conversation. "Why I should talk to you?" some say. We've been threatened with rocks, hit, spit upon, flipped off, and mooned. But we're constantly astonished at how many thieves talk to us. Why do they do it? We don't flash badges at them, and we don't dangle handcuffs. Yet, the outlaws don't know who we are or what's behind our front. Might we be undercover cops? That must be hard to imagine, with our flimsy body structures and frequent lack of local language.

Bob can usually find a common language for an interview, though he or the perp may have limited ability with it. Sometimes we have a translator with us or we are able to find one, impromptu. Most importantly, Bob has a unique advantage: he has worked for forty years as a pickpocket.

Inside knowledge, familiarity with moves and challenges, and level dialogue allay our subjects' suspicions. Or perhaps they're highly suspicious, nervous, and confused. Ultimately, they don't know what to make of us.

Okay, so Bob's a stage pickpocket. He steals from audience members in a comedy setting and always returns his booty. But the physical techniques are the same, the distraction requirement, the analysis of body language, the sheer balls. And Bob has that other illicit necessity: grift sense. He can sense a con, he can play a con.

No doubt our interviewees intuit that in only moments. Next thing we know, they're buying us a beer, accepting our invitation to lunch or, in our favorite case, offering us lucrative work as partners.

While victims relate their anger, inconvenience, and bemusement, their perpetrators tell tales of persecution, desperation, an unjust world, or alternative beliefs in the rights of ownership.

Research
Before You Go 2

It was Cecily's dream vacation: she and her family had rented an ancient stone farmhouse near St.-Paul-de-Vence on the French Riviera. Recently renovated to luxurious standards, it stood between an olive orchard and a lavender farm, strolling distance from the sea, and it came with a Renault.

For their first morning, coffee, baguette, and fresh farm butter had been delivered by the agent. Cecily feasted lightly on the terrace, then drove into Nice and shopped for groceries. So far, excellent. She loaded the Renault feeling spiffy, pleased with her success, and rather . . . *je ne sais quois*. Perhaps rather *French*.

Just as Cecily got into the car, a nice-looking man approached and asked her something: where could he buy a newspaper? Where was a petrol station? Cecily's French had rusted since high school, but she struggled to understand.

"Don't worry," the man said in English. "I am not going to steal from you."

What? Cecily swiveled in her seat just in time to see another man dash off with her purse, which, sadly, still contained her entire family's passports and return airplane tickets. The nice-looking man at her window was gone.

Cecily had spent weeks researching French villa rental companies and poring over their offerings. After deciding on the four-hundred-year-old farmhouse, she read up on the nearby perfume factories, the Musée Picasso, and where to tour an olive oil processor. She compiled a list of every enticing restaurant she'd read about within a one-hundred-mile radius of the farmhouse, whether it was Michelin starred or a village secret. Crime reports were the furthest thing from Cecily's mind. She'd focused on weather reports.

Educate Yourself

When you research your destination, check on crime and security issues, too. Knowing what commonly happens and where gives you the edge. The goal is to be mentally prepared and to understand the local risks. You can then adapt your awareness level to the specific situation. If, for example, you know that sneak thieves prey on tourists watching street entertainment, you can enjoy the entertainment with a hand on your valuables or your backpack on your chest.

Most travel guidebooks include a section on crime and safety. The Internet has a wealth of information, limited only by your search skills. Advice found on the Internet is unregulated, so the reliability of the source must be considered. The United States Department of State Bureau of Consular Affairs (*www.travel.state.gov*) posts annual reports on the conditions in every country a traveler might visit, and many we wouldn't dream of visiting. These so-called Consular Information Sheets are politically flavorless; the U.S. government does not massage information in order to pander to advertisers or foreign ministries of tourism. The U.S. State Department is unbiased and tells it like it is, ruffled feathers be damned. Special updates are posted between annual reports whenever conditions change.

Consular Information Sheets are not exhaustive on the subject of crime, but they do cover numerous subjects of interest to a visitor. In addition to current crime trends, a typical report describes: the country and its major cities; its entry and exit requirements (including visas, departure taxes); safety and security issues (political and ethnic tensions, existence of anti-foreign sentiment, land mine dangers); medical facilities and health issues (vaccines, diseases, water quality); traffic safety and road conditions; aviation safety; railway safety; customs regulations (bringing electronic equipment in, antiquities out); currency regulations; child issues; criminal penalties; embassy locations; and more.

Reading the U.S. government's report on France could have saved Cecily her anguish. "Thefts from cars stopped at red lights are common, particularly in the Nice-Antibes-Cannes area, and in Marseille. Car doors should be kept locked at all times while traveling to prevent incidents of 'snatch and grab' thefts. . . . Special caution is advised when entering and exiting the car, because that offers opportunity for purse-snatchings."

The government reports trends, not singular events. The few specific techniques that make it into the Consular Information Sheets should be taken seriously.

Reading the brief, fluff-free reports pertinent to your itinerary will put you miles ahead of potential trouble. Surprisingly few travelers take advantage of this free educational service. If misfortune befalls the unwary and swindlers seek the weak, enlighten yourself and raise your awareness.

Overconfidence is the enemy of travelers in unfamiliar lands. The know-it-all risks loss and embarrassment. Henry started his story with the wistful remark we've heard countless times:

"I didn't think it could happen to me," he said, shaking his head. "I never even sensed the other guy was near me."

Henry and Kathy were world travelers. We met them in the third month of their current foreign travel adventure. Only in their forties, they

Travel Advice
Courtesy of the U.S. Government

Odd, but possibly vital, information can be found in the Consular Information Sheets regularly posted by the U.S. Department of State (DOS). For example: "It is illegal to bring into Japan some over-the-counter medicines commonly used in the United States, including inhalers and some allergy and sinus medications. Japanese customs officials have detained travelers carrying prohibited items, sometimes for several weeks. Some U.S. prescription medications cannot be imported into Japan, even when accompanied by a customs declaration and a copy of the prescription." Staggering advice! But the report doesn't stop there. It includes links to English-language Japanese sites with prescription look-ups, because "Japanese customs officials do not make on-the-spot 'humanitarian' exceptions."

In a recent Peru information sheet, "Travelers are advised to seek advice from local residents before swimming in jungle lakes or rivers, where alligators or other dangerous creatures may live. All adventure travelers should leave detailed written plans and a timetable with a friend and with local authorities in the region, and they should carry waterproof identification and emergency contact information. . . . Peruvian customs regulations require that many electronic items or items for commercial use be declared upon entering the country. Failure to make a full and accurate declaration can lead to arrest and incarceration." Better mention your laptop or digital camera.

If you "get sand in your shoes," that is, fall in love with island life on your Bahamian vacation, you'll be glad to have read that "U.S. citizens should exercise caution when considering time-share investments and be aware of the aggressive tactics used by some time-share sales representatives. Bahamian law allows time-share purchasers five days to cancel the contract for full reimbursement. Disputes that arise after that period can be very time-consuming and expensive to resolve through the local legal system."

Going to see the pyramids of Giza and Cairo's exotic Khan el Khalili bazaar? The U.S. DOS tells us that "Egypt is one of the world's leaders in fatal auto accidents. Traffic regulations are routinely ignored. If available, seatbelts should be worn at all times. . . . Sidewalks and pedestrian crossings are non-existent in many areas, and drivers do not yield the right-of-way to pedestrians." Knowing this will certainly alter your behavior whether driving, taxiing, or walking in Egypt.

The U.S. Department of State isn't in the scare business. Each of its reports is rich with phone numbers and links to official Web sites to help travelers get the information they need. Instruction is included on how to deal with problems and emergencies while abroad, including after-hour phone numbers. The State Department's information is invaluable, free, and available via phone, fax, pamphlet, and Internet.

U.S. Department of State

Bureau of Consular Affairs

Washington, D.C. 20520

For recorded travel information, call 202-647-5225

For information by fax, call 202-647-3000 from your fax machine

Internet Address: *www.travel.state.gov*

were quite young compared to others with the time and resources for extended travel. Both were physically fit and mentally sharp. To Kathy's alert, quiet reserve, Henry radiated self-assurance and arrogance.

On this day, as usual, Kathy carried their cash in the deep front pocket of her tight shorts. Henry carried nothing but the plastic boarding card issued to him by his cruise ship.

The couple was standing on a street corner near the *souk* in Casablanca when a large local man approached. Glancing at Henry's Blue Jays cap, the interloper leaned into Henry, lightly knocking his shoulder.

"You from Canada?" he slurred, in a drunken act.

Henry, always on his toes, second-guessed the ulterior motive.

"Keep your hands off me, pal," he said threateningly.

The stranger backed away and glanced across the street. Kathy followed his look and watched as a second man approached them. He was the big guy's partner.

"Sorry, I have no use for this," the partner said, and held out Henry's boarding card. The couple had never even noticed him near them, yet somehow, he had been.

I like this story for its considerate thief. Most, with hopes of snagging a credit card quashed, would drop the worthless plastic in a trash bin or, more likely, on the ground. The notion of a quixotic thief appeals to my wispy romantic being. Luciano, that ever-present menace on Naples' trams, told us that because he doesn't use the credit cards he steals, he drops them into a mail box so they can be returned to their owners.

Had Henry Smartypants read the State Department's report on Morocco, he would have known that "criminals have targeted tourists for robberies, assaults, muggings, thefts, purse snatching, pickpocketing, and scams of all types," and that "most of the petty crime occurs in the medina/market areas. . . ." Perhaps he would have thwarted the thief who snuck up behind him; his antennas would certainly have been up.

The detailed Bob Arno Travel Advisory on our Web site (*www.BobArno.com/BATA*) is devoted exclusively to travel scams and con games, and only in those cities of which we have personal knowledge. But what we cover in BATA, we cover thoroughly, so that is another treasure trove of tricks to beware.

Of course, no source can cover *everything*, no traveler can be hypertuned constantly, and scamsters are ever inventive. Thieves will continue to succeed, but you can destroy their advantage and let them move on to an easier target. Who, then, is likely to be that easy mark?

Let's look at the anatomy of a victim. I'm thinking of a couple I saw in Barcelona not too long ago. They had the word "gull" plastered all over them, a perfect lesson in what not to do. They just looked affluent: the woman wore a slinky black dress, a big blonde wig, and garish diamonds from here to there, real or not. Her watch was thin, gold, and diamond

Stung by a Wasp
Scooter-Riding Bandits Buzz Bob and Bambi

I didn't think it could happen to me.

There was no warning. One moment, Bambi and I were walking down a narrow, cobblestone alley in Naples' *Centro Storico,* having just looked back at an empty street. The next moment, I was grabbed from behind, like in a Heimlich maneuver—except I wasn't choking on chicken. I was being mugged and there were three of them.

There was nothing slick about it; they were just fast and singularly focused on my thirty-year-old Rolex. Without finesse, it was merely a crude attempt to break the metal strap. What these amateurs didn't know was that they had selected a mark who had, himself, lifted hundreds of thousands of watches in his career as an honest crook.

Until now, I had never been on the receiving end of my game, even though I'd often strolled through ultimate pocket-picking grounds in Cartegena, the *souks* in Cairo, and La Rambla in Barcelona. I'd been pushed and shoved using public transportation like the Star Ferry in Hong Kong and rush-hour subways in Tokyo, London, and New York—yet I'd never been a victim.

Finally, my luck turned—I'm not sure for the good or bad—during a visit to Naples, Italy. Though I hadn't been there in some fifteen years, I knew full well about its slick pickpockets, and particularly about the infamous *scippatori.* The latter is a unique style of rip-off that involves speeding scooters and short Italians with long arms. Little did I know that I would finally become a statistic in what must be one of the world's highest concentrations of muggings and pickpocketings in an area of less than one square mile: *Quartieri Spagnoli,* a district even the police avoid.

Scippatori are marauding teams of pirates on motor scooters. The scooter of choice is the Vespa, a nimble machine with a plaintive buzz that, when carrying a pair of highway bandits, delivers a surprising sting. *Scippatori* ply their vicious bag-snatching chicanery on unsuspecting tourists in Italy, but particularly in Naples. Handbags and gold chains are plucked as easily as ripe oranges by backseat riders in daring dash-and-grab capers.

It was, therefore, with extreme caution that Bambi and I walked these streets, popular with tourists primarily as a gateway city. It's the starting point for ferry trips to Capri, bus tours to Pompeii, and drives along the spectacular Amalfi-Sorrento Coast. Let me emphasize *starting point.* Even Naples' car rental companies urge tourists to drive directly out of town.

Though it hardly matches the beauty or historical magnitude of Rome, Venice, or Florence, Bambi wanted to photograph the colorful *Quartieri Spagnoli.* Its old section, the *Centro Storico,* has a seedy, rustic, old-world fascination, with its dismal balconied apartments stacked on dreary, minuscule shops. As we walked, I reminded my wife that this was the birthplace of pickpocketing, and I scrutinized every scooter that buzzed by, making sure we were out of reach.

It was mid-afternoon, *siesta* time, as Bambi and I strolled the deserted lanes. Little light filtered down through the seven or eight stories of laundry hanging above the narrow alleys. Almost all the shops were shut, their steel shutters rolled down and padlocked, and it was quiet except for the snarl of traffic on Via Toledo, the perimeter street.

(continued)

The ancient "Spanish quarter" of Naples, Italy, where streets are narrow and scooters dominate the roads.

A lone shellfish monger remained, amid shallow dishes of live cockles, clams, snails, and *cigalo* glittering in water. Though we were practically alone in the area, we frequently glanced behind us.

Still, they caught us completely off guard. With silence their foil, they rolled down a hill: three young thugs on a Vespa scooter, its engine off. One guy remained on the scooter, ready to bolt; another held me with my arms pinned to my sides, and the third tried to tear the watch off my wrist. It was sudden, quick, and silent. No shouts or vulgar threats.

It's a joke, I thought in that first crucial instant, expecting a friend or fan to say, "Gotcha!" I'm quite often grabbed by people who've seen me perform; they like to make me a faux victim as a sort of role-reversing prank. Although this vice-grip felt deadly serious, my thought process, instant and automatic, cost me several seconds. I didn't fight back with a sharp elbow or kick. And because my reflexes never got into gear, I didn't have a chance to coil my muscles into a protective stance.

Fortunately, pickpockets are generally petty criminals who can easily be scared off. They prefer stealth, diversion, and speed to violence as their *modus operandi*. Bambi reacted a moment before I did, bravely smashing my captor on the head with her umbrella. Other than breaking the umbrella, this had no effect at all.

As soon as my adrenaline kicked in, I yelled at the top of my voice, *"Polizia, polizia."* Years of stage speaking enabled me to project my voice throughout the neighborhood. Instant reaction! They scrambled away as fast as they had appeared.

We walked away, lucky but shaken. My steel watchband didn't give despite considerable force applied in attempting to snap its pin. All I had lost was my own track record. I could no longer claim that pickpockets had never tried to steal from me.

Bambi still tenses at the buzz of a motorcycle behind her—not a bad legacy, perhaps. And both of us now strip down to skin and cloth when visiting this most colorful district. The proof of my own stupidity—namely, wearing a Rolex in Naples—was a scratched up wrist. I should have known better.

First rule for avoiding pickpockets: don't attract them. Don't signal you're worth their while. Second rule: acknowledge that it can happen to anyone. Whether you're strong, confident, aware, or careful, you are not immune. Even a veteran pickpocket can become a victim.

encrusted. She carried a designer purse and a recognizably expensive shopping bag. The man wore a floppy black suit, trendy black T-shirt, and a gold Rolex. He carried a large camera bag with a Sony label on it. They stood, utterly bewildered, with map in hand, staring at street signs. I had an urge to educate them, but what could they change right then and there? I'd only manage to scare them. Bob and I want people to enjoy their travels. We mean to raise awareness, not paranoia.

If this couple were the ideal paradigm of oblivion, they'd plop down at a sidewalk café. She'd sling her purse (unzipped) over the back of the chair by its delicate strap and he'd put his camera bag on the ground beside or under his chair. He would not put his foot through the strap. He'd hang his jacket on the back of his chair. Is anything in its pockets? They'd both relax and watch the people parade, as they should. When the bill arrived, he'd leave his thick wallet on the table in front of him while he waited for change. Eventually he'd realize there would be no change because he hadn't counted on a cover charge, a charge for bread, a charge for moist, scented, plastic-wrapped napkins, a built-in tip, and water that cost more than wine.

How many mistakes did they make?

"Tourists are more vulnerable than anyone else on the streets," Bob says. "And not only because they often carry more money than others. Their eyes are everywhere: on the fine architecture, the uneven pavement, shop windows, the map in their hands, unfamiliar traffic patterns, unpronounceable street signs. They don't know the customs of the locals and don't recognize the local troublemakers. Con artists and thieves are drawn to tourists for the same reasons. Tourists are unsuspecting and vulnerable."

Don't Be Self-Ripped

That means: do your research. Besides knowing the tricks and scams prevalent in your destination, you should be up-to-date on currency. Look up the exchange rate, be familiar with the denominations of foreign currency and what each note is worth in dollars. Low-value currency can be baffling. Menus and price tags can blind you with zeros in Istanbul, for example, with the Turkish lira at over six hundred thousand to the dollar. Will you pay 21,875,000 lira for your dinner, or 218,750,000? It's easy to make a mistake. We got so many Zambian *kwachas* for our ten dollars once, we kept them and stuck wads inside our prop wallets. (That was before we realized that cut paper thickened a wallet just as temptingly.)

So, know the currency. Also, consider how much cash you need to carry. Bob and I recommend carrying as little as possible. We're great proponents of credit cards. Sure, you need enough local currency for small purchases.

The Tasteful Tourist

Bob and I looked at each other in disbelief. Only we knew the incredible odds we'd just beaten. To stroll into Rome's Termini, the main train and subway station, pick a platform, peg a pair of old men as pickpockets, position a victim, and have it all work as if to a script in under twenty minutes on our first take . . . we were flabbergasted and giggly. The fact that the film crew's hidden cameras captured it all was merely the cherry on top. This had been our hope and our plan, but we never dreamed we'd pull it off so quickly, if at all. Our prey were Italians; ordinary-looking, regular citizens. Not ethnic minorities, not immigrants, not identifiable outcasts. We'd begun the project for ABC's *20/20* with this, the toughest challenge of them all.

The first night, at dinner in a wonderfully touristy *trattoria,* investigative reporter Arnold Diaz and segment producer Glenn Ruppel had expressed their severe doubt. They wondered why ABC had allowed this frivolous endeavor, invested the time and significant expense in so improbable a venture. Hidden camera expert Jill Goldstein, serious videographer though she was, just seemed pleased to be along, on her first trip abroad. The five of us ate an innumerable procession of courses any Italian would have pared by half, toasting luck first with Prosecco, then wine, grappa, and finally little glasses of thick, sweet limoncello.

Bob and I had worried for the previous two weeks, fretting over a myriad of potential obstacles. How could we be certain to lead the crew to thieves, get Arnold Diaz pickpocketed, and get it all on film? How would we find the perps in all of Rome?

Our hopes slipped a little when we first met Arnold. With his refined Latin looks and flair for fashion, he blended right in with the local Italian crowd. He didn't look like a typical American tourist, who may as well have the stars and stripes tattooed across his forehead. Arnold didn't look like a tourist at all; rather, he looked like a European businessman. So we gave him a five-minute makeover. We slung a backpack on him, put a guidebook in his hand, a camera around his neck, and a "wife" by his side (me!) and, poof—there he was: a tasteful tourist, ready to be ripped off.

Taxis, delightful sidewalk coffee and exotic street food, craft markets, tips, and all those expensive luxury items you want to buy without a paper trail all require cash. But for the rest of it, credit cards are a better deal.

When you buy foreign currency, the money dealer makes a profit. You may be charged a poor rate of exchange, a fixed fee, a commission, or all three. Believe it or not, many money changers will negotiate. You might get a better rate or lower commission if you exchange more money. Some dealers prefer U.S. notes in certain denominations and will give you a better rate for them. Many won't take old, tattered, or damaged U.S. notes. Most won't take torn or taped bills at all.

Before you buy foreign currency, compare the posted prices at several booths or banks. Find out whether they charge fees or commissions. Compare and ask for better deals.

Never change money on the black market. *Never* change money on the street.

How much local currency should you buy? You'll definitely get a better rate if you change a larger amount, say, over US$400. But if you don't use it all and have foreign currency left over at the end of your trip, you'll lose again changing it back into U.S. dollars. You can get local money from ATM cashpoints, but they are notoriously expensive, often charging fees at both ends (your own bank and the local bank) on top of poor rates. Not to mention the numerous tricks, scams, and thefts associated with ATMs, which I'll discuss later.

Bob and I say change a little money. Enough for small purchases (whatever that means to you), depending on where you are. Use a credit card for everything else.

Credit cards are accepted in the most remote and exotic places. (But not all. Research first.) Some taxi drivers take them, as do shops, restaurants, tour companies, and hotels around the world. Not all, of course. And cash does give you bargaining power. Your research will help you decide how much cash you need. Here's the advantage of credit cards: they charge the prevailing rate plus 2 or 3 percent on foreign purchases. That means, as currency prices fluctuate, you'll be charged for today's purchase at today's exchange rate, plus that small percentage, which varies by company. Compare that with the 10 to 15 percent commission you'll pay to buy foreign cash. As to the fluctuation in price of foreign currency, well, unless you're planning to spend a lot of money over a period of weeks or months, or during turbulent times, that should not be a huge consideration.

And there are more advantages to using credit cards. Many credit card companies offer wonderful perks, including guarantees for loss or damage of your purchase, doubled warranties on items purchased, and assistance with disputes or shipping problems. Only you know what fringe benefits your credit card attaches. Of course, they're easy to carry and use. If you should lose one, a timely phone call to the sponsoring bank will relieve you of liability should the card be fraudulently used. There will be more coverage on this in chapter 9.

If you're organized, you can monitor your charges and pay your bill on the Internet, wherever you are. You can also pay by phone, and many countries have a local number that patches you through to a U.S. company representative.

We recommend having three separate credit card accounts from three separate companies: Visa, Mastercard, and American Express. At least one is likely to be accepted wherever you go. Always leave one of the cards locked up in your hotel room. In the worst-case scenario, if you lose your wallet and need to cancel your cards, you'll still have one, *on a different account,* that you can use for the remainder of your trip.

Suppose you do lose your two credit cards and need to cancel them. Do you know the phone number to call? No. It's printed on the back of the card and the card is gone. Do you know your account number? Hopefully you do. But before you do anything else, prepare yourself: fill out our Theft First Aid form in the back of this book and put it with your passport. When you travel, leave the Theft First Aid form in your hotel room.

And while you're preparing yourself, make a photocopy of the first page of your passport. You can carry the copy around for identification while your passport is safely stowed in your hotel room. Only a few countries actually require you to carry your passport around on a daily basis, although situations change with the political winds. If you're not required to carry your passport around, don't. Unless, that is, you're staying in a grass hut on a beach with no locks on the door. You must judge the security of your home away from home.

When you have to carry your passport in a risky or unfamiliar place—say, from the airport to your hotel—carry it on your body, not in a purse. That means in a tight pocket, in a pouch under your shirt, or in some other travel-safe container. I'll discuss some of these later.

Debit cards are about as convenient as credit cards now, at least for extracting cash from ATMs. The major difference is if you should lose it. A credit card has a liability cap of $50 in fraudulent charges, and, in many cases, the credit card company won't even require you to pay that much. Debit cards, however, come with stricter responsibilities. You are expected to report its loss or theft within a day or two. The longer your delay, the higher your financial responsibility for fraudulent charges. Your bank will ask you about your password. If you used your birthdate, or some other easily discovered combination, you'll have greater responsibility. You'll also be asked how you safeguarded the card.

Travelers' checks are a good safety measure for some people. Bob and I find them a hassle. We don't use them. If you do, remember to keep a list of the check numbers separate from your wallet, and cross them out as you use them.

You're There

So you've done your research, studied up on foreign currency, and made the long-awaited journey to elsewhere. After touchdown, you trudge through immigration with no surprises. You have whatever visas are required, perhaps your yellow immunization card, return ticket, proof of transfer tax, or visa fees paid—whatever foreign officials can throw at you. Now you need a taxi.

It's hard to know if you'll find an organized taxi queue or a pack of hustlers. Chances are, your research has suggested that you only use official taxis and agree on a rate before stepping in. Taxis can be a traveler's first rip-off. Try to get a vague idea of what the charge should be from the airport to the hotel. Your hotel or travel agent may be able to tell you

Taxi Trickery

"Visitors should be alert to the potential for substantial overcharging by taxis, particularly in areas frequented by tourists."
—U.S. Department of State Consular Information Sheet
Czech Republic, January 18, 2002

After an eventful overnight train journey, we were disgorged into a very foreign Sunday morning. Not a single sign in Prague's main train terminal was in friendly English or in any other language we could make out, not even an exit sign. The station was haunted by solitary figures standing, smoking, watching, waiting. It took us half an hour to find a dismal tourist information booth. The grouchy attendant, stingy with his every word, pushed a map at us through a slit in his glass barrier and considered himself done. Averse to bribing a public servant, we persisted with our questions, formulating the same query in endless ways. Finally, we extracted this gem: taxi fare to our hotel ought to be two hundred koruna, about six dollars.

The taxi drivers had something else in mind.

"Meter," they said, "more fair." Finally, our bags were loaded into a trunk and we got in.

"*About* how much?" we asked.

"Meter," the driver insisted. Again we pressed for an estimate, and the driver finally said seven hundred. Seven hundred! Out we got, and out with our bags. The driver said something to the other waiting taxi drivers, and we were certain we wouldn't get a ride from any of them. So we walked.

A few blocks down the street, we flagged down a passing taxi. He, too, suggested the meter. We said, c'mon, *about* how much. Three hundred, he said. Okay. We watched the meter start spinning. No way was it a legal spin. As the meter crept to four hundred, we protested, and the driver agreed to a flat three hundred.

"The taxi drivers wanted seven hundred koruna!" I exclaimed in outrage to the hotel receptionist.

"They are thieves," was his simple reply.

before you leave home; at the least, ask at an information booth in the airport when you arrive. Still, you can't always protect yourself from unscrupulous practices.

The tired traveler flies into flower-filled Changi Airport and instantly feels at ease. It's neat, clean, functional, and aesthetic. Rules are adhered to in Singapore. The streets are as safe to walk as the tap water is to drink. What sort of thief can operate in such an ostensive utopia?

The traveler collects his luggage and changes a little money at the airport booth, then jumps into a taxi to his hotel. "Fifteen dollars," the driver might say as he pulls up to Raffles or the Regent or the Mandarin; and in most cases, the visitor pays and that is that.

Many American tourists' first sense of Singapore is not at all that of an exotic Oriental land, but rather, that the place resembles the modern city in which they live. Therefore, a surprising number of American tourists happily, ignorantly, and accidentally pay their taxi fare in U.S. dollars. What taxi driver will refuse an instant bonus of more than forty percent? That tourist has been self-ripped, so to say, and the driver is hardly to blame.

More cunning, though, is the driver or shop clerk who recognizes your naiveté and slips some worthless or worth-less money into your change. This happened to me once in Singapore. A taxi driver put a few Malaysian bills into the stack of Singapore bills he gave me. The pink Malaysian bills look remarkably similar to the pink Singaporean ten-dollar notes. So similar, in fact, that the passing of them could have been just an accident. But the ten-ringgit Malaysian notes were worth only half the value of the Singaporean tens.

Other self-rips include pavement wagers, which I'll discuss later. These include the three-shell game and three-card monte. Like casino games, you bet against a house advantage. Unlike casino games, you cannot win.

I'll also describe a prevalent, greed-based self-rip called the bait-and-switch scam. This one occurs when you're offered a deal too good to be true; a camera, for example, at *such* an irresistible price. You think it *might* be stolen, but that's a detail you just don't want to know. You test and scrutinize the item, you hem and haw, you buy it, and you get self-ripped. More on that one later.

What about tipping policies? Are you prepared? Do taxis and waiters expect a hefty 20 percent? Do locals typically round up to the whole number? Are tips considered an insult? Are they included in the bill? Are they included in the bill with a blank total on the credit card slip, encouraging you to not notice and add more (or, to be fair, allowing you to lessen the included tip)? Tipping ignorance may lead you to self-rips. The State Department won't help you here, but Internet research and travel guidebooks will.

Bob and I are travel enthusiasts. We adore the variety of being in London one day, and Johannesburg, Mumbai, New York, Florence, Sydney, Cairo, or Buenos Aires the next . . . all in a year's work. The last thing we want to do is frighten travelers.

We believe that awareness and forewarning put a serious dent in the number of needless thefts that occur. One wallet stolen: it's a small crime, not devastating, and its likelihood and consequences do not spontaneously occur to people traveling to unfamiliar destinations for business or pleasure. Since the threat never enters their minds, they are not prepared to protect themselves.

Yet the after-effect is annoying at the least, troublesome and humiliating at worst, with the added potential of identity theft, which begins with stolen documents.

Bob and I say awareness is your best weapon. We say do your research, raise your antennas, and go forth: explore and savor the natural and cultural differences that make each country and city unique. Rejoice in your fortune to be able to travel. *Bon voyage* and travel safe!

Theft Thwarters #1: Research and Readjust Your Attitude

When you go on vacation, don't forget to pack your common sense. But while that's a great beginning, specific knowledge can turn your safety concerns into confidence and give you the advantage in travel safety and security. From the obvious to the sophisticated, the commonplace to the innovative, these essential tips will prepare you for a trip abroad or into your hometown subway.

First, understand: yes, it *can* happen to you.

- Awareness is your best weapon. When you research your destination, check on crime and security issues, too. Learn what commonly happens and where in order to gain an edge. Understand the local risks and adapt your level of alert to each situation. Example: Sneak thieves prey on tourists watching street entertainment. Remedy: Enjoy the entertainment, but keep a hand on your valuables or your backpack on your chest.

- Telegraph signals of confidence and awareness; con men and thieves are quick to distinguish the vigilant from the vulnerable. They look for the easiest mark. In crowds, keep physical contact with your belongings. Example: The rush and jostle of boarding a crowded bus or train is a pickpocket's favorite opportunity. Precaution: Take a look at the faces around you and keep a hand on your purse or wallet.

- Maintain a low profile in public. Dress down. Try to blend in. Extreme example: Carry a local newspaper.

- Don't attract thieves by looking like a wealthy tourist. Don't wear flashy jewelry. And remember—the thief can't tell that your Rolex is fake or your jewelry is costume. Leave it in your hotel.

- Familiarize yourself with the foreign currency you'll be using and its exchange rate.

- Never carry more cash or valuables than necessary. Use a credit card for most purchases. You'll save on currency exchange commissions, too.

- Travel with three different credit cards, but keep one in your hotel safe.

- Write down your credit card account numbers and the phone numbers to call if your cards are lost. Use our Theft First Aid form, and keep it in your luggage, not in your purse or wallet.

- It is rarely necessary to carry your passport once you've arrived at your destination. Keep it locked up with your airline tickets, and carry a photocopy of the first page instead.

- Make photocopies of all travel documents, including tickets, passports, and itinerary. Carry the copies separate from the originals.

- As an ultimate back-up plan, send an e-mail to yourself with attached copies of all your travel documents, including tickets, the first two pages of your passport, and itinerary. You might also include your hotel information, traveler's check numbers, and other important phone numbers. If you lose your documents, vital information is as close as the nearest Internet access point. Be sure not to delete the e-mail message during your travels!

- If your destination is considered volatile or unpredictable by the U.S. State Department's travel advisory Web site (*www.travel.state.gov*), take ultimate precautions. Countries that are popular tourist destinations for Americans, yet are unpredictable in terms of travel safety, include: Indonesia, South Africa, Kenya, Brazil, Peru, and parts of the Middle East. This is by no means a complete list; international security is always fluid.

Getting There— with All Your Marbles

3

By Plane

"Did you know you're wearing mismatched shoes?" a well-dressed Englishman said to our friend, Brooks, at London's Heathrow airport one day.

Brooks was talking on a pay phone, frantic at finding out that he was supposed to be at London's other airport, Gatwick. He locked eyes with the stranger. "I am not!" he said, refusing to be distracted. "And you'll not succeed in grabbing my briefcase!"

Brooks had become security-obsessed after hearing our tales.

"Pardon me, then. But you are." The man walked away, intentions defeated, whatever they were.

Brooks finished his telephone call, feeling rather smug that he'd thwarted a thief who tried to distract him. Then he looked down at his shoes, only to see one tasseled, one buckled loafer.

Everyone knows not to leave bags unattended in airports and, lest we forget, we are relentlessly reminded by annoying announcements. Bag-stealing strategists are devious, though. Even if you aren't looking away from your things, you may be connived into doing so. Questions by an apparently confused or puzzled foreigner touch our good-natured core and we want to help. A moment's distraction is all an accomplice requires. Who would suspect that the pretty girl asking to borrow your pen is merely a diversion as her colleagues snag your bag? Or, here's a good one: you're suddenly paged. Who would page you at an airport? Who even knows you're there? You rush off to find the white courtesy phone, befuddled and worried. The accented voice on the line sounds unclear, yet urgent. You may be asked to write down a number, requiring some gymnastics while you extract a pen and find a scrap of paper. Have you looked away from your briefcase? Have you lost physical contact with it? Where is it, anyway?

Earlier, the thief had examined the object of his desire, your bag. Its luggage tag informed him of your name. The strategist paged you. He distracted you. He created his own plausible situation. Or, as Bob would say, he created a shituation.

Airports give the illusion of safety, especially now with increased security. The swirling crowd of dazed travelers, lost or rushed or tired, makes a perfect haystack for the needle-like thief. Your bag might disappear before you even get inside, in all the curbside commotion. Long, tedious, check-in lines can be disorderly madness in some airports, inducing inattention when you need it most.

Computers and purses disappear, too, at airport security checkpoints. Guards have their hands full keeping order at the chaotic bottlenecks, and they're watching for bigger fish than bag thieves. Don't assume they'll safeguard your bags.

Practically every television news program has shown this ruse. The scam occurs just after you've put your items on the belt. Before you walk through the metal detector, a stranger cuts in front as if in a hurry. The equipment buzzes and he has to back up and remove his watch, his coins, something. Meanwhile, you're trapped in limboland and your bags are free-for-all on the so-called secure side.

If you're traveling with another person, make a habit of this: one person goes through security first and collects her and your bags as they appear. The other waits to see that all bags go fully and safely into the x-ray machine, and watches the belt to see that it isn't reversed, leaving your items vulnerable on the other side. If you're alone, wait for any crowd at the checkpoint to pass, if you can, or be alert to anyone who barges in front of you after you've let go of your things.

So you've made it through security. Does that mean you're in a secure area? Not secure enough to relax your attention. Thieves have been known to buy multi-leg plane tickets and work the gate areas in each airport, never needing to pass security after their initial entry into carefree-land.

You wouldn't look twice at the couple sitting back-to-back with you in the departure hall. Smartly dressed, stylish bags, composed manner: they look like frequent international travelers—and they are. The troupe arrested in Paris' Charles de Gaulle Airport was not French, but South American. They, and other sophisticated gangs of thieves take the same international flights as their victims, stay in the same hotels, and attend the same trade shows, sporting events, and operas. "They're clever, don't take chances, and do a lot of damage," a French police officer said. "They keep the cash and sell off everything else—credit cards, passports."

"These gangs systematically comb all major international airports on both sides of customs," said an undercover police officer at Amsterdam's Schiphol Airport. "They often fly between five or six airports on round-trip tickets," explained the crime prevention coordinator for the military police there.

Many airports around the world have installed camera surveillance, which has cut theft of bags and theft from bags. In Cape Town, for example, while an inbound visitor stood at a car rental counter with his luggage

Kharem's Lucky Haul

Kharem, a pickpocket in Spain, sometimes chooses Barcelona's airport over the rich pickings of the city. When Bob and I last found Kharem at work on La Rambla, nine months after we'd previously interviewed him, we asked how he'd been.

"Supremely good!" Kharem said. He swept the tip of his thumb against his forehead, fingers fisted, in a quick, subtle gesture.

"He actually said, 'son-of-a-bitch good,'" our translator clarified. Our friend Terry Jones was tagging along on our prowl that day. His own street crime expertise was more in the bag-snatch discipline than the pickpocket branch. Although he'd watched the local thieves with fascination and sometimes wrote about them, he'd never interviewed one. Now he translated our conversation, intrigued and electrified by the novelty.

"But haven't there been fewer tourists?" Bob asked. We'd last met Kharem just a few weeks before September 11. "Let's get away from the crowd and talk."

"The work is good at the airport," he said. "I robbed an Egyptian there. It was son-of-a-bitch good. But yes, there are fewer tourists and it has affected my business. Also, there are more policemen around."

The four of us ambled up a narrow side street in Barcelona's Gothic Quarter. I tightened my grip on our camera bag. Bob was filming Kharem openly.

"Do the police arrest you more than they did last year?"

"No, they don't arrest me. They just take the money and let me go," Kharem said, flipping his thumbtip against his forehead again. "The police are not very good; they don't have much experience. I'm better than they are, in the street." He smiled bashfully and looked at the ground.

"Is there more bag-snatching?"

"Yes, but they're young people who don't know how to work. If all you want is a wallet, you can take it without violence. But these people don't know how to work clean.

Kharem, thirty-seven, from Algeria, works in Barcelona

They're young, and some of them are on drugs. Many children have come from Morocco this year, since Spain and Morocco are side by side. These Moroccan children work in a crude and unsophisticated way."

"I think he's a little proud of his own skill and style," Terry added.

"Besides La Rambla, I work in the metro and sometimes at the airport. The Egyptian I mentioned—it was a briefcase I took from him just last week in the airport. It had thousands of dollars in it."

"How did you take it?" Bob asked.

"I threw some money on the floor," he said. "Let me show you." He bent to take our canvas bag from the cobblestones where it was safely lodged between my feet. I looked at Bob, but he didn't seem

(continued)

concerned about letting this known thief and now confessed bag snatcher handle our $15,000 sack of stuff.

Kharem lifted the bag and took two steps away. As if in slow motion, I watched our camera, mixer, mic, and tapes of fresh footage retreat, and waited to see Kharem lunge and dash away with a fine fee for a little chat. We'd greeted him like old friends, I recalled; we hadn't criticized his way of life. Must we show *this* much trust? He's *not* our friend. And we certainly are not his. But the alternative was unpredictable. I could have stopped him from taking our bag, or snatched it out of his hands, or just said, "Sorry, I don't think so." And what might Kharem have done then? Did we care about preserving a relationship for the future? Or did we just not care to insult a person who'd revealed to us the most intimate secrets of his life?

Kharem set the bag down gently at Terry's feet, steadying it so it wouldn't tip. He tossed a couple of 10 Euro notes and Terry twisted to watch them flutter to the ground.

"He bent to get the money and I just walked off with his briefcase," Kharem said, lifting our bag once again. He smiled, swiped his thumbtip against his forehead, and handed the bag to me.

behind him on a trolley, a thief simply lifted one of his bags, popped into a men's room, changed clothes, and walked out with the stolen property. After leaving it in a waiting car, he returned to the baggage hall to scout for more goodies. It was all caught on tape.

Trains between concourses are another area where personal property goes missing. On these, as well as in airport shops and restaurants, one must maintain vigilance. This is especially difficult for people who don't travel often and live in small towns where safety is almost a given. Thieves hone in on relaxed attitudes like heat-seeking missiles. What works: keep physical contact with your property.

I'm sure it sounds obsessive to mention the necessity of onboard watchfulness. The likelihood of theft while on an aircraft is low, granted, but it's unpredictable, and that's the problem. If you're carrying valuables, such as cash, jewelry, or credit cards, you may as well continue with your precautions. The risks are to the carry-on items you can't see: those in the overhead compartment can be ransacked practically under your nose—or above your nose. Those under the seat in front of you are vulnerable if you sleep or leave them while you get up. I want to stress that these are low-probability scenarios, especially if you're not traveling alone. Your degree of precaution must harmonize with your comfort level and the value of the items you carry.

Sadly, suitcases are occasionally compromised while in the airlines' possession. The odd unscrupulous employee needs only the moment of opportunity. It's well known that most luggage locks are next to useless. Keys are generic, and even combination locks have certain pressure points that free latches.

The Stick, the Shade, and the Wire

Johnnie Downs, an American "whiz player," travels to all the top sporting events in the United States. His favorite tool is a garment bag, which he calls his "shade," a prop to hide his theft of a "sting," or a wallet. Dressed in a suit from the wardrobe he's proud of, he flies to his destination penniless. He described his recent trip to Las Vegas.

"I made $900 coming out of the airport. When the plane lands, I start work. I got to get my money to get out of McCarran airport. Play strictly on skill, that's how I play—on the plane. Yeah, plane lands, people have their arms up getting their bags. See my man, get up on him, *pow*, I spank him, off the front leg.

"It was a pappy—a man—right? He got a sting—a wallet—in the front slide, but he also got cash. I played this for his credit card. I got a guy with me we call a writer. He writes the work, writes the spreads. He's a stick—what *you* call a stall, what we call a stickman writer. He's stick and shade. I do the wire. The wire is the one who takes. We split up when we get on the plane, he gets in the back and I get in the front.

"Right now, I can go to McCarran airport and go to baggage claim and beat some stings. Because security is, evidently, lax, and the people are rushing to get their bags, and the bags are coming off the trolley, and I got my garment bag. . . .

"And when he's stooping down to get his luggage—'Oh, is that mine, sir?' Shake him up. 'Oh, is this mine? It looks like mine.' If you're moving, and I got someone with me, and you're in the airport, I'm going to play you. If I feel like I can work you I'm going to play you.

"Every play is different, so you can never really set the motion for the play. All I need is my garment bag, or the coat called London Fog. It's wintertime, and the London Fog coat, it's got a split in the pockets. So your hands are coming out from inside, while the coat is buttoned up. It's hard for someone else, or even a camera, to see close up. When the hand come out like this, you use the other part of the coat to hide it."

Bob and I believe in hard-sided luggage. The ones we use are aluminum, made by Zero Halliburton. They're not for everyone, being both heavy and expensive. But when our bags were forced with a crowbar or other tool somewhere on the nether tarmac of the Miami airport, the locks and hinges held tight. Shiny scars in the seam, as if gnawed by a metal-eating mouse, were the only evidence of serious tampering.

As we watch our silvery Halliburtons trundle off toward baggage handlers in Lusaka, in Santiago, in Mexico City, filled with sound and video equipment, or perhaps with our favorite shoes from Florence, we're eternally grateful for and confident in their sturdy locking mechanisms. Even more so after trying desperately and failing to break into our own locked suitcase when it jammed once in London.

Of course, bags like these do call attention to themselves and an argument can be made for using inexpensive luggage. One world-traveling couple we met swears by the cheap stuff. After repeated thefts from their Louis Vuitton cases at Heathrow airport, they resorted to department store brands, buying new bags every year or so. A small price to pay, they say, given the cost of their trip and value of their belongings. That's their argument, but I don't buy it. I say, buy the best bags you can find and afford, and use their locks. Budget extra time into your airport experience so you can see that your bags are properly locked after they are scanned.

Now I'm going to reveal the raggedy edge of my latent obsessive-compulsive propensity. I actually run a strip of tape—something similar to duct tape—around the seam of my suitcase. Yes, I really do. I began doing it in order to keep condensation and rain from leaking in and staining my clothes, which had happened more than once on long-haul flights. But I soon realized the security value of the tape. Although it takes only a moment to stick on and I use the same strip over and over, it adheres strongly to the aluminum. It's very much a deterrent to tampering and, for better or worse, makes the bag appear quite shabby. Look: I travel hundreds of thousands of miles every year. Some things I just know.

It's rare, nowadays, to find an airport that checks bag tags. Our policy is to get to the baggage claim area immediately. We don't allow our suitcases to ride the carousel unattended, where they might "get legs". In Las Vegas, a man was recently arrested for serial luggage theft. He stole only black bags, simply lifting them off the conveyor belt and walking out as if they were his. When challenged by a rightful owner, he'd apologize and say the bag looked just like his own. This unsophisticated system worked well for quite some time, until he walked off with a bag that belonged to an FBI agent. When the thief was arrested, his apartment was found to contain racks and racks of sorted clothes: men's, women's, and children's. He'd been selling it to second-hand stores in $300 lots, the maximum cash-in-advance the stores would give him.

To prevent your luggage going intentionally or accidentally missing thanks to someone who thought "it looked just like mine," decorate your bag with something that won't fall off. I have green tennis racket wrap around the handle of my generic black roll-aboard. Who could mistake it for theirs?

And speaking of falling off, when we retrieved our three suitcases from the carousel recently, two were missing their sturdy handles. Not only did this make lifting them difficult, we were lucky to get them at all. With the handles went our ID tags and the airline's luggage tags listing the bags' destination. What would United have done with the bags, on this multi-leg flight, if we hadn't had adhesive labels with our name and phone number stuck to the outsides? I praise United for determining the correct end city, but I'm amazed at its arrogance. "Our employees throw bags," a United representative said when we complained. "All baggage handlers do." Tough luck.

A final word on luggage choice concerns the size and weight of carry-on bags. It's been drilled into passengers forever: carry on your valuables, your delicates, your medications. Of course—the airlines don't want to be responsible if your checked baggage is damaged, delayed, lost, or stolen. So you choose your carry-on bag carefully to accommodate your necessities, keeping FAA size regulations in mind. It's panicky, then, on your connection abroad, when gate agents heft your bag and say uh-uh, it's too heavy. Most foreign airlines allow a carry-on bag of only six kilos—that's just thirteen pounds. My FAA-regulation roll-aboard weighs more than that empty!

Filled with your valuables, your delicates, your medications—and perhaps your bag doesn't lock or can take only a toy padlock on wimpy zipper tabs—it's with a thumping heart you watch your precious vitals pass into the care of airline baggage personnel.

The goal is to avoid that scenario. You could call in advance and ask the airlines with which you'll be flying what their cabin baggage allowances are and then stay within their limitations. Or you can take your chances with an FAA-regulation bag, overweight though you know it might be, and hope gate agents will let it pass. You could choose a lockable hard-shell carry-on that you'd feel secure about relinquishing, which is what Bob does; or you could keep a small canvas bag or tote inside your carry-on, so that if you're forced to hand over the bag, you can first remove a few choice items, which is what I do.

Americans often assume that FAA regulations are international. Strangely, you can get a fifty-pound carry-on out of America, but you may find yourself stuck with it elsewhere, suffering separation anxiety as you board a foreign flight. Airlines' rules vary; airlines' adherence to rules varies; airline employees' moods and sympathies vary. Rhyme and reason are out the window, along with consistency.

Once we collect our suitcases and load them onto a trolley, we keep them in front of us. That is, at a customs inspection, a car rental counter, in a taxi queue, or arranging any airport transportation. While waiting, making phone calls, or whatever, keep your luggage in front of you. This is not difficult to manage.

As a neat segue from planes to trains, let me quote a stern warning from the U.S. State Department's Consular Information Sheet on France. This scenario, sad to say, is ubiquitous and the warning is applicable worldwide. "Gangs of thieves operate on the rail link from Charles de Gaulle Airport to downtown Paris by preying on jet-lagged, luggage-burdened tourists. Often, one thief distracts the tourist with a question about directions while an accomplice takes a momentarily unguarded backpack, briefcase, or purse. Thieves also time their thefts to coincide with train stops so that they may quickly exit the car. Travelers may wish to consider traveling from the airport to the city by bus or taxi."

Nigerian Nightmare

The moment Michael Griffith turned his back, his wife let out a blood-curdling scream. He whipped around to see Nancy jumping up and down, crying, her face contorted with panic and disgust. They were at the immigration desk at Lagos airport with barely an hour left to suffer Nigeria.

Michael now knew for sure he shouldn't have brought Nancy along on this short business trip. She'd been so warned, so exhorted, so horror-storied, that she was utterly paranoid and never even left the perceived safety of the hotel.

A few days earlier, as Nancy browsed the hotel gift shops, she'd had a brief conversation with another hotel guest.

"I hope you're not leaving this godforsaken country on Friday," he'd told her.

"I don't know for sure," Nancy said with alarm. "Why?"

"They steal passports on Fridays," the man explained. "Goddamned immigration officials at the airport."

"Why on Fridays?"

"Because they know you'll pay anything to get your passport back so you can get the hell out of Nigeria without waiting all weekend until Monday."

When Michael returned to the hotel that evening, Nancy asked him what day they were leaving. Friday, Michael said. So Nancy related her newest tale of terror and, together, she and Michael came up with a plan. Nancy would carry their remaining cash in a flat leather pouch attached to her belt and slid inside her jeans. One hundred nairas, the exact amount of departure tax for two, would be put into Michael's shirt pocket. Nancy would tuck an American $20 bill into each of her two front jeans pockets in case bribes were necessary, and Michael would carry a 20 naira note in each of his two front pants pockets. Never let go of your passport at immigration, they'd been warned. Michael would hold onto their passports during examination and stamping.

As a lawyer who represents Americans arrested abroad, Michael was no novice at foreign travel. He'd been to almost eighty countries, through hundreds of airports. It was his business to know the laws and procedures of other countries, their customs, and dangers. He'd been through the notorious Lagos airport many times before, but never with his tall, blond wife. Nancy, too, had traveled extensively. She had just retired from her career as a supermodel. Nancy's jitters came from the endless nightmare experiences she'd heard and read about travel through Nigeria. Even the U.S. State Department considers it one of the most dangerous, corrupt, and unpredictable territories on Earth.

So it was not a pair of travel virgins who meticulously prepared themselves for the perilous journey through Nigerian formalities. These were travel warriors. From New York. Michael, at least, thought he'd pretty much seen it all.

They approached the immigration desk as planned, Michael in the lead, Nancy dragging their rolling bag. It was not crowded, and they stepped right up to the official's high desk.

"Airport tax fifty nairas each," the government official demanded.

Michael reached into his shirt pocket and extracted the prepared cash, five 20-naira notes. As the officer's fingers closed around the money, Nancy shrieked. She yelled with a shrillness and urgency Michael had never heard before. In an instant, a heartbeat, a fraction of a moment, Michael heard intense terror and overpowering repulsion, desperation, and primeval fear. He felt it in the hollow of his chest. In his bones. On his skin.

He spun, already flushed and slick with instant sweat.

(continued)

Nancy was screaming, but she was also jumping and twitching. And Michael saw that she was covered with cockroaches.

Covered might be the wrong word. There were only twenty or thirty cockroaches. But they were huge, shiny as glass, and black as terror. They skittered up Nancy's jeans, down her blouse, and along her bare arms. One had become entangled in her hair, and kicked frantically at her ear. A few dropped onto the floor, where Nancy crushed them as she leapt spasmodically.

A uniformed immigration officer strolled away from the hysteria, indifferent. At his side, he casually swung a large-mouthed jar of grimy glass. It was empty.

Michael, accustomed to extracting people from sticky situations, was at a loss. He'd pulled people out of South American prisons, choreographed an American's escape from a Turkish jail, rescued the wrongly accused and the clearly guilty. Now, as he grabbed his delirious wife by her shoulders and tried to steady her, he saw the same overwhelmed eyes he saw in many of his clients. They bulged with a desperate plea for a savior and of unspeakable horrors.

Michael swatted and kicked away most of the creatures. Then he opened the lower buttons of Nancy's blouse and removed one more. He pulled one from her hair, and then removed the serrated legs that had remained stuck there. He asked her if there were any more. Then he held her.

"Let's get out of here," he whispered in her ear. "We're almost home."

He turned back to the immigration officer, still placid in her high booth.

"You only gave me four twenties," she said. "I need one more."

"Lady, I'm from New York," Michael said dangerously, "and this is the best I've ever seen. You know and I know that I gave you a hundred nairas. You're getting nothing more from me."

The officer waved them through, expressionless.

Nancy, catatonic with shock, began to regain her composure when they arrived at the gate for their flight.

"If I ever get out of here, I'm going to kiss the ground of America," she said with conviction.

And she did so, eighteen hours later at JFK airport, though it was technically not ground, but the dusty terrazzo floor thirty feet above it.

A U.S. Customs Officer must have seen Nancy bend to the floor in the busy baggage hall.

"Ma'am, you must be just back from Lagos!" he grinned. "Welcome to the USA! Welcome home!"

By Train

Traveling by train requires even more watchfulness than flying. Stations can be seedy. They're open and available to anyone, with or without tickets. They attract a varied population of travelers and nontravelers alike. Vigilance is vital.

Stations with the biggest theft problems are those that are connected to, or nearby, bus or subway stations, which are often hangouts for gangs, drug dealers, and other undesirables. Thieves are able to loiter unchallenged within the stations without attracting attention. Then they can take advantage of congestion for cover and easy escape.

Train stations and daytime journeys are covered in chapter 6. Here, I'll discuss overnight trips. Certainly not all overnight trains carry such risks as the following, which are some of the worst cases. They're a popular and logical mode of travel that are not to be dismissed. If you plan well, you make the most of your vacation days, see a bit of countryside, meet some other interesting travelers, and save the expense of a hotel night.

My Swedish friends called me "exotic" because I had never been on an overnight train. It's easy to find a European who has never been on an airplane, they told me, but *everyone's* been on an overnight train. So when Bob and I found ourselves in Venice, Italy, ready to visit Prague in the Czech Republic, we decided to go by rail, overnight.

We boarded in late evening, and it seemed we would encounter our first train scam immediately. A large, slobbish, dreary man blocked the aisle and demanded our tickets.

"Tickets!"

He wore baggy black pants and a soggy white shirt. Nothing official—no monogram, badge, cap, embroidery, or name tag, nothing to identify him. Yet, as his bulk impeded our path, we had no choice but to give him our tickets. He pointed to our reserved compartment. Thankfully, he didn't demand money. But he didn't return our tickets, either.

We could have been assigned to an Italian-owned wagon, or an Austrian one, possibly even a Swiss one. But we got a wagon owned and maintained by the Czech Railroad. We entered our dismal compartment and tallied up the security risks.

First, though, what happened to our tickets? Bob went to find the big sour slob who had confiscated them. I could just imagine the moment a uniformed conductor would come to punch our tickets.

"But . . . but . . . we've already given them to the conductor!" we'd say.

"What conductor?"

"The man in black pants!"

"No tickets, no travel! Get off the train!"

Bob and the Czech ticket-taker argued in mutually exclusive languages. Bob returned without the tickets. We had nothing, not even a receipt. My turn. I tried another way. I found a Czech lady who explained: the man is our "attendant". He keeps the tickets to show officials at border crossings. He'll wake us in the morning, and will return the tickets then.

Okay.

Back in our dusty quarters we assessed the realistic hazards and dismissed the rest. We would not, for example, worry about knock-out gas being snuck under our door as a precursor to robbery. *Bob said* we wouldn't worry about it. I merely insisted we keep the window open. Where, then, shall we put our luggage? Under the window is the obvious place, but not if we leave it open. The only other possibility would block the door.

Block the door.

We had not brought anything suitable to secure the door, but its flimsy chain would be enough. Bob said so.

I couldn't sleep.

The gentle rocking I had imagined would seduce me to slumber was instead a rude awakening. It was jerky and ruthless, like being aroused by an earthquake. If I slept, I could be rolled like a drunk and never parse the violence of the assault from the brutality of the jolting train.

The noise from the open window was deafening. The rhythmic, metallic percussion of the tracks combined with a menagerie of whistles, screeches, and shrieks when we stopped at stations and borders. It was torment, but I wouldn't shut the window.

Just a few days before, we had interviewed a railway police officer in Milan whose detail was theft. He claimed that most, if not all, the "gassing" tales are made up by victims too embarrassed to admit that they had slept through their own robberies. I had read an interview of a young Czech train thief who described exactly how he enters a compartment, watches his sleeping victim, slices open the victim's pocket, and lets the wallet drop into his hand. Without gas or drugs. That sounded unbelievable to me; impossible. Surely the victim would awaken? But having experienced the dreadful noise and ceaseless motion of an un-air-conditioned overnight train, I realize how horribly possible it is.

Atul and Smriti Shah experienced it firsthand. "It happened during the night," they concluded. "The entire compartment was sprayed with some sort of gas that knocked us out. Then our suitcase was slowly extracted from under our seat, the lock twisted loose and, with all the time in the world, the suitcase was looted."

Atul and Smriti live with their small daughters in Mumbai, India, where railway is the customary way to crisscross the country. For the occasion of a relative's marriage, the family traveled to the town of Kanpur, in Uttar Pradesh. As tradition dictates, they brought along their finest clothes and jewelry to wear to the many matrimonial celebrations and ceremonies. As a high-caste woman from a wealthy family, now married to a successful businessman, Smriti carried an enviable display of gold and diamonds.

"She had diamonds on her fingers and in her nose and ears," Atul explained with pride, "and gold bangles and necklaces. Also, she wore the good-luck vermilion mark on her forehead that Indians always wear when traveling away from home."

After the wedding and family visits, the Shahs boarded the train for the twenty-hour journey home. They had one suitcase, but it was a large one: fifty kilos, Atul estimated. It contained all the family's finery, including Smriti's jewelry, and had a small padlock on the zipper tabs. Atul forced the suitcase under Smriti's seat in the train compartment, where it was tightly lodged. They did not open the suitcase for the duration of the journey.

The Shahs boarded in the evening, had a meal packed by Smriti's mother, and settled down for the night.

"The strange thing is that none of us woke up during the night," Smriti told me. "Even the children slept the night through, and they never do."

She remembers a vague sensation of bitterness in her mouth during the night, then the desire for water. But she also remembers the lethargy she felt, the heaviness of her limbs.

Food- and drink-drugging has long been a problem on trains, but could knockout gas really be in a thief's arsenal? In my early research, doctors had doubted the likelihood of a thief acquiring the right gas and the victims not waking from the smell. I went back to the doctors, and this time they all agreed it could happen. Chloroform is often used in primitive surgical conditions and has no smell at all, some said. An anesthesiologist mentioned Halothane, which would be readily available from any surgical facility or veterinarian. Halothane has a slight odor but not enough to wake an already-sleeping person.

"Within twenty or thirty minutes," Dr. Jared Kniffen told me, "someone could be in a deep enough sleep so that you could enter the room without his awareness. The danger of this is you could kill someone if too much were used. There's a second possibility—a gas called Cevoflurane. It's odorless, but much more difficult to obtain."

But wouldn't the robber himself be knocked out? I asked.

"There are ways to avoid that," Dr. Kniffen said. "A certain travel-supply house sells a smoke hood that gives twenty minutes of oxygen." It's meant for use in escaping from a burning building, but a clever thief might employ one for another use.

It sounds too sophisticated to me, too troublesome and risky. But if the reward were a treasure chest like Smriti Shah's, it must be worth one thousand times the risk of simply snagging a laptop from a business traveler.

Despite the Shahs' conviction, gassing on an overnight train is only a remote risk; my paranoid apprehension on our journey to Prague was out of proportion. Breaking into and stealing from compartments is a real risk though, and so is food- and drink-drugging. Nembitol, scopolamine, and benzodiazepine are the drugs most commonly slipped into food or drink, but only after the thief builds trust and confidence with the mark.

A common ploy involves young men who claim to be students of English or students at a tourism school, who volunteer to accompany you to historical sites and act as your guide or translator, and who may

Central and East European Train Crime

Railway mafia groups fight over territory along the thousands of kilometers of track across central and eastern Europe. The most lucrative connections are those between major cities that are most frequented by foreign tourists who are filthy rich, naïve, gullible, and can afford to shed some of their wealth, in the eyes of the criminals who specialize in robbing sleeping victims.

"The mafia groups fight amongst themselves for territory and they use sleeping gas to subdue their victims," said the sheriff of a Polish railway station on the Polish-Czech border with over thirty years of experience in his job who requested that his name be withheld. "They are very skilled and use the ventilation system to gas their victims or quietly inject the fast-acting gas into their cabins through a slightly opened door."

Foreign tourists are followed and carefully watched. There is no easier place to rob them than in a train, which they essentially control on some tracks way out in nowhere. They attack you when you are asleep, that's their style and that's their specialty.

—Central and East European CrimiScope
www.ceeds.com/cee-crimiscope [defunct], April 27, 1998

That read, we traveled exceptionally lightly for our week-long research trip to Prague: one change of clothes, computers and camera equipment, money, passports, and plastic watches each.

We boarded the Venice-to-Prague overnight train at 8 P.M. on a Saturday. After being forced to surrender our tickets to an unidentified man (who we eventually learned was our "attendant"), we were shown to a gritty compartment. Dust clumps the size of rats swirled around the floor. Sad brown floral curtains of a coarse material hung above mismatched cushions and general grime. The bunks had been opened and made up for sleeping, with bed linen that seemed fresh and clean enough. But it was stifling hot in the un-air-conditioned train, and the stale air was of suffocating stillness.

There was no choice in the sweat-smelly and sweltering compartment but to leave the window open for air, despite the deafening, rackety-clackety clamor that made sleep all but impossible. In the dark hubbub, aromas told a tactless tale. The smell of sweet wood smoke rushed in, then fresh-cut hay, and, later, cow manure. At every stop, the train's brakes sliced the rhythmic clatter with ear-piercing shrieks. I clamped my palms to my overly sensitive ears in agony.

Then, stationary in a depot or switching yard, sometimes for half an hour or more, I worried about that open window. Could someone reach in and grab a bag? Voices shouted, neighboring trains clanged and clattered, but even in the relative quiet, I was afraid to drop off to sleep. And without the circulation of air, our somber cell quickly grew hot and sour smelling.

We had read so much about East European train robbers I was, frankly, petrified.

Bolt your door from the inside, I read.

One common, square-hole key opens all compartment doors, I read somewhere else.

Bring wire with which to secure your door, and tie down your belongings.

(continued)

Sleep on top of your bags.

Don't sleep!

What scared me most were the tales of the gassers, who knock you out in the dead of night by fumigating your compartment from under the door. Then they break in and help themselves to your belongings. My doctor friend Ann had said there was no gas she knew of that wouldn't wake you up with its smell, or make you gag or throw up, or kill you. Was that supposed to be comforting?

I was primed for panic when aroused from a light and fitful nap by the quiet rattling of our door. I heard a key jiggle in the lock and the bolt was thrown. The door was yanked open an inch and stopped by the safety chain, which held. A flashlight shined at me through the crack and several male voices mumbled quietly.

Not very sneaky, I thought. But maybe they have knives! They couldn't have expected as light a sleeper as me. Or—I sniffed the air—maybe they've gassed us, not expecting an open window to dilute the chemical.

"Passports," Bob murmured from the bunk below me—not the night-train novice I was. We were at the Austrian border.

Thus experienced, I was prepared for the repeat performance several hours later at the Czech border. We were not well rested when we arrived at Prague at nine in the morning.

But arrive we did, with bags and tickets intact.

---

befriend you for several days before springing their trap. These thieves are con men in the truest sense. Clearly, it's unwise to accept consumables from strangers, even really nice strangers. And, sad to say, one should also be wary of leaving any food or drink unattended on a train (and other places too).

It's a sad commentary on the state of the world when one must look at every stranger with distrustful eyes, and in some ways, it defeats the whole purpose of leisure travel. Spectacular landscapes, ruins, markets, shops, and food are only the skin of a culture. Its people are its core. Around the world, people are attracted to people; locals are warm and welcoming to travelers, and swell with national pride. In many countries, to refuse a gift is to insult your host. In some countries, insulting your host is provocative indeed.

Encounters with locals can offer the deepest, longest-lasting memories of a trip. But when cultures collide, sensitivity and caution must be in balance. Judgment is critical, but how can we determine what our own behavior should be, with little understanding of foreign sentiment? A majority of Americans, cocooned as we are in our huge world of a nation, have a myopian global perspective, as limited as that of an Amazonian tribesman or a Mongolian herder. Our collective ignorance of political issues stuns smaller nations, which can't afford to know only their own business.

Our naïveté may occasionally lead to confrontations. It can also foster dangerous hostility, and it allows us to walk into scams, swindles, and set-ups. Bob and I walked into several in South Africa, which brings me to the cautions necessary when driving in unfamiliar places.

By Car

You'll already have considered the obvious potential differences before taking to the road in a foreign land. They may include driving on the left side of the road, a right-hand drive car, a standard transmission, shifting with your left hand, road signs in foreign languages, and navigating the hair-raising traffic circles of British-influenced territories. If you're driving a rented car, know the limitations of your insurance and be prepared to pay the extortionist rates the rental company charges for its policies. These are clear but measurable risks. Others are nebulous.

In Egypt, for example, cars are driven extremely fast, often without headlights at night. In some parts of Italy, drivers consider stoplights merely suggestions. Red lights are run frequently in Canada. South Africa has no seatbelt law, and cars may not even be equipped with seatbelts. Portugal has poor roads, worse drivers, and one of the highest rates of traffic fatalities in Europe. Australia's Northern Territory has no speed limit. On-the-spot fines are imposed for failure to display a road usage tax sticker, which is required to drive on major highways in the Czech Republic. In Bermuda, horn honking usually means hello, not watch out.

In Cape Town (and elsewhere), boys and men trying to eke out a living commandeer public parking spots all over the city and provide unsolicited assistance to drivers as they park. The driver is then expected to offer a coin for the "protection" of the car.

"What if we don't pay?" I asked a Cape Town business owner.

"You might come back to find some new scratches in your paint," she told me. "But we always give to them. This one," she pointed to a scruffy boy across the street, "he's there every day." The boy had taken off his shirt and was using it to polish one of his charges.

In Hawaii, property theft rates are some of the highest in the United States. Theft from parked cars is a particular risk to visitors, who are discouraged from leaving anything in cars. That's difficult nowadays because at some sites—the Arizona Memorial in particular—visitors are not allowed to bring in any bulky items, including strollers and backpacks. If you must leave items in your car, put them in the trunk before you arrive at your destination.

In southern Europe, Costa Rica, Morocco, and elsewhere, a good Samaritan-type scam occurs on highways. Rental cars are targeted—some of which can still be identified by their license plate numbers (although

Car Thieves Teach an Ugly Lesson

It was somewhat of a shock to find nothing but white lines on asphalt in the place we knew we left a van. We couldn't help but wonder whether our minds were slipping and the van stood undisturbed in a forgotten location. But there it wasn't, high noon and sixty feet from the entrance of Rustenburg's busiest supermarket. We stood two and a half hours, groceries dripping and spoiling, staring morosely at our empty parking space as we waited for the South African police. They never bothered to show up.

So the van was stolen; we shouldn't have been surprised. We'd read in the local papers how often these vehicles disappear into the taxi trade, and our own experience had provided us with enough warnings. Once we'd returned from an hour in a Johannesburg mall to find the ignition busted by a would-be thief who'd easily entered the vehicle but couldn't get it started, presumably due to the special electronic safety key system with which the van was equipped. Weeks later, in the same parking lot, a less-skilled perpetrator was foiled, ruining only the door lock. Then, the week before Christmas, we were jabbed by the foul fingers of crime in a more personal manner.

Winding up a long stay in South Africa, we had packed a few boxes to mail home. The year had seen a natural accumulation of files, notes, photos, and clothing purchased to shield us from a winter for which we were ill-prepared. Though we weren't sending anything of major value, we were distressed to learn that it wasn't possible to insure any mail to the United States. We never completely trust international mail, especially in nations rife with poverty. In addition to sloppy and careless handling, we worry about stamp stealing, prevalent in many parts of Africa. Postal workers are known to steam stamps off envelopes, discard the letters, and earn pennies for the stamps. But as we couldn't justify sending everything air cargo, we packed up four twenty-pound boxes of a year's slough.

In Rustenburg, an hour's drive from where we lived, we rushed to the post office, as we knew it closed for lunch at one. We parked at the busy entrance, directly in front of the public telephones. I waited in the van with the parcels while Bob went to buy tape for a final touch on the labels. I was engrossed in *Newsweek* when a sullen man materialized at my open window. He asked where some street or shop was; I couldn't quite understand, as he spoke in the submissive, barely audible mumble so many South Africans used. I asked him several times to repeat himself—we were always so sensitive about being friendly and courteous to everyone there.

Meanwhile, a second man appeared at the open driver's side window and asked another unintelligible question. With a stranger on either side of me, open windows, keys dangling in the ignition, I felt frighteningly vulnerable. I casually lowered a hand to my bag and shoved my watch-wearing wrist down and out of sight, trying to look at both men at once while politely saying I don't know, sorry, no. I was definitely nervous.

Both the lost souls wandered innocently away in seemingly separate directions and Bob returned with his purchase. Being an unpredictable land, the post office closed at twelve-thirty, not one that day, so we missed it after all, and only by two minutes. While we taped labels, I told Bob what had happened, and we discussed how close we'd come to being ripped off.

We locked and left the van and walked to our usual lunch place two blocks away, grumbling about what a shame it was that we had to suspect people who are most likely decent and honest. We felt certain we were almost robbed, even though the gentlemen

(continued)

merely asked for directions. Did they appear shady? By our cultural standards, yes. But in South Africa, the downcast eyes, low mumbled speech, and meek stance seem to be the product of generations of oppression and domination, if not their own aboriginal behavior. As we analyzed the origin of the character traits, we felt guilty. Were we prejudiced, or merely wise?

Not wise. We returned forty minutes later to find only one of our four boxes left in the locked-tight van. Yes, in retrospect, leaving the boxes in the unattended van was stupid. We should have known. But, in broad daylight, on a crowded street, right in front of a government building, who would think they'd have the nerve? We half expected to lose a box or two in the mailing, but not before.

Of course, none of the people at the telephones or post office saw anything. Off we went to the police station, where officers assured us we'd never see our things again. Our clothing would be put to good use and our files, photos, and books would most likely fuel an evening's cooking fire.

We'd had the privilege of using a borrowed van for weekly treks into town from where we lived in the bush. Careful and conscientious, we treated the van as if it were our own; that is, we parked it in the busiest, closest, and best-lit places, and always ensured it was locked securely. Despite this, the statistics were shocking. In forty-five weeks we borrowed the van about forty times, almost once a week. With our four occurrences, we were victimized 10 percent of the times we drove. This would translate to thirty-six times a year—an intolerable figure—if we had driven every day, as we do at home.

Bob and I left that country with a unique South African souvenir tucked safely away, an unfortunate by-product of the chronic crime we experienced there. Not rare, but valuable; we took away a useful and lasting kernel of cynicism, planted by thieves. As we continue living the lives of expatriots, and, even in our own country, we're more suspicious of and aloof to everyone who approaches us.

---

these are slowly being phased out)—or tourists are identified and followed. A tire may be slashed or punctured, eventually forcing you to pull over. Alternatively, you could be driving along when a passing motorist gestures urgently that something is wrong with your car, so you pull over to investigate. On the shoulder, the good Samaritan arrives to offer his assistance; moments later, you are robbed. The highway bandits take purses from the front seat, luggage from the open trunk, and sometimes the car itself.

Depending on who and where you are, you might just drive on rather than stopping to investigate mechanical problems. Drive all the way to a service station or other public place, even on a flat tire. But do not, however, stop at a roadside rest stop without open services. If something really seems wrong and you feel you must pull over, remove the keys from the ignition and lock the car, even if someone remains inside it. If assistance is offered by a passer-by, request help in making a phone call to police or a legitimate auto repair service.

One common Mexican scam occurs in cities or towns. At a stoplight, someone, perhaps a child, offers something for sale or attempts to wash your windshield. This is an excuse to get close enough to look inside your car. If he sees something grabbable, he marks the car with chewing gum, say, on a taillight. The next time you're stopped in traffic, a partner reaches in, smashing the window if necessary, grabs, and runs.

When we interviewed Luciano in Naples, Italy, our translator, a Napolitano, explained how Rolexes are stolen off the wrists of drivers in the summer. The team targets expensive cars and scopes out the drivers' watches from the vantage point of a motorcycle. It's hot. The windows are up and the air conditioner is on. Traffic is heavy as always in Naples, and there are no such things as lanes. Cars squeeze into whatever interstices exist.

There's a Mercedes that fits the bill. A scooter slips alongside it; the scooter driver folds down the Mercedes' side mirror in order to pass, and winds away through the gridlock. The Mercedes driver opens her window and readjusts the side mirror with her left hand. That's the moment another scooter zooms up, rips the Rolex or Cartier or Piaget right off the extended wrist, follows the first scooter between stagnant cars, and disappears into an alley.

South Africa, an exotic and exciting travel destination, is fighting a seemingly insurmountable crime problem. While most visitors will have a superlative experience at top-rated game parks, lush wine country, and vibrant Cape Town with its spectacular Table Mountain, plenty of potential for problems exists. It may be tempting to rent a car and crisscross this diverse country; and, with a local guide or escort, that's not out of the question. Unfortunately though, robbery and car theft are giving way to more violent crime such as rape, mugging, and carjacking. "Pseudo-cops" (police impersonators) and some real police practice roadside extortion.

Mike Fuller, an entertainment promoter in Johannesburg, wasn't the first to tell us about police corruption in South Africa, and how locals have learned to avoid roadside extortion. "One day, I was driving on the highway and missed my exit," Mike told us. "Instead of continuing and backtracking as I should have done, I put the car in reverse and backed up the short distance to the exit, even though I knew that was illegal. Sure enough," Mike said, "a police car pulled up behind me, and I knew I was going to be ticketed and made to pay him off. So I said, 'Sorry, Officer, something dropped off from under my car. I was just looking for it.' The officer helped me search, then sent me on my way."

A friend of his, Mike went on to tell us, was driving 180 kph when he went through a speed trap. "Knowing the police would come after him, he sped up. When he got around a bend he pulled over, jumped out of the car, and locked himself in the trunk. When the cops pulled up behind him, he started banging on the trunk door, as if he'd been locked in by carjackers." This tale implies that carjacking is so common in South Africa, it's more believable than simple speeding.

"We don't have to pull over when a police car flags us down on the road," the father of a friend said, "as long as we drive directly to the nearest police station. The officer, if he really is one, can make his charge there."

Mickey, an operations manager at a casino just outside Johannesburg, told us that, by necessity, women have their own set of driving rules. "At night, we never stop at red lights if no one is around. We treat robots [traffic signals] like yield signs and keep moving if the way is clear. Bandits often put up fake roadblocks, but we locals can always tell the difference and we drive right through.

"A friend of mine saw a man lying in the road," Mickey went on, "but he sensed it was an ambush. Instead of stopping to help the man, he swerved off into the bushes to get around him, then continued on his way. When he got to his destination, he called the police to report the scam. The police said yes, they knew, and that by driving off the road to get around the man, he had run over three ambushers lying in wait."

This is daily life for ordinary South Africans, and they've learned how to live defensively behind their razor-wire-topped electric fences, guard dogs, and armed patrols. For a visitor, venturing outside established tourist zones is unquestionably risky. A rental car comes with hazard lights and an owner's manual, but it doesn't come with a book of rules on the daily activities of life. The independence that comes with a car is, in South Africa, a hazard itself.

Other countries have equal driving perils. Mexico is especially worthy of warning because many Americans choose to drive there. Dangers include highway bandits, "pseudo-cops," and corrupt officials. Buses and taxis are unsafe in Mexico, and, in particular, in Mexico City, with robberies, often violent, common to both forms of transportation. In Rio de Janeiro, Brazil, motorists are allowed to treat traffic lights like stop signs in order to avoid being robbed. Colombia and Nigeria, among others, are definitely no-drive zones, but it's far less likely that one would want or need to drive in those countries.

Travel by private car (your own or a rental) offers the ultimate freedom for independent travelers, but it's prudent to be aware of both the peculiarities and risks of the road in your chosen territory.

Theft Thwarters #2: Getting There

Planes

- Your home address should not be visible on your luggage. List an office address or post office box, or use a luggage tag that must be opened to read the information.

- Find a way to attach a permanent ID to the outside of your bag. Use an adhesive label, or glue, or sew one on. ID attached to the handle of your bag is not enough. Again, do not include your home address.

- To prevent someone from mistaking your bags for his, personalize your suitcases with something obvious that won't fall off.

- Perk up if you're paged; it could be a ruse. Keep your eyes or a body part on your bags at all times.

- Be particularly vigilant at the security checkpoint. Do not put your valuables on the conveyor belt until you are certain you can walk through the metal detector. If someone suddenly cuts in front of you, beware! A common criminal strategy swiftly separates you from your goodies when the interloper is required to back up and empty his pockets. While you are delayed, your belongings travel to the other side of security where, of course, they instantly acquire new owners. In this team sport, your purse or laptop is both goal and prize.

- Keep physical contact with your property.

- Lock small bags stowed overhead on planes, or make them difficult to get into by putting their openings down or toward the back of the bin.

- Be aware that carry-on allowance may be severely limited on flights originating outside of America. Roll-aboards allowed within the United States may be required to fly cargo on foreign flights. Choose a lockable carry-on, or keep a canvas tote handy for your valuables and necessities in case your bag is taken away for cargo.

- Promptly retrieve luggage from the baggage claim area.

- Pay particular attention to your property on airport-to-city trains.

Overnight Trains

- Try to secure the door and window before you sleep.

- Keep bags away from an open window. They can be grabbed when stopped at stations.

- If possible, tie or lock your luggage to something using wire or a cable lock.
- Sleep on top of your cash, passports, and small valuables.
- Don't flash your stuff. Don't advertise what you have.
- Behave cautiously toward overly friendly strangers.
- Don't accept food or drink from strangers.
- Don't leave your food or drink unattended.

Buses

- Luggage storage is tricky: if your bags are stowed beneath the bus, keep an eye on them at every stop to be sure they don't walk away. Roof storage is risky and potentially wet.

Cars

- Research peculiarities and potential risks before driving abroad. Ask locals at the car rental company about common dangers.
- Don't leave bags, packages, or luggage in an unoccupied car.
- Keep bags and purses out of sight even while driving, if possible, to prevent smash-and-grabs.
- In unpredictable areas, drive with all personal property locked in the trunk.
- In dangerous areas, drive with windows up and doors locked.
- When you park your car, don't open the trunk. Lock items into the trunk before you reach your destination.
- When the driver gets out, remove keys from the ignition, even if the car remains occupied.
- Be suspicious and cautious if you must pull off the road for mechanical problems; it could be a set-up. Try to drive on to a service station.
- If approached by police, ask to see ID; "pseudo-cops" rarely have documentation.

Hotels: Have a Nice Stay

4

"No thanks, I'll carry that bag myself," Marianne Crossley said to the porter as she stepped out of the London black cab, "it's too valuable." She handed a fistful of pound sterling to the driver, hefted her designer tote, and followed the porter into the cool marble lobby of the Langham Hilton Hotel.

Elegance embraced her. Marianne straightened her posture. The Langham was exclusive. She was privileged. She imagined herself belonging to the "UC," as she thought of it, the English Upper Class. Her entire European vacation would be the height of luxury; the black cab and Langham lobby were just the beginning.

Marianne chatted brightly with the reception staff as she checked in, a fresh veneer of energy covering the exhaustion and jet lag of her journey. Emotionally, she had already slipped into something comfortable, something contrived, perhaps a bit pretentious. Cloistered within the confines of the lobby, she felt protected, shielded from the rudeness of the real world.

You know what's coming. Marianne took her room key in one hand and reached for her tote with the other. It was gone.

The Langham's two lobby cameras caught the crook, but the video was not monitored by security officers and was only viewed after the fact. When the larceny was discovered and the tapes reviewed, an interloper could be seen in Marianne's proximity; but the front desk blocked the camera's view of the tote. Neither the hotel, nor the police, recognized the suspect as a known thief.

Hotel lobbies are common sites of bag theft. To the guest, they offer a false sense of security, with doormen in their guard-like uniforms, desk clerks facing outward, and bellmen looking after luggage. In reality, most anyone can enter a lobby, and who's to say whether or not they have legitimate business in the hotel? At peak hours, reception staff are harried and the lobby swirls with the incoming, the outgoing, guests of guests, and lookyloos.

Some small hotels keep their entrances locked and visitors must be buzzed in, but many of these have no security staff or video surveillance. Large hotels, with shops and restaurants open to the public, may have guards and cameras, but are as exclusive as a post office: anyone can come and go without suspicion. Which are safer?

There is no answer to that question. The responsibility for personal belongings is the traveler's—period. We may give our luggage to bellmen and that is fine; but if we don't, or if we have a carry-on, a roll-aboard, a purse, or anything we prefer to handle ourselves, its safekeeping is our responsibility. Hotel staff don't know whose bags are whose or who is traveling together. Perhaps a Langham employee saw a man take Marianne's bag. Perhaps he assumed the man was Marianne's husband.

The Langham is not particularly prone to lobby lifts, and neither did it suffer a rash of them. Perhaps an opportunist overheard Marianne's general announcement in the portico that her bag was "too valuable" to entrust to a hotel employee. Perhaps not.

Marianne was luckier than most victims. Her bag was found intact by a London businessman who went to the trouble of phoning her home in America. Relatives there told him where she was staying and he personally delivered the bag to her, refusing a reward or reimbursement for the international phone call. Only cash had been taken from Marianne's bag. Yet, in the interim days, she'd had to replace her passport and airline tickets, cancel her credit cards, arrange to get cash, and file a police report.

If the Langham were on busy Oxford Street, this lobby lift would make more sense. But it's not; the Langham is on a relatively quiet street several blocks off Oxford. Hotels smack on a main tourist drag have many more lobby thefts; those on La Rambla, in Barcelona, come first to my mind. But if it can happen at the Langham, it can happen anywhere.

And if it can happen in seemingly safe Scandinavia, it can happen anywhere. Certain frequent visitors during Stockholm's summer season have been dubbed "breakfast thieves". They don't steal breakfast; they lurk on the fringes of sumptuous buffets at upscale hotels, waiting for a moment of inattention.

"They lie in wait for a businessman to fetch a second glass of orange juice," said Anders Fogelberg, head of the Stockholm police department's tiny pickpocket detail, "and in that instant of opportunity, they and the businessman's laptop, briefcase, or mini-computer skip out the door."

Breakfast thieves are certainly not unique to Stockholm, but the city, and others in Scandinavia, are ill-prepared to deal with them. The phenomenon is most commonly perpetrated by visiting gangs from South America. Scandinavia, long an insular society, was not used to droves of foreigners, at least until fairly recently. While it had always played host to independent, well-to-do tourists and shoestring travelers, it had never experienced tourism on a grand scale, compared to other European countries.

Cruise ships, affordable flights, and a shrinking world have finally brought tourists *en masse* and they, along with innocent, trusting locals,

How Stealing Came to Sweden

"When one thinks of Sweden, images of tall blond women, sullen Bergmanesque behavior, and cradle-to-grave state support come to mind," Bob explains. "After the Second World War the Scandinavian nations experienced stable economies, long periods of socialist government, and huge tax obligations. For travelers, these were some of the safest countries in the world, with low crime rates compared to other industrial nations.

"But lately, something has gone askew. Paradise has been rocked by some of the highest unemployment figures in the developed world. True figures are hard to pinpoint because of employment 'gray areas' and entire segments of the workforce being subsidized by the government. The published figure hovers at 11–12 percent, but is probably closer to 15–16 percent. The tax burden is becoming ever harsher to embrace by a working population that previously complied with the world's highest taxation. To maintain financial stability and fulfill obligations to the aging population, there have been tremendous cuts in public services. Now a gloomy feeling persists that, sooner or later, the system will go bust. The socialist experiment of the 1950s seems to have imploded.

"With unemployment comes a natural increase in crime—yes, even in Scandinavia. To the homegrown strife, add a foreign influx: the fall of Communism in the East and border controls within the European Union have let loose an avalanche of crime that had previously been under control. Smuggling, prostitution, drug dealing, money laundering, car theft, and pickpocketing are on the increase all across Europe, and governments cannot squeeze out more tax revenues to fund the necessary counter-offensives.

"In Sweden, police reorganization, cutbacks, and a reduced budget have come at the wrong time. The Swedish social structure is changing: due to the drain of a negative birthrate, the country has, to national criticism, thrown open its borders to welcome a new generation of immigrant taxpayers, new citizens with foreign values.

"With unfortunate timing, criminal gangs from South America have discovered Scandinavia as an ideal territory within which to practice their trade. Locals are timid, trusting, and unsuspecting of their neighbors' intentions if lightly bumped or squeezed in a crowd. They wander around completely oblivious to predators in their vicinity. Pickpockets have a heyday. There simply is not enough manpower to control the sudden burst of criminal activity.

"What does this mean to the visitor? In the past few years we've seen an explosion in personal robbery. August's 'Water Festival' is thievery's peak season in Stockholm, and the problem persists all summer on buses crowded with Swedes and tourists going out to the animal sanctuary Djurgården, the big amusement park Gröna Lund, the outdoor museum Skansen, and the Viking boat Wasa Museum. Pickpockets know that Bus 74 is the main public transport to these fine attractions, and that's where the picking is ripe.

"Given that Sweden is considered a highly organized and efficient country, it must seem an odd contrast that police in Stockholm are not on top of this problem. After all, the crime is chronic and has a discernible pattern. But in Sweden, there is a national abhorrence of anything that could be mistaken for prejudice. It's particularly difficult for police to couple any form of profiling to established patterns of crime.

"To travel in Scandinavia today with your guard down would be foolish. Yet, it would be wrong for me to paint a picture of danger lurking behind every corner. The Scandinavian nations are still among the safest in world."

attract thieves. The net effect is Scandinavia's loss of innocence. Although it remains comparatively safe, one can no longer go about carefree. "T-Banan," Stockholm's subway system, now warns of thieves operating in its main stations, and with hand-drawn posters, busy restaurants remind patrons to hold onto their bags.

Bob and I sleep more nights in hotels than in our own home and, to date, we have never been ripped off in a hotel room. True, we use a certain amount of care, but our laptops are usually left out and sometimes valuables are more hidden than locked. We stay in hotels ranked from six stars to no stars, depending on our sponsors and our intentions. In each hotel room, we make a quick and automatic assessment of risks and adjust our behavior to correspond. We have never walked out of a hotel because of safety issues; we simply adopt the necessary precautions.

We evaluate several pivotal points:

The room key: we prefer electronic card keys. Old-fashioned metal keys can be copied, and where might copies be floating around? Electronic locks are usually recoded after each guest. Most electronic locks save records of whose keys have recently gained entry. Authorized keys are registered to their users. So if a guest reports a problem, security can tap into records stored in the lock's mechanism and see the last ten or so entries, be they housekeeping, an engineer, a minibar man, or the guest himself.

Electronic key cards should not be marked with a room number. They're usually given in a folder that identifies the room. Leave the folder in the room when you go out and carry just the un-numbered magnetic card. If you lose the key, the safety of your room won't be compromised.

Some hotels still use metal keys attached to a big fat ornament and expect guests to leave keys at the front desk when going out. I'm not fond of this method for several reasons. First, I prefer privacy and anonymity rather than announcing my comings and goings. In some hotels, anyone can look at the hooks or pigeonholes behind the desk and know if a room is occupied or empty. Second, I don't care for the delay entailed in asking for the key on returning. I could just take the thing with me, but its design discourages that. So third, I don't want to haul around a chunk of brass the size of a doorknocker. And finally, these keys are usually well identified with the name of the hotel and room number. Losing it would expose me to substantial risk. When possible, Bob and I remove the key from its chunk and just carry it, reattaching it before check out. At other times, we go traditional and turn in the key as the hotel suggests.

Deadbolts and door latches: we like these for security during the night, but they aren't universal. In Paris once, two men entered our room in the dead of night. Luckily, we woke up and Bob dramatically commanded them to get out. *"Pardon,"* they said, *"c'est une erreur,"* it is a mistake. The strange thing was that they had been standing there whispering for a moment. If it had truly been a mistake, wouldn't they immediately back out of an occupied room? We should have placed a chair in front of the door beneath the knob.

Peephole in the door: I always look out at who's knocking on the door, and if there's no peephole, I ask through the closed door. Minibar? No thanks. Window cleaner? Wait until I check out. Engineer? I'll call the front desk and find out who and why.

Connecting doors to adjoining rooms: I always double check to make sure they're locked. They always are.

Windows: this is what I look at first, mostly because I hope they open. If they do open, I need to know about outside access. Is there a balcony? If so, there's probably access to mine from a neighboring balcony. I've spoken enough with Frank Black, a career burglar, to never leave a room with an open balcony door. Frank specialized in burglarizing high-rise apartment buildings, but twenty-one years in prison has, apparently, retired him from that business. He's now a respected tattoo artist and children's book author.

In Florida (and I presume elsewhere, too), a certain subset of cat burglar is called a pants burglar. These creep in at night through open lanai doors while the occupants are sleeping. They're named for their beeline to men's trousers, where they hope to find a wallet. They also visit the dresser top hoping to find, perhaps, a woman's ring taken off for the night.

I love an open window, but before I sleep with a breeze, I need to analyze window access. If my room is on the ground floor, on an atrium floor, or if it has a rooftop out the window, I won't sleep with it open. If there are nearby balconies, forget it. Of course, it also depends on the overall ambiance and character of the property. At a safari lodge in Tanzania, I'll worry more about baboons. In a thatched-roof teak tree house in Bali, I figure I've paid enough to expect good security. At an all-inclusive beach resort with rooms that don't lock—well, I planned for that when I packed.

After a quick appraisal of the room's security combined with its overall quality, we know how careful we want to be. In truth, we leave our laptops out in full view in about 85 percent of the rooms we stay in. Digital cameras? Never. Wallets and jewelry? In the safe.

Some travelers believe in using duct tape to fasten their valuables to the underside of a bedside table, or other furniture. I can't endorse that practice, unless it's a last resort.

"During peak travel seasons, hotels tend to use a lot of transient help," Bob says, "and sometimes the screening of these temporary employees is not as high as it could be. So, yes, one always has to be concerned about hotel room theft." The only way to protect your small valuables is to lock them in the hotel room safe.

But is the safe safe? We generally feel secure with electronic safes that allow us to key in our own code or swipe our own magnetic strip. For a

Key Issues

We love King George's House hotel, an atmospheric fourteenth-century building in Prague's Staré Mesto district, the old town. The ground floor of the building houses three boisterous, late-night pubs—a noisy negative perhaps, but we remind ourselves that Prague's lively beer culture is part of its charm.

We stay in the attic—or penthouse, depending on how you look at it. Getting to the room, three long, creaky flights up, requires passing through three doors, each of which locks with a separate key. Secure, but prison in an emergency. The airy suite feels old. Huge black beams across the ceiling and steeply slanted walls have Bob perpetually stooped after one or two head-crackings. Large dormer windows on three sides offer spectacular views of the tiled rooftops and medieval spires of the ancient city.

The room key, like the other two, is an old iron skeleton key. The door lock is a double barrel: the same key locks and unlocks it from inside and out. Bob and I each get a set of keys. At night, we leave one set hanging in the door.

After several days in Prague one time, Bob needed to leave for a show in Sweden. I stayed to continue our research. Bob slipped out before dawn, leaving his keys in the door. I got up later and took my own keys down to breakfast. When I came back upstairs, I couldn't unlock the door. Bob's key, still in the door on the inside, occupied the lock. The hotel charged me a pretty penny for a locksmith, kept me out of the room for most of the day, and belittled me for my stupidity. In fact, we have double barrel locks in our own home, and often leave a key hanging on the inside.

magnetic strip, we use an airline or telephone card, not a credit card. The old-fashioned type of safe that takes a regular metal key we do not consider safe and do not use. We've surveyed police officers, hotel security, and FBI agents on this issue, and they agree with this reasoning.

Safe-cracks are extremely rare, although a man was recently arrested in Palma de Mallorca and charged with a spate of hotel safe robberies. Somehow, he had come into possession of a master tool that hotel security uses to open certain jammed electronic safes. (Other electronic safes can be opened by security using numerical bypass codes.) Presumably, then, the man also had the tools to get into the hotel room itself. The burglar posted his female accessory at the elevator. They each had a cell phone and kept an open connection between them. When people came to the elevator, the woman would delay them for one minute. The burglar would hear the conversation, tidy up, and get out of the room.

As long as they're electronic, Bob and I always make use of hotel room safes. "They're extremely safe if they're used," says Sergeant Tim Shalhoob of the Las Vegas Metropolitan Police. "Problem is, 90 percent

Bali Safe Sting

Natalie Carper is a tour sales manager for one of the major cruise lines. She's an experienced world traveler and accustomed to advising others on travel dos and don'ts. Natalie and a girlfriend, both Australian, took a trip to Bali, Indonesia. A wide range of hotel options exists there, from luxury six-star resorts to shacks on the beach that rent for two dollars a night. Natalie and Linda booked a "decent" hotel: one with a lobby, private bathroom, rooms that lock, and a sense of organization. In America, it would fall into the three-star range.

At check-in, the two women were each given a manila envelope in which to put their valuables. They sealed and signed the envelopes themselves and gave them to the reception clerk, who put them in the front office safe.

Admittedly, they had a splendid holiday on the exotic isle, carefree and uneventful.

At check-out, the two were given their envelopes and they turned to get a taxi. But as they were leaving, they overheard another guest complaining at the front desk. Cash was missing from her envelope.

Natalie and Linda tore into their envelopes and also found cash to be missing. Yet, their envelopes did not appear to be tampered with in any way. The hotel denied any responsibility and, after a brief argument, Natalie and her friend chose to leave in order not to miss their flight home. Later, Natalie wrote to the hotel, but never received a reply. She didn't take the issue any further.

Did the hotel make a system of this nasty theft? If so, it's particularly underhanded with its intentional implication of security. As in the "pigeon drop" scam, the villain suggests and the victim voluntarily complies with the transference of valuables to the bad guy. A con if ever there was one.

The timing, too, is strategic. Most guests, like Natalie and Linda, will have a plane to catch. They'll often plan to fight the matter later, but rarely follow through.

So how was the envelope opened? Could it have been a magician's trick?

In my former career as a graphic designer, I occasionally used wax to fix a graphic element to a page. Rarely, because most page design was completely electronic. The wax I used was in stick form. It looked and acted exactly like a glue stick, except that it never dried.

If hotel guests were handed a wax stick with which to seal their envelopes (I don't know that they were), they'd likely never realize the temporary condition of the closure. A duplicitous staff member could later open a supposedly sealed envelope, then glue it shut properly. Who'd know? Who'd even notice?

Alternatively, the bottom flap of the envelope could have been lightly glued, then later opened and resealed.

There are just too many people in this world who cannot be trusted, and it's best to avoid the necessity at all, if possible. Then what to do?

Travel with hard-sided luggage and use your largest as your safe. True, the entire suitcase can be stolen, but we feel that would be highly unlikely in most situations, while a small tempting object might, on occasion, "get legs."

of hotel guests don't use them." Sergeant Shalhoob has never had a complaint about a hotel safe break-in. Well, what about thieves with illicit keys, as in Palma, I asked him. "Here we don't use keys or tools; we use override numerical codes. If a thief had a key or a code, he would specifically target high rollers. But this simply doesn't happen in Vegas."

The major danger in using hotel safes is remembering to empty them before you check out. When I expect a hurried or groggy predawn checkout, I scrawl a bedside note to myself.

What if your belongings are larger than the size of the safe, for example, a video camera or laptop? Or what if your room doesn't have an electronic safe? Here's another argument for top-quality hard-sided suitcases. You can use one as your safe. The chance of a hotel thief walking away with a camera or jewelry box exists. The likelihood of that same thief walking out with an entire suitcase is slim. The possibility of his breaking into the bag while it's in your room depends on the quality of the bag. Again, for serious travelers, Bob and I recommend aluminum cases made by Zero Halliburton. We have many of them, of all shapes and sizes. As a temporary safe, we always use the largest one we have with us.

If our suitcase safe has a combination lock rather than a key lock (we have both kinds), we have to remind ourselves not to leave the dials set to the correct combination when the case is left unlocked. For a determined

The authors with some of their Halliburton luggage.

or clever thief, this would give away the game. Then again, we might be going a bit overboard.

What if you don't travel enough to justify buying aluminum luggage? What if your bags close with zippers? Are tiny padlocks good enough? No, they are not. Tiny padlocks used to fasten zippers may give pause to a casual opportunist, but they'll not stop anyone who really wants to get inside your bag. It's nothing to twist a zipper tab right off. Use them, by all means, but don't expect them to stop even a mildly determined thief.

And those thin, attractive, combination cable locks? Even worse. Bob recently bought one to test. As a joke, he fastened it around his brother's neck—it just fit, snug but not tight. It was funny for a minute, then the joke was over. The lock jammed, and Bob couldn't get it open. Brother Claes had an appointment and didn't want to go with a steel cable around his neck as if he were some sort of punk rocker or bondage freak. As Bob located a wire-cutter, we considered the serious potential consequences of a cheap lock like this one. Imagine you're on a train and have locked your backpack to the luggage rack. As you near your station, you discover the jammed lock. What do you do? Stay on the train to struggle with the lock, miss your station, miss your connection, pay a fine for staying on the train beyond your stop?

Bob eventually cut the cable off Claes's neck, and thus emerged the real joke. With the gentle snip and the tiniest twist of Bob's wrist, one end of the steel cable detached from its metal sleeve. We needn't have bothered cutting the cable—all it required was a little tug.

I also consider the relaxation factor. If you stay in a hotel for several days, a week, perhaps more, you get comfortable. Maybe you get to know the staff. Maybe you let down your guard. If I were a hotel employee bent on stealing from a guest, I'd wait until the guest's last day in hopes she might not miss the item. Then she'd leave. Are thieves that analytical? I don't know. But I like to make a policy and stick with it.

"Door-pushers" are a huge problem in Las Vegas. These thieves saunter down the long corridors of giant hotels with their arms outstretched, methodically pushing on every door on each side of the hall. Some doors open. Las Vegas police get three hundred to four hundred reports of theft due to door-pushers every month.

"But we know there are more," Officer Priscilla Green told me. "Some hotels prefer not to report them to us, but door-pushers we catch tell us they work there." These are huge Strip hotels that don't want negative publicity.

The risk is completely preventable. Just make certain your door closes tightly when you leave your room. Why wouldn't the door close tightly? Air pressure in hermetically sealed hotels is one possible reason; alignment of door latches or frames are others. We recently stayed in the phenomenal Davenport Hotel in Spokane, Washington, where the doors to suites

Should Have Left It in the Hotel

Gisela and Ludvig Horst checked into their Barcelona hotel and immediately got into an argument. Gisela did not feel comfortable leaving their valuables in the room, though Ludvig was insistent that they should. They'd just arrived from Germany for an Herbalife convention. With thirty thousand international participants in town, each sporting big "I-heart-Herbalife" buttons, every Barcelona hotel was fully booked. The Horsts ended up in the same small, semi-seedy inn Bob and I had chosen for our semi-seedy research. We met them at breakfast the morning after.

The Horsts went out for their evening exploration with everything in Gisela's purse. They joined another Herbalife couple for drinks at an outdoor café on La Rambla. The *avenida* was lively, the June weather delightful. Gisela was enthralled by the entertaining parade of strollers, yet she never forgot caution. Conscious of the value her purse contained, she held it on her lap. The foursome ordered sangriá and let the Spanish nightlife swirl around them.

If the Horsts' cash and passports had been stolen from their hotel room, one might fault them for leaving their things unsecured. Had Gisela hung her purse from the back of her café chair, one could chastise her severely. Had she put it on the ground, out of sight, out of mind, she could be blamed. But Gisela's handbag was securely cradled right under her nose.

Thinking back, Gisela remembered a middle-aged man seated alone at a table behind them. Was it him? She also sensed the bulk of a man moving behind her and had assumed it was a waiter. Without warning, her bag was snatched right off her lap.

The Horsts lost everything. Besides the tremendous paperwork hassle, the mood of their trip was ruined and Gisela was badly traumatized. She blamed herself and lost confidence in her judgment, though she was hardly at fault.

Personal security is an art, not a science. Information and awareness are everything. In the Horsts' situation, I may have done exactly as Gisela did, had I been lacking a suitable suitcase to use as a safe. However, I'd try to split up my goodies, and put as much as possible on my body instead of in a grabbable bag.

took almost a full minute to close, due to hydraulic systems. We couldn't pull the doors closed or hurry them along in any way. Patience was the only option. (Ours always closed properly, eventually.)

One Vegas hotel had a problem with faulty door jambs, which a gang of female thieves, not hotel employees, discovered. With lateral pressure applied, the jambs allowed the doors to be easily forced open, as long as the deadbolt wasn't thrown. How could one protect against such an unforeseen risk? Again, it's a case for locking up small valuables. Use the in-room safe or, as an alternative, your largest luggage.

Drink-drugging is a growing problem in nightclubs, and many nightclubs are located in hotels. Las Vegas is experiencing a serious epidemic of drink-drugging, its police officers told me. The motive is usually rape rather than robbery, but to my mind, rape is the theft of priceless intangibles. As young women are the most frequent victims, Sergeant Shalhoob advises them to look out for one another. "If you're three in a group, two dance, one stays and guards the drinks." It's just too simple to drop a bit of powder into a drink—it takes a fraction of a second.

Robbery is the motive in a "trick-roll," when a prostitute drugs her customer in a hotel room. This, too, is on the increase, as drugs are ever easier to obtain.

Sadly, valet theft is on the rise, primarily at swanky restaurants and nightclubs, many of which are located in hotels. I say sadly because the thieves are employees with a special, fiduciary duty to their customers. We voluntarily entrust our cars to them, assuming they're trustworthy. Must we strip the cars of every valuable possible before handing over the keys? Apparently, we must. An unofficial investigation in Los Angeles found that cash or small items were stolen from one in four cars given to valet parking.

At check-out time, you call a bellman to collect your luggage. You pay your bill, then tip your bellman for loading your bags into a taxi. Did you count your bags? Bellmen at Las Vegas hotels tell me that suitcases are frequently left behind, even when guests are asked to check and sign a luggage release form. Bellmen don't know whose bags are whose. And cabbies often drive to the airport with bags that don't belong to their passengers. "What happens then?" I asked Ed, a bellman at Mandalay Bay. "Some cabs will bring them back to us. Some leave them at the airport, but give us a call and tell us. Others just leave them. Then we have to trace them."

Most hotels offer some sort of bag storage for guests. Say check-out is noon and your flight is not until night, or you visit Las Vegas and want to take an overnight bus trip to the Grand Canyon and leave your club-wear behind. Bob and I frequently take advantage of hotel luggage storage, but only after examining the facility.

A large hotel may have a dedicated room with limited access, possibly kept locked, possibly dispensing luggage tags. This is common in, say, Nairobi, where guests headquarter themselves, then take off on safari with light duffel bags. In small hotels in Venice, Istanbul, and Westport, Connecticut, for example, we've left bags in the hotel manager's office, behind his desk. In Athens recently, the storage option we were offered was out of the question; we opted to rearrange our plans instead. A motley heap of suitcases were piled in the lobby, with nothing but the desk clerk's "eye on them". We've passed on adding our bags to rows of others with rope through their handles, and messy mountains of luggage with netting tossed over them.

Group travelers arriving early, before rooms are available, are urged by their tour leaders to leave their bags and go out. We're often amazed at the unclaimed masses of miscellaneous suitcases in hotel lobbies, extracted from the underbellies of tour buses and left unguarded. Just who is responsible? A young dancer in a show in which we worked lost her lap-top this way. "Just leave your bag there," she was told on arrival, after flying into Stockholm from New York. When she found her emptied back-pack, she got plenty of sympathy, but the nebulous question of accounta-bility was never answered.

Judging the safety of hotel bag storage, whether it's a locked room behind the front desk or organized chaos spread across the lobby floor, means making a personal decision based on your own comfort level. What's in your luggage? Dirty clothes, or expensive electronic equipment? What kind of luggage is it? Hard-shell with generic locks? Soft-sided with zippers? What about lobby traffic, and how many employees exist to oversee the situation? Like most personal safety issues, only you can weigh potential risks against your particular circumstance. The idea is to make an informed decision, not allow happenstance. At some time or other, you're bound to make compromises, but with evaluation, you cut your losses.

Theft Thwarters #3: Hotels

Hotels

- Hotel lobbies are not secure enough to leave bags unguarded.

- Bags entrusted to bellmen are safe. All others are the traveler's responsibility.

- Business travelers: don't leave your laptop or briefcase unguarded at hotel breakfast buffets. "Breakfast thieves" specialize in stealing these at upscale hotels.

- PDAs, cell phones, and laptop computers are particularly attractive booty in foreign countries. If your handheld computer is full of juicy information you'd prefer to keep private, treat its password with extreme care.

- Even seemingly safe cities play involuntary host to roving criminal gangs.

- Make a quick evaluation of safety in your hotel room. Analyze outdoor window access in particular.

- Do not carry your electronic card key in its folder marked with your room number.

- Identify unexpected visitors to your room. Call the front desk to verify the identity of unexpected hotel workers who want access to your room.

- Use your door's deadbolt or chain latch at night. Place a chair in front of the door if there is none.

- Do not leave small, tempting valuables lying around in your room.

- Use the in-room safe for small valuables. (Caveat: safes that use metal keys are not as secure.)

- Make a note to yourself to remember to empty the safe.

- As an alternative safe, use your largest hard-sided luggage that, preferably, has a quality lock.

- Don't expect miracles from tiny padlocks on zipper tabs. A zipper tab is easily twisted off. Yet, in some cases, any lock is better than no lock.

- Always make sure your door closes completely when you leave your room.

- Don't slack off vigilance near the end of your stay just because you feel comfortable and know the staff.

- When forced to carry valuables, split them up in different pockets and carry whatever you can on your body in pouches, money belt, or even in pockets.

- In nightclubs, try not to leave your drink unattended. This is especially important for women. Drink-drugging is a growing problem.

- Count your bags at check-out and be certain everything is loaded into your taxi.

- Assess the risks of lobby luggage storage before taking advantage of the service.

- Make informed decisions about where you leave your belongings and to whom you entrust them.

Luggage

- Lockable, hard-sided luggage is best, preferably made of aluminum. Attach two labels listing your name, country, office or e-mail address, and phone number. At least one label should be adhesive. Do not affix your home address to your luggage; that would tell a perpetrator the location of your empty home. Thieves can inform their partners-in-crime that your home is open for business. Stick a third label inside the suitcase.

- Consider an alternative case for your laptop. A bag that doesn't shout "computer inside" will camouflage an item highly desirable to thieves. Try carrying your laptop case inside another bag.

- You can never obtain 100 percent total security, but aim for a compromise that is comfortable for your travel style.

- Remember: the idea is to increase your awareness and decrease the opportunities for an unfortunate incident.

Rip-Offs: Introducing the Opportunist

5

Speed

A dozen boys swarmed around Gary Ferrari in front of the Sheraton Hotel in Lima. At least, it seemed like a dozen—they'd appeared out of nowhere and were gone in just a few seconds. In that cyclone of baby faces and a hundred probing fingers, they got Gary's wallet and the gold chain from his neck.

"We call them *pirañas*," said Dora Pinedo, concierge at the Sheraton. "They are everywhere."

"I don't know how they got my chain," said Gary, rubbing the red welt on his neck. "It was under my shirt." He didn't realize that the boys had learned to recognize the telltale ridge of fabric that covers any chain worth stealing.

"They're usually seven-, eight-, nine-year-old boys," Dora told us, "and they mob their victim in groups of six to ten. There is nothing one can do with so many little hands all over."

We interviewed Petter Infante, twenty-eight, and Wilmer Sulca, seventeen, both grown-up *pirañas*. We found them at Lima's University Park, where a comedy presentation was taking place in an entertainment pit, rather like a small amphitheater. Hundreds of people surrounded the pit, transfixed. Others loitered around the audience, more sat on cement benches, and many were asleep in the grass. Petter and Wilmer looked at us skeptically but agreed to talk to us after Gori, our interpreter, paid off a policeman patrolling the park.

"But not here," Wilmer said.

"Anywhere you want," said Bob. Right, let's enter their lair, and let's take our fancy equipment in with us. The five of us piled into a taxi and Wilmer instructed the driver in staccato Spanish. Where were they taking us? I looked at Gori for assurance but our fine-boned archeology-student interpreter was not a bodyguard.

Wilmer led us into a garage-like cantina, dark, deserted, music blaring, disco lights flashing. The boys ordered huge bottles of Cristal beer. Bob wired Petter with a microphone and I set up our video camera, hyper-conscious of our vulnerability—read that: scared. My eyes were

Petter, at twenty-eight, is a grown-up piraña. Piraña is the word for Lima's street children who go marauding in packs.

Wilmer, seventeen, has been living and stealing on the streets of Lima since he was five years old.

glued to Petter's left arm, a mass of parallel scars, layer upon layer of them. A cut on his wrist was gaping open, infected. I used the gash to focus the camera.

"The first thing I ever stole was a chicken," Petter said. "I was twelve years old, alone, and hungry. I had small brothers to take care of." Petter's expressive face told a many-chaptered tale of violence: his snaggle teeth were edged with gold, his cheeks cross-hatched with scars.

"I'm best at stealing watches. I just grab it off someone walking, then run. I'm a very fast runner. The victim could never catch me. We call this *arreba tar*. It means run-steal."

He stood to demonstrate his expertise. Bob stood to be victim. "You can see there's nothing in his front pocket, it's flat," Petter said. Then he did a lightning-fast dip and grab into Bob's back pocket. The wallet flew upward with a grand flourish, like the follow-through of a tennis stroke.

"We'll steal anything," Wilmer said, "nothing in particular. It's all easy. It's like a game." Wilmer then showed the same method from Bob's front pocket, finishing with the same exuberant flourish. "*Cocagado*—I'm already gone. By the time the victim realizes, we're *cocagado*."

The knife scars on Petter's arm are like stripes on an officer's shoulders: you have to respect him. You see he's tough and dangerous. He started cutting himself a few years ago.

"If the police catch you, you cut yourself and they release you. They don't want you if you're cut and bleeding."

(A police officer later explained that an injured arrestee must be taken to a hospital, which requires *hours* of paperwork. If an arresting officer is near the end of his shift, he may not want to pursue such lengthy formalities.)

"I'm on the street nine years and I never cut myself," Wilmer said. "I don't like to do that. We don't have the same philosophy, Petter and I. He likes to cut himself, I do not. We think differently."

Petter and Wilmer are opportunists, *pirañas* grown into hardened thieves. Petter thinks nothing of threatening his victims with a knife. I don't know if he ever has or would use it. The boys' main operative is speed.

"We wait at the bus stops and look for someone with a good watch, or something else to take. We wait until the bus doors are ready to close then grab it and run. And sometimes we grab things through the open windows of the bus. We reach inside and grab cell phones, watches, glasses, purses, anything."

Opportunists look for sure bets, for temptations, for the fat wallet protruding from a back pocket "like a gift," as a pickpocket in Prague told me. "We call it 'the other man's pocket,'" a Russian thief revealed; "the sucker pocket," said another. "Tourists make it too easy," complained a man in Prague whose family members were admitted thieves.

Barcelona pickpocket Kharem guided us on a thief's tour of La Rambla. "Just point and talk," Bob instructed him.

But he did more than that. Brazen and fearless, he actually tapped on men's pockets as we fast-walked through the crowd. No one seemed to notice. Nobody gave him a second glance. Kharem, the professional thief, slipped in and out of strangers' personal spheres like a gnat through a window screen.

"Most important is to figure out where the money is. Pants, jacket, waist pouch, backpack. That man has a fat wallet in his jacket pocket,"

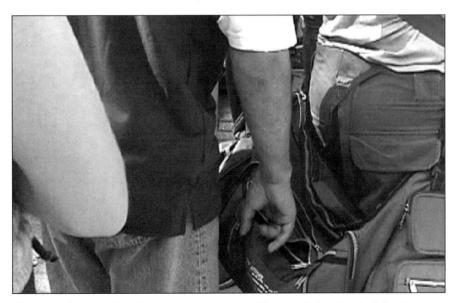

Kharem works a crowd watching street entertainment. He opened, then closed, all the zippers on this bag.

Danger at the Derby

"We do what you do," Bob told the poker-faced pickpocket. "Same job."

From his blank expression, it wasn't clear that he understood. Perhaps he didn't speak English. If he did understand, his mind must have been racing. What could be worse for a pickpocket than being confronted by a stranger? Even one who claims to be a colleague.

"Here, I'll show you." Bob put his hand on the young man's shoulder, dipped into his pants pocket, and extracted a woman's wallet, the same one we'd just watched—and filmed—the pickpocket snag from someone's handbag.

Bob opened the wallet. There was no money in it. The pickpocket watched in stunned silence as Bob turned away with it.

"Excuse me, madam. Is this yours?" Bob offered the wallet to the victim, who still stood just a few yards away, engaged in the spectacle she'd come to witness. The woman accepted the wallet gratefully, but puzzled. She hadn't realized it was missing.

"You see?" Bob asked, returning to the pickpocket. "Same job. You understand?"

"I understand," the young man said. Clearly, he didn't know what was coming. Best to say little, he seemed to think. Speak only when questioned.

It was our first visit to Durban in many years. The climate had changed drastically since the abolishment of apartheid and the switch to a black government. Violent crime in South Africa was frighteningly high now, to the extent that the U.S. State Department, as well as Britain's and Australia's governments, recommended that business travelers to the country employ armed bodyguards. Visitors were warned to stay in their hotels after dark and use extreme caution at all times.

It was a warm spring Sunday when Bob and I landed in Durban's city center. We had intended to wander through the outdoor market when our attention was drawn to a huge crowd on the edge of Central Park. Though we couldn't see beyond the spectators, roaring engines soon informed us that they were watching car races. We hung back a bit and studied the rapt audience.

"Watch those three," Bob said, and I followed his eyes. "Watch their body language."

Within two minutes of our arrival, our eyes were fixed on a trio of suspicious characters. These three did not strain to look over or between the heads of the crowd. They seemed to be as interested in car races as Bob and I were. Instead, they looked at the backs of the spectators. They lingered and loitered a few minutes, then moved on and looked for opportunities among new backsides.

Engines roared and tires squealed. Loudspeakers blared some exciting results. One of the young men had a plastic shopping bag in his hand as, in fact, many people did. But his bag was folded flat in half twice, which gave it a bit of firmness. It could have contained a greeting card, or a small pad of paper. On closer inspection, I noticed the red advertising copy printed on the bag was worn off to the point of illegibility. The folded bag must have been held in a sweaty grip for hours.

The three men positioned themselves around a woman whose purse stuck out behind her. One man moved in on each side of the woman, blocking her purse from the views of anyone to her sides. The third man slowly crowded into the woman from behind, stretching his neck as if trying to watch the race. Slowly, his left hand raised the flattened bag to the purse, where his right hand crept up to meet it. Then, with

(continued)

the plastic bag as a shield and his right hand poised above the purse, he gave the woman a little jostle. A gentle, natural jostle, appropriate for a tightly crowded audience engrossed in vicarious thrills. His skinny elbow raised and lowered then, and Bob and I caught a quick glimpse of brown leather before it was folded into the flattened bag and plunged into the thief's deep pants pocket.

he said, while the would-be victim was still several yards away. "See how his jacket is hanging unevenly." He swept his thumbtip across his forehead in that odd gesture of his. "And this man," Kharem touched the thigh of a stranger. "He has loose cash. Very good. Very easy."

No reader who has even skimmed this book should be the victim of an opportunist. Attitude and awareness are key. Smart stashing is simple. Make it a little difficult and the opportunist will move on to an easier victim. After all, the opportunist isn't the rocket scientist of his profession. (The strategist is.)

Luciano, the Italian tram thief from Naples, is a case in point. Without using the term itself, Luciano described himself as a classic opportunist, and an unsophisticated one at that. He operates exclusively on stealth, not cunning. Although his technical skills sound significant, he never tries to capitalize on his ability. He admits that he rarely makes any special effort to target tourists, although he finds them easier to steal from. The advantages of victimizing tourists had never even occurred to him. That a tourist is unfamiliar with the customs of the city, that a tourist often carries plentiful cash, that they are less likely to find or identify a perpetrator, and that they will rarely return for a court appearance were all facts far beyond his thought process. Neither had he ever noticed a difference in character among nationalities, a factor used to advantage by more analytical thieves.

"When you spoke with Luciano," said Raffaele, a competitor of his, "you spoke with the most stupid of all." No one need be Luciano's victim. Yet, he makes a living from stealing.

What does the opportunist look for? The visibility of a thick wallet is a magnetic attraction. Back pocket, front pocket, it doesn't matter. There are specialists of both. "They think whatever you carry in your pocket is theirs," says Lothel Crawford, New York subway cop, recently retired. A gaping front pocket is an open invitation, as is an open purse, or a purse easily opened. Purses in general are favored targets since they are not part of the body. Purses don't have nerve endings; they can be tampered with.

Speed-driven grabbers like Petter and Wilmer in Lima are crude, unsophisticated, effective thieves. Rather than read the signals sent by flashy jewelry ("this person, compared to you, is wealthy beyond reason and carries riches you can smell, riches you can *have* . . ."), they just snatch the jewelry. There's even a word for it. "*Pescueso* means neck," said Wilmer. "It is also the name for a guy like Petter, who can take a lady's necklace or earrings and she wouldn't have a chance."

Seizure

The bag snatcher who accosted Mary Chipman in Barcelona wasn't so innocuous. When he yanked the Canadian tourist's purse from her shoulder, she fell to the ground and broke her hip. It was the first day of Mary's vacation; the next ten were spent in a Spanish hospital. Nurses there informed her that she was currently their fourth broken-hip bag-snatch victim on the ward! I'm sad to report that bag snatchers in my beloved city have become ever more prevalent and increasingly brutal. The broken arms and collarbones are lodged in another ward of the hospital, and deaths go to the morgue.

How does one die of bag snatching? More than a few women have smashed their heads on the pavement when roughly pushed to the ground by a snatch thief. A woman on an overcrowded trolley car in London was killed after a brutal bag snatcher caused her to fall into traffic. A Dutch businesswoman died after being stabbed by bag snatchers at the Ben Thanh market in Ho Chi Minh City, Vietnam. In a highly publicized case in London, a woman was run over by the car of escaping bag snatchers. Naples, Italy, has seen its share of fatalities thanks to its scooter-riding bandits and their drive-by bag-snatch style.

Tragedies like these can never be foreseen, and the only prevention, short of staying home, is to dress down and refrain from carrying a bag at all. This, I admit, is not always practical.

I must interrupt myself to say that, although Barcelona is currently one of the world's hot spots for bag snatching, I sincerely hope that I don't dissuade anyone from visiting. I am miserable about repeatedly naming this creative, eclectic, cultural capital as the scene of so much crime, but therein lies the paradox. With so much to offer, Barcelona is a tourist Mecca. Geographically and politically, it's a gateway for illegal immigrants. The result is an intimate mélange of haves and have-nots, distraction, desperation, and desire. I say, *go* to Barcelona, but go forearmed with attitude and awareness.

Bob and I advise specific precaution if you know that bag snatching is among a destination's risks, and even if you don't. Walk on the side against the traffic, meaning toward it. If you must carry a purse, use a wide-strapped one worn across your chest, or a short-strapped one with the purse tucked under your arm. Women with handbags should be away from the curb.

Live and learn. I had not yet formulated this rather obvious advice on the day of my own incident. I found myself dazed and wondering, rather inappropriately: was it instinct or anger that made Bob chase my bag snatcher?

He rocketed down the street brandishing the famous umbrella weapon that was so ineffectual in Naples. I had managed nothing more than "Hey!" but my weak protestation was like the starting gun at the Monaco Grand Prix. Two grown men went from zero to sixty in an instant.

I can't say I was caught unaware when the bag snatcher stepped up to meet me, face to face. He calmly looked me in the eyes, seized the strap of my purse with both hands, and yanked it hard enough to break the leather against my shoulder. It happened much faster than you can read that sentence.

I gave my little shout and the creep was off and running, with Bob on his tail. It took me several seconds to realize that I still had the purse clutched tightly in my hands. I could have laughed, but for the fact that my husband was in pursuit of a potentially dangerous criminal in a decidedly unsafe neighborhood.

The street we had walked was full of the necessities of life in this non-touristy part of Barcelona, lined with tiny hardware, shoe repair, and paint shops. We had been directed there, without any specific warning, in search of a few pieces of wood. Peeking through doorways seeking the lumberyard, we revealed ourselves as obvious outsiders. As we strayed ever further from the relative safety of La Rambla, we sensed a vague but growing threat of danger.

My antennas were out way before the interloper trespassed so suddenly into my aura. I didn't see his approach, but I had already assumed a protective posture. Both my hands held the small purse I wore diagonally crossed over my chest.

Bob was a few steps ahead of me and didn't see the confrontation. It only lasted two seconds. It's astonishing what analysis and conclusions the brain can manage in those instants. I thought the man looked ordinary but grave. He stood uncomfortably close and made uncommon eye contact. I thought he would speak. I thought he would ask a question, or offer advice. Against my will, I slipped into the trusting attitude of a traveler in a foreign land. And that was my mistake.

Perhaps I'd have reacted quicker or with more suspicion if the bag snatcher had looked sleazy, mean, or desperate. But he didn't, and I gave him the benefit of any doubt. In those two seconds, the gentleman had all the opportunity he needed to seize the strap of my bag and yank.

My feeble objection was enough to get Bob's attention. He whirled around and leapt into pursuit, his long stride a clear advantage. When the perp dashed into a crowded alley, I thought it was all over. Bob bellowed *"Policia!"* at a volume that would fill an amphitheater. I, far behind, expected to see the escaping sprinter blocked or tripped by the local loiterers.

On the contrary. The sea of people opened for his getaway, then closed up again to watch the tall guy run. They didn't exactly block Bob's path, but seemed to plant themselves firmly as obstacles. Bob had to give up.

Revelations of a Rolex Thief

"You remember that famous movie, the one shot in Naples?" shouted Officer Daniele Conse. "In this restaurant, they filmed that movie. The whole world knows this section of Napoli." He gunned his motorcycle and he, with Bob on the back, left me in the dust on the back of Officer Marco's bike.

Daniele and Marco are *Falchi*—Falcons—two of Naples' anti-theft plainclothes motorcycle warriors. The squad was launched in 1995 to fight, among other criminals, *scippatori,* the pickpockets and purse snatchers who operate on motor scooters. Patrolling the city on souped-up motorcycles, the Falcons fight speed with speed, power with power, and strength with strength.

Our motorcycle excursion through Quartieri Spagnoli was not exactly a wind-in-the-hair power ride, but it was a bracing cop's-eye view and guided tour of one huge crime scene. Hugging the backs of these brawny, spiky-haired, Levi-clad, cool dudes, we felt immune to danger—*there,* at ground level, but in a protective bubble.

Bob and Daniele had stopped to talk with a guy on a Vespa as Marco and I caught up with them.

"This is Antoni, one of the best *scippatori,*" Daniele said. "He's an expert with Rolexes." The cop turned to Antoni: "These are two journalists from America. They want to interview you."

"What are you doing here?"

"We're making a touristic tour," Daniele said with a sweeping gesture.

"How many Rolexes do you take?" Bob asked. He had a video camera in his hand but it was pointed at the ground.

"In a week? It depends. Where are they going to show this movie?"

A street in Naples' Quartieri Spagnoli.

(continued)

Undercover officer Daniele introduces Bob to Antoni, a Rolex thief in Quartieri Spagnoli.

"In America. In Las Vegas. Hey—this man is better than you at stealing!" said Daniele. Antoni didn't react. "Are you filming this? Are you filming me and everything?"

"How many watches do you take in a week?" Bob persisted.

"I take maybe ten Rolexes in one week. Hey, I don't like this movie you're making. You're going to show a bad image of Napoli."

"This guy makes films about crime in all different cities. Quartieri Spagnoli will be famous in America." Daniele said.

"Antoni, how much do you get for one Rolex?" asked Bob.

"Sixteen thousand dollars. For, you know, the one with diamonds all around."

"Now we are friends with Bob. We can visit him in America!" Daniele started his bike.

"Can I call you on the phone?" Bob asked. "Later, when I find someone to speak Italian for me?"

"No, I don't want to give you my phone number."

"Bob is okay, we've known him for many years." Daniele said. Translation: give him your number.

"Okay, you can call me. Here's my number."

"Why is it different? Is it new?"

"Ah, I changed the SIM card." Translation: I'm using a different stolen phone.

Bob and I had wanted a good look at Quartieri Spagnoli ever since our unexpected introduction to a trio of *scippatori*—from behind. We'd heard from other officers that the police don't even go into this district except in squads of four or more. It was a war zone, they told us. Neapolitans disown Quartieri Spagnoli as other Italians disown Naples.

As we rode through the narrow lanes, Daniele told us about his symbiotic relationship with Antoni.

(continued)

"Antoni has a lot of respect for me, that is why he gave you his number. He gives me information about the criminals here. We cooperate."

Antoni is an informer—he rats on major drug activity. In exchange, the Falchi close their eyes to Antoni's vocation. Unless, that is, a tourist comes complaining to the police about a Rolex theft. In those cases, Daniele can have a chat with Antoni, and Antoni can do some digging, find out who did the swipe, and try to recover the item. Not that it always works. . . .

Daniele stopped his bike to point out some of the quarter's highlights.

"Look at all the laundry hanging from the balconies. Typical for this area. And here, this is one of the squares where the mob is very big, the Camorra. They all have their own areas and their own crimes—drugs, prostitution, stealing. . . ."

"Do the grandmothers really sit in the upper windows watching for Rolexes?" I asked. It sounded like a myth, but I'd heard many times that theft here was a family affair.

Someone whistled—the piercing, two-finger type.

"That means police," Daniele said. "They're warning their friends that we're here. Yes, the women sit on their balconies, and when they see something to steal, they call their sons or grandsons to come by on their scooters. It's true." He twisted around to look at Bob. "You must be careful with your video camera. These are gangs of thieves we're passing and they're looking at it. They can steal it."

We paused in front of the funicular, the very one that inspired the classic Neapolitan song "Funiculi, Funicula."

"Here in Piazza Montesanto there are many pickpockets near the underground station. They steal many wallets in this area. And the *funiculare* is here. We have four video cameras watching this Piazza. There's a lot of drug dealing here, too."

Most tourists never venture into these areas of Naples' old town, and it's a shame. Napolitanos are warm and welcoming toward visitors; Bob and I adore their casual, urbane tradition. With its lively outdoor culture and its heart on its sleeve, Quartieri Spagnoli is the heart and soul of the place I call the city of hugs and thugs.

For me, the humiliation suffered by the would-be thief was almost enough. Like a cat with a mouthful of feathers, he ran with nothing more than twelve inches of torn leather strap in his fist. Yet, I was shaken and weak-kneed immediately following the experience, and the after-effects lingered for months. Despite the fact that I wasn't hurt, I lost nothing of value, and Bob hadn't been tripped in the chase, I felt victimized.

After our travel safety lecture one day, a woman came up to me to share some advice. I repeat it here for its comedic value only, since I find it ridiculous to the point of hilarity. "A police officer came to speak to a group at my condo," the woman said, "and he recommended that women carry a purse of this type." She held out her floppy leather bag that zipped across the top. "And we're supposed to carry it like this: strap over the shoulder, but upside down." She donned the bag with its long strap in a normal position, then up-ended just the purse-part, zipper down (which folded the strap), and cradled it on her forearm as if it were a newborn.

"Then, if you think someone's going to snatch it," she continued, "you unzip it—still upside down—and everything falls on the ground."

The absurd image of this scenario delighted me, but I didn't know how to respond politely. I asked the woman: how many false alarms before you give up that tactic? How many times does one chase rolling lipsticks, blowing papers, and scattered parts of smashed cell phones intentionally dumped to the ground? And how would one explain such behavior to a witness who might ask why?

Easy pickings. A woman hangs her purse on the back of her chair at an outdoor café. A woman at the table to the left did the same, then walked away.

You can hardly call it bag snatching when a handbag is left hanging on the back of a chair, free for the taking. We regularly warn people about this unsafe habit. Worse yet are bags placed under chairs. These appeal to opportunists who operate on stealth, rather than speed.

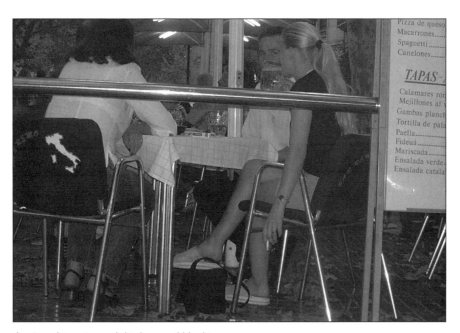

A minor distraction and this bag would be history.

We met the Hansons in Barcelona's American Express office. They were reporting their loss when Bob and I popped in for our irregular count of stolen credit cards, a useful barometer and an excellent excuse to visit the nearby Il Caffe di Francesco on Consell de Cent for superb cappuccino.

The Hansons had been enjoying a lesser brand of coffee and watching the passing-people parade at Tapas-Tapas, a popular sidewalk café near Antoni Gaudi's innovative Casa Mila apartment house.

"We were in the corner and felt safe," Mrs. Hanson said. "There was no apparent risk. Our carry-all was on the ground between us as we sat side by side. The bag contained my purse, our camera, and some small purchases."

Bob and I went directly over to Tapas-Tapas, just a few blocks away. Umbrellaed tables were grouped invitingly on the sidewalk. Surrounding them on three sides, a row of potted ficus trees lent an air of privacy and coziness to the setting. The Hansons had been sitting in a corner, where the dense foliage gave the impression of walls and a sense of security. Rather, it gave a *false* sense of security.

Behind the potted plants, traffic buzzed on Passeig Gracia, and a dim stairway descended to the subway. Can you see the risk now? A person crouching behind the planters might not be noticed. He could simply reach through the "wall," possibly with the aid of a crude hook, snag the bag, and disappear into the subway.

"About five a day," the manager of Tapas-Tapas said, when we asked him how often patrons complained of stolen bags. *Five a day!* Yet management saw no need to change the set-up, and police paid no extra attention to the area.

Many an outdoor dining area is bordered with potted plants—it's a typical arrangement. The close proximity of a subway entrance makes Tapas-Tapas particularly attractive to thieves, but the risk is universal. The solution is to maintain physical contact with belongings. Then you can relax, enjoy your meal, people watch, and appreciate your surroundings without worry. You can tuck a strap under your thigh, put your foot or the chair leg through it, or keep your bag between your feet. Most thieves would rather work on a less-vigilant mark.

As much as we love the city, there's no denying that street thievery is rampant in Barcelona. Yet, bag snatching, in one form or another, is a universal crime.

Bag snatchers, like pickpockets, can be divided into two categories: the opportunists, who include desperate novices like my perp, and the strategists, who create their own advantages.

Even Stockholm, rightfully considered one of the world's safest modern cities, has its share of street crime. Kajsas fish restaurant in Hötorget Saluhallen, which serves the ultimate fish soup, posts warnings of bag takers. Thieves use their own coats to cover a bag hanging on the back of a chair or on the floor, then walk away with it concealed in the folds of the fabric.

Bob and I once demonstrated these moves for the Swedish press. I hung my bag on the back of my chair as photographers focused and Bob prepared to play the perp. Immediately, a woman came to my side and scolded me, in Swedish, for hanging my bag behind me. She admitted to having been a victim only three weeks before, in this very location. She had seen the man take her bag and she shouted. The man dropped her bag and got away.

Pointing out the photographers, I explained that we were actually demonstrating the crime, and invited the woman to be our model victim. She agreed, and told her story with authority.

In St. Petersburg, Russia, we saw a camera ripped right out of a tourist's hand. This was inside a rather nice department store on Nevsky Prospekt, a presumed safety zone, where tourists and locals alike are apt to let their guard down. In parts of South Africa, even drinks are fair game. If you walk along the street sipping a juice or soft drink, a young man may very well take possession of it.

"Why?" I asked a South African in Durban. "Because they can? To show dominance? As a threat?"

"Probably they're thirsty," she answered. "They can't afford to buy a soda."

Wristwatches are a classic subject of seizure. The problem is not widespread, but concentrated largely in specific locales. Naples, Italy, is only one of them.

José, a day visitor there, stopped on Via Toledo to photograph a colorful produce stand. As he walked away with his wife, his Rolex was snatched from his wrist. He turned in time to see a teenage boy running up into the narrow alleys of Quartieri Spagnoli, bystanders watching with no apparent concern. A cruise ship captain had his Rolex ripped off from the perceived safety of a taxi stopped in traffic, as he rested his arm on the open window. And a grocer we met, a *Napolitano,* said the motorcycle bandits, *scippatori,* had tried to grab his Rolex four times, and finally succeeded. He had a new one now, but showed us the cheap watch he switched to before leaving his store every day with the Rolex in his pocket.

In Caracas, seventeen members of an organized tour paused in a square to view a statue of Bolivar. While the tour guide lectured, a pair of men in business suits jumped a Japanese couple who stood at the back of the group. They were wrestled to the ground, their Rolexes pried off their wrists, and the well-dressed thieves were out of sight before anyone could spring into action.

After watching Bob demonstrate watch steals in his show, people come up to us with wrists outstretched. "But they couldn't get this one, could they? It's even hard for me to unclasp." Bob's theatrical techniques are totally unlike the street thieves' methods. Bob's stage steals are designed to climax with the surprise return of an intact watch. The thief, on the other hand, does not care if the victim notices or if the watch breaks. In the street, a watch thief gets his quick fingers under the face of the watch and pulls, snapping the tiny pins that connect the watch to its strap.

The readily recognizable Rolex is a universal symbol of wealth. Its instant identification factor makes it not only a conspicuous target, but also highly desirable on the second-hand market. Even a fraction of its "hot" price brings big bucks to the thief and the fence.

Outside of Naples, in South Africa, Brazil, and England, for example, seizure of Rolex watches is big business, often perpetrated by Nigerian gangs who send shipments of these status symbols to eager dealers in the Middle East. Who would guess that watch snatching is so organized, so global?

Stealth

On her recent trip to London, Diane Breitman went to see the hit musical *Mamma Mia* at Prince Edward's Theatre in Soho. She had seat number one in a row near the front: the seat was all the way against the left wall. The row in front of Diane was empty; the row in front of that was occupied.

During the overture, a lone man took the seat directly in front of Diane. He irritated her by humming along with the songs, so she noticed him. He also moved a lot, first slouching back, then leaning way forward, back and forth. After a while, he got up and left, bent over so as not to block others' views.

Some time later, the woman in front of Diane, two rows ahead and also in the seat against the wall, looked back. Shockingly for a lady at the theater, she clambered over the back of her seat and got into the empty row between her seat and Diane's. She turned to Diane.

"Did you see the man who was sitting in front of you?"

"Yes, sort of."

"He stole my wallet!" she hissed. "My purse was on the floor at my feet, against the wall. When I looked for it, it was under and behind my seat. I only noticed because I needed a tissue."

What sort of thief would buy an expensive ticket to the hottest play in London? Possibly one who expected to collect many rich and neglected wallets. Could he have snuck in without a ticket? Highly unlikely. Prince Edward's Theatre is one of the few with a security staff. Guards and video surveillance, however, only monitor the lobby and chaotic sidewalk area in front of the theater. My theory is that the perpetrator bought a ticket for pittance after the show had started from one of the resellers who loiter in front of the theater. He may have changed seats several times, and stolen several wallets. There are no cameras inside the theater. Security officers acknowledged this incident but said reports like this one are extremely rare.

They may *not* be rare at the Mariinskiy Theatre in St. Petersburg, Russia, where our friend Vladimir had arranged to take us to see Verdi's *Forces of Destiny*. Well-meaning Vladimir, who wanted to treat us, had purchased "Russian" tickets, which cost a fraction of "foreigner" ticket prices. At his suggestion, we stopped speaking English as we entered the theater and tried to effect gloomy Russian expressions, but ticket-takers instantly recognized us as foreigners and rejected our tickets. Vladimir was mortified. We tried to pay full price then, but didn't have enough rubles and the box office didn't accept American Express, the only card we had on us. Eventually Vladimir found a sympathetic ear and we were allowed to sneak in. He'd obtained excellent seats in the historic theater.

At intermission, we mingled among the audience on the mezzanine, in the lobby, and in the stairwells. We were off duty, but Bob's trained eyes leapt to a pair of thieves in the stairwell bottleneck. It was an ideal situation for them, and what opera-goer would be on guard inside the gold-leafed glory of the Mariinskiy?

"We have many theaters and museums in St. Petersburg," Officer Alina Kokina told us in the St. Petersburg police station. "Pickpockets love to work inside them. They like to work on foreigners. They judge from a person's appearance how much money there might be." She paused. "To be

The Nocturnal Sting and the Bite

Skansen, Stockholm's outdoor museum, suffered a nasty spate of pickpocketing incidents one midsummer. Up to eight known incidents per day occurred within the dark confines of the nocturnal animal exhibit, a part of Skansen's aquarium.

Jonas Wahlström, owner of the Månskenshallen (Moonshine Hall), had an idea. He placed a particularly irritable five-pound Australian beaver rat into the shoulder bag of an aquarium employee, and had her mingle with visitors at the exhibit.

An earthy smell permeated the cave-like area, and the only light came from the dimly lit habitats. Visitors tended to murmur softly, as if they might otherwise disturb the animals. Therefore, it was shocking to everyone when a deathly human scream erupted and a heavy animal shot up toward the low ceiling before thudding to the ground.

There was havoc, of course. Visitors screamed and clumped together as far as possible from the hubbub, too curious to flee. When the poor animal fell, the aquarium employee who had been wearing it dropped to the floor and trapped it with her shoulder bag before it could cause further harm to anyone else or itself. No one saw the man who screamed.

The badly bitten pickpocket left a trail of blood on his way out, and it is a testament to Swedish mentality that he escaped so easily. The trap was laid, the bait was fresh, the exits unguarded.

Mdubuzi, a pickpocket in Durban, South Africa, stole a wallet from a woman watching a car race. Bob stole it from Mdubuzi and returned it to the victim.

a pickpocket was a prestigious profession during the war. Now they just do it out of desperation."

That thievery has crept into the realm of privileged society should remind us that a habit of prevention will serve us well. It would help in department stores, too, where female pickpockets often specialize in lifting wallets from purses on the shoulders of victims. We've seen this in many department store surveillance tapes. It usually happens at a busy cash register, where the pickpocket uses a coat over her arm to cover her stealthy moves.

I've discussed opportunists who operate on speed and seizure. A more sophisticated subcategory depends on stealth. Mdubuzi, a pickpocket we spoke with in Durban,

Two friends of Mdubuzi examine a wallet they just obtained. It had no money in it.

South Africa, uses stealth to steal from women's purses, his forte. So does Plaid, a thief drawn to men's trouser pockets—front, back, and cargo-type.

We watched Plaid prey for an hour before we spoke with him, but understand: although a pickpocket's behavior may give him away, the close proximity in which he works and the cover he uses to shield his business often make it impossible to verify his vocation. This is precisely what makes them so difficult to arrest. Many penal codes require a witness to the act, a clear view of a hand in a pocket. Obviously, a pickpocket won't steal when a uniformed cop is in the vicinity, and plainclothes police are often easy to detect. Bob makes a game of it. He looks for a strong build, observant eyes, confidence and authority in body language, shoes suitable for running, the bulk of a radio and other equipment. Savvy street thieves make the same analysis.

"Plaid Shirt," forty-six, patiently preys on distracted La Rambla tourists. He specializes in the back and cargo pockets of men's pants.

"I can see them with eyes in back of my head," Kharem told us. He turned and ruffled his salt-and-pepper hair to show his chimerical eyes. "I can *smell* them."

"Are there more plainclothes police now, after September 11?" Bob asked him.

"It doesn't matter what they wear, I recognize them. Anyway, the same officers work in uniforms and in regular clothes, so I know them."

Yikes. How will Barcelona ever solve its problem?

When it comes to catching thieves in the act, Bob and I have an enormous advantage over law enforcement officers. We don't fit any of Bob's profile points except for observant eyes, which sunglasses cover. Plus we're a couple. Plus we hold hands.

We have disadvantages, too. We often don't speak the local language. We have no authority to arrest. We are not prepared for a physical scuffle. And Bob, with his narrow 6'5" build does not exactly blend into a crowd. But, pictures we get. Video footage, we get.

On observing the behavior of someone like Plaid, we label him a suspect. We follow and film, yet we can't be certain he's a thief.

"He could be a pervert," says Detective Crawford. "Watch his eyes." Plaid's eyes said wallet. His furtive fingers opening buttons said pickpocket. We stayed glued to his back until he gave up.

"Let's go talk to him." Bob was already trotting toward him. I had to run to catch up.

A Perimeter Pocket Parade

La Rambla: the ramble. To ramble is to move about aimlessly, casually, or for pleasure. To follow an irregular course. As a noun, it's a leisurely, lengthy walk.

The marvelous promenade by that name is in Barcelona, Spain. The behavior of its populace is predictable. Individuals know where they're going or they don't. They're hurrying or meandering, focused or spaced-out. They're tourists and locals, business people and vacationers, jetlagged, wondrous, drunk, bored, frustrated, and everything in between. People are strolling, watching, sitting, eating, and drinking. Large and small clusters of people gather and disperse like afternoon clouds, watching artists at work, living statues, musicians, street performers, and one another.

On one crowded summer Sunday, Bob and I patrolled the perimeters of the street performers' audiences. Of all the thieves and con men we watched that day—and there were many—"Plaid Shirt" was the slickest. I locked onto him because of his smile.

A Spanish folksinger had attracted an audience of hundreds. Backpackers were camped long term on the ground, and people stood four and five deep behind them in a giant circle, enjoying the free concert.

Plaid Shirt was neatly dressed, and I almost eliminated him on the basis of the thick wallet in his back pocket. His gray plaid shirt tucked into dark blue jeans did not grab my attention. The windbreaker he carried over his arm was a tip-off, but not a dead giveaway. I had considered a sweater myself that morning, and wished for one in the evening.

What raised my antennas was his behavior. Plaid Shirt sidled up close into the back of the attentive audience. After a minute, a man beside him turned and glared at him. My suspect smiled in response and took half a step back. But that smile! It was the paradigm of shit-eating grin.

Plaid Shirt slowly and calmly relocated, pressing himself into another section of the crowd. He did this repeatedly, never staying more than two minutes in one spot. I tagged onto him, stepping right in behind or beside him. Whenever he turned to leave, I swiveled away or moved in the opposite direction.

Later, Bob joined me with his camera. Plaid continued his pattern of getting close, then backing off. When he was glared at, he proffered his cat-ate-canary grin, but more often, he was not noticed at all.

'Round and 'round the periphery we went. After Bob got some footage of Plaid, I moved even closer and learned his secret specialty. With absolute stealth and fingers like feathers, Plaid lifted the flaps on men's cargo pockets—those low-down side pants pockets—and unbuttoned them. Despite his use of a jacket for cover, I saw him unbutton three cargo pockets and one hip pocket on four men. He probably opened many others I couldn't see.

I did not, however, see him steal any wallets. If he'd gotten anything, he would have left, at least long enough to dump the leather.

Why did he leave each mark after only opening the button? Did he sense the men had felt him? Was he just setting up for a later approach? Most of his targets seemed not to have sensed anything amiss.

Amazed that he hadn't wisened to me, I began to think of Plaid as a hapless fool. We'd circled and circled the audience together, moving in, pausing, moving on. For forty-five minutes I followed Plaid's balding head while he failed to notice me. With my bright white dress and big curly hair, it's not as if I were totally inconspicuous.

(continued)

Meanwhile, Bob dared not get close, although he may as well have. Plaid was concentrating so intently he wouldn't even have noticed a six-foot-five videographer hovering over him. But Bob hung back while Plaid and I traced a flower-petal design around the hand-clapping fans, curving in and out at irregular intervals.

Plaid moved in behind a man with a child balanced on his shoulders. The man swayed gently with the music and the child tapped her thigh. Plaid lowered his jacket and positioned his body, attempting to block sight lines. I snuck in closer, in time to watch Plaid lift the flap of the father's cargo pocket, and slowly open the button. I motioned for Bob to come near. This was a good opportunity with enough of a view.

Plaid worked meticulously. Stealth was his main operative, with nerve and patience tied for second and a goofy smile his ace in the hole. He kept his face forward and head straight; only his eyes flicked down now and then. Father and child were oblivious. The music swelled.

Plaid took a half step away. No reaction from the mark. He moved back in and lowered his jacket again. Bob slipped up behind me and I edged away, letting him have the sightline. In the background now, I went crazy not knowing. Was Plaid extracting the wallet? Was Bob getting it on camera? What would we do afterward: alert the father or try to talk to Plaid? I crept up, trying to see. . . .

Interruption!

Have I described La Rambla's comical chair patrolman? He controls the rows of chairs on the upper end of the boulevard, collecting a few pesetas for the privilege of resting tired feet in prime people-watching seats. With his many-pocketed vest, visor cap, and change purse at his waist, he looks like a circus clown's imitation of a policeman. For years we've seen him waddling around his territory, a stern eye on his lucrative concession, quasi-defender of all he surveys.

A shrill whistle blew, not far from our ears.

The superintendent of chairs marched toward us, pointing.

"Pick-pock-et!" he said, the whistle dropping from his mouth to his chest. "*Attencione!*"

The concert continued. The father and child still swayed to the music. Only three people reacted to the pretend officer's accusation, and we three rearranged ourselves into an eccentric perimeter parade.

Plaid beat it around the circle and we followed. He *still* didn't seem to be aware of us, the witless dolt. Like Plaid, I dodged cars in the street where the crowd stretched to the curb, but Bob was slower with a heavy camera bag on his shoulder. I waited for him, keeping an eye on Plaid, who had abandoned the game and now stood at a closed lotto booth.

What was he doing there? He was facing an inward corner, a niche in the wall of the kiosk, very close, but looking away, toward me. He was doing something with his hands. I stared at him, not worried now about being noticed. As before, Plaid looked innocently away from his busy hands.

Bob reached me. "Where is he?"

"One o'clock—at the kiosk. I bet he's dumping a wallet!"

Plaid finished and strode away. I ran to the kiosk and, raising my sunglasses, peered closely into the dark shadow of the niche.

Foul fumes hit me in the face.

"He was peeing! Disgusting!"

"*Scusa,*" Bob called, "*por favor . . .*" He was mixing up his languages in the excitement.

Plaid stopped and bestowed an empty grin on us.

"Do you speak English?"

"No, no English. I speak French. And I speak Algerian." Plaid held up his hands as if he were off the hook and turned to continue on his way.

"*En francaise, c'est bien,*" Bob said, dredging up his French. "We want to talk to you." He tossed the video camera to me.

"Okay, nice to meet you." Plaid offered his hand. Bob shook it without hesitation, neatly stealing Plaid's watch at the same time. I was still fumbling with the camera so half the watch steal was filmed upside down.

"We'd like to ask you some questions." Bob dangled the watch in front of Plaid, who glanced at his naked wrist then back to Bob. He broke into a bewildered smile.

"That's superb. Please . . ."

Bob will often steal something from a thief then return it for a reaction. His unique talent instantly establishes rapport with an outlaw and, more often then not, they'll talk to us.

Plaid, an opportunist whose method is stealth, is a lone wolf. He works solo, without a partner. His neat clothes and haircut, decent shoes, and polite manner are calculated to blend into a crowd. He's a chameleon. We call him a gentleman thief, a type almost impossible to detect.

"I want you to explain for me—"

"Why me?"

"Because we have watched you work." Bob tried to explain that he is an "*artiste,*" a stage performer, but Plaid couldn't grasp the concept of stealing as entertainment.

"Please, don't tell anyone what I do. I know this is bad work. You know, this is Spain, and there is no job for me. I have no papers . . . that's why I'm doing this. Because I have a child to feed. See, I have reasons to steal, because I need to feed my baby."

He tried to give Bob a little advice, one pickpocket pal to another. "Use your brain, be smart. You don't need violence. Use your mind."

Plaid took a few steps backward, itchy to make his escape. "You need patience to do this. Now I must go. Let me say good-bye."

And the gentleman thief was gone, an invisible germ in an oblivious crowd.

Motion

The foot of Charles Bridge, in Prague, is alive with movement. People come and go, lounging and looking, snapping pictures, sipping sodas, eager not to miss a thing on their own personal agendas. Souvenir kiosks

Is Nothing Sacred Anymore?

Anthony Powell hovered on the fringes of Princess Diana's funeral, lifting wallets from the handbags and pockets of devastated mourners. *At Princess Diana's funeral!* He edged up to his grieving marks as they waited in line to photograph the brilliant floral tributes piled against the Kensington Palace gates. Powell had a female accomplice to whom he passed his ill-gotten gains. She exchanged sorrowful glances with each intended victim before stuffing their cash and valuables into a bag suspended from her waist.

At thirty-two years old, Anthony Powell may have been at the height of his specious career. Or perhaps he'd have gone much further, making international "business trips" in order to attend major world events where pickings are plentiful.

Like all successful pickpockets, Anthony Powell knew the operating maxim put so succinctly by Detective Crawford of New York: *distraction before extraction.* It's fair to assume that most of the funeral crowd were upset, distressed, and experiencing emotional turmoil. What a perfect milieu for a pickpocket.

In court, a witness described watching the thief "twitch his fingers like a gunfighter in a cowboy film" as he reached toward a mark's bulging hip pocket. The observant citizen had used her cell phone to call police. She forfeited the formalities of the funeral and kept her attention on the pickpockets until the police arrived. The couple was arrested and found to be carrying a large amount of cash in sterling and at least ten foreign currencies, several wallets, and credit cards not in their names.

Their apartment in southwest London was searched later on that unfortunate September 6th, and the evidence was damning. Well over a hundred empty wallets were found, and, under the mattress, a rainbow of currency from around the world. It was quite obvious that the couple had been doing this for a while.

What kind of person could prey on distraught mourners at a funeral, I wonder? How heartless must one be to prowl and pilfer on such a heart-wrenching day of international sadness? Was the man entirely lacking in compassion? Was he deranged?

"Totally unscrupulous parasites," a judge called Powell and his partner, as they were each sentenced to three years in jail.

attract tight knots of tourists who admire glass animals, wooden puppets, and mad-hatter hats.

Bob and I were staking out a pair of well-dressed women with two teenage boys. One of the women carried a blazer slung over one shoulder. As we surreptitiously observed the foursome, we pantomimed the restless and fidgety movements of people waiting for tardy friends, impatiently glancing at our watches and scanning the streets. Simultaneously, we strained to see over and around the milling mob.

The team showed us numerous repetitions of the same choreography—thievery in motion. As pedestrians waited to cross the street, the young boys positioned themselves in front of the target victim chosen by the women, and the women closed in behind. When the light changed, the

The two women on the left and the two boys on the right are a pickpocket team in Prague. Their most recent victim is at center, with her hand on her purse.

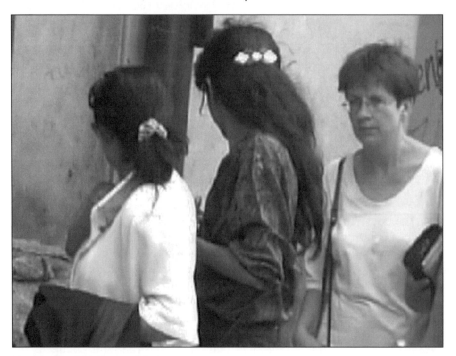

Two women pickpockets and their accuser.

When in Prague, Czech Your Wallet

Despite a sleepless night on the train, we hit the cobblestones as soon as we had dropped our bags and admired our room. The late-summer crowd of cheap tourists absorbed us into their mass migration.

Since pickpockets operate where tourists congregate, we allowed the happily drifting crowd to sweep us along the narrow lanes. It wasn't easy to peel our eyes away from the intriguing marionette shops, enticing beer joints, and the Renaissance-costumed concert touts. But our mission meant scrutinizing people, not souvenirs and architecture. We disciplined ourselves to study the throng and began to get used to the faces, rhythm, and tempo around us.

When we emerged into a sunny clearing, we found ourselves at the foot of Charles Bridge, a magnet for tourists. The many graceful arches of this medieval bridge step across the broad Vltava River to the Mala Strana area. Mala Strana is a popular pub and restaurant district, and a little further up the hill is Prague Castle. So Charles Bridge is heavy with pedestrian traffic all day and into the night. Among its eighteenth-century statues, artists and craftsmen ply their wares and musicians play everything from classical to klezmer. The bridge is a destination itself.

We realized at once that the square at the foot of Charles Bridge offered a unique opportunity for pickpockets. A street of wild traffic and speeding trams separates old town from Charles Bridge. Everyone wishing to get from one place to the other must cross the street here at a stoplight. Crowds of a hundred or more people, mostly tourists, quickly accumulate on both sides of the street. Pickpockets have ample time to locate a mark, get in position, and work them while they cross.

An affectionate couple on the street corner caught our attention in a big way. When the light changed and the traffic paused, they crossed the busy street among a mob of gawking tourists. But three quarters of the way across the street, they abruptly turned and crossed back to where they had begun.

There they stood, again waiting to cross with the next gathering crowd. The man's hand casually rested on the woman's right shoulder. The woman had a blue blazer hanging from her left shoulder. They were better dressed than any of the summer tourists, but somehow didn't quite look like local business people, either.

The woman sidled up to a man waiting to cross. The light changed. The pedestrians stepped off the curb and surged around the nose of a tram, which had come to a stop in the crossers' territory.

The man shifted his hand to the woman's left shoulder, where he anchored her blazer. The woman used her left hand to extend the blazer, completely shielding her work. As we all reached the opposite curb, I fought through the crowd and tried to speak with the elderly gentleman who was the woman's target.

"Where are you from?" I asked him.

"Greece," his wife said. The man was old and hard of hearing.

"Does he have his wallet?" I asked.

The wife didn't understand.

"*Portofoli?*" I asked, pointing to the old man's pocket and hoping I remembered the correct Greek word for wallet.

(continued)

> The wife felt her husband's pocket and looked up at me in alarm. I looked wildly around for the affectionate couple but they were gone. Thinking frantically for the Greek word for pickpocket, I tried Spanish and Italian. Finally, *klepsimo*. The woman understood, but why not—the wallet was gone. She hurried away from me before I could say anything else, as if I were the thief.

boys stepped off the curb, then hesitated—*stalled*—causing the mark to bump into them. The women naturally crashed into the mark and, in the moment of physical contact, dipped into the victim's pocket.

Over half an hour, as they repeated their scripted moves, the two women occasionally lifted their heads to scan the crowd but, for the most part, they laughed, chatted, and gently scolded the boys as they worked. They appeared as natural and at ease as every other individual on the square, and possessed the intersection with confidence. Nothing would give them away to the casual observer, unless one noticed that they never left the intersection. What tourist, or local for that matter, crosses and recrosses the same street, again and again?

I used the words *choreography* and *scripted moves,* which usually do not apply to opportunists. While this outfit utilized a minor strategy, I wouldn't call them strategists. They went for the easy marks, made many efforts, and had a high rate of failure. They didn't invest much in each setup and were not noticed by a newly replenished crowd.

Often, the team targeted women with large handbags. Under the cover of the jacket-tool, they delicately dipped and groped for treasure. We saw them get nabbed twice in that half hour. Once, when they crossed late, the foursome got stuck on the narrow median strip with their victim. Trapped together, the victim and her husband accused the women in German. Cars, trucks, and trams careened wildly around them. Appearing frustrated, the victim repeatedly opened the flap of her own bag, demonstrating what she knew the two women had done. The thieves pretended ignorance and refused to respond.

When the light finally changed and the opponents were freed from their traffic island prison, they stormed off in opposite directions. Bob and I caught up with the victim and learned that nothing had been stolen. But she had felt a hand in her purse. She was alert, she was quick, and she was furious.

So many gangs like these prey on visitors to Prague that, combined with well-known taxi scams and restaurant overcharges, the city's reputation for tourism has been seriously damaged. Group tour leader Graham Bell, of London, traveled to Prague with a group of twenty-one. Of those, nine were pickpocketed. Nine who left themselves open to opportunists—

a totally unnecessary state. Bob and I would encourage any of our readers to visit Prague for it's stunning beauty—*you* will go prepared.

Impedence

Similar to the Prague teams, but even more sophisticated, was a South American gang regularly devastating an intersection on Fifth Avenue in New York City. A famous jewelry store on that corner mounted an offensive that starred several high-powered video cameras. The gang was made up of Jenny (the dip), three blockers, and a stall. They worked the intersection for hours at a time with brazen confidence and utter impunity. Each time Jenny made an illicit withdrawal, she counted the money in her hand—right out in the open—and divvied it up among her cohorts while crossing the street behind their victim. That way, NYPD Detective Crawford said, if accused, no single member would be carrying too much cash. Well, they might be, considering they made up to $8,000 per day, according to Crawford.

Like the Prague gang, Jenny's danced an intricate choreography practiced until it appeared effortless. Their maneuvers impeded the victims' forward progress, but they often performed in motion as well, tightly clustered around a victim as they crossed the street together. Jenny's hand groped in a pocket or purse, and her assistants positioned to block the views of other pedestrians. They did not, however, block the view from above, where mounted surveillance cameras tracked them like hawks tracking mice. The gang was arrested and Jenny served three years in prison.

While impeding employs a brilliant strategy that is simplicity itself, an opportunity must present itself. Therefore, I consider it an avoidable theft. None of us need be victims of impeder-thieves. We've seen the impedence technique used at doorways, including bank and department store doors, at turnstiles, at the entries of trains and buses, and at already-existing bottlenecks on sidewalks. Prague's Wenceslas Square has a beauty: a subway stairway in the middle of a sidewalk, which forces pedestrians into a narrow passage. Thieves are known to prey there. Revolving doors are also frequent settings, and there, the door itself does the impeding. A purse is snagged just as a woman disappears through the doorway, leaving her stuck and her valuables exposed.

Subcategories of impedence include those who work on public transportation, which I'll discuss in chapter 6, and those who script their teams like thirty-second plays—tight as a television commercial—which I'll expose in chapter 7. In all impedence thefts, though, three ingredients are required: a stall who hinders the victim, a dip who extracts the goods, and *accessible valuables*. In other words, it's preventable.

Playing the Whiz

Johnnie Downs came from a good family but got his education on the streets.

"I used to go on what they call—you know, every town got a Broad Street, a Main, or Canal Boulevard. I used to go there. I met a guy down there. His name was Blue and he was a trolley car man. That's what he called himself. He loved the trolley cars because you could jump on and jump off when you wanted to.

"When I first got out there, he would ask me to get a crate. And he'd stand me on this crate, and I'd look into this bank window, and I'd watch a guy. On a certain day of the month, I'd watch this guy get an envelope with money. And wherever the guy put the money at, Blue'd tell me to tell him.

"Then he'd give me a whole bunch of pennies, and he'd tell me that, when the guy gets on the trolley car, on the second step of the trolley car, drop the pennies. And when I hear the kiss sound, step to the side, let the guy get up, make sure the trolley door closes, and walk off. . . . That's all I had to do." Johnnie was a stall.

"Eventually I realized Blue wasn't paying me enough. And I said, I can do this and pay myself. I can, what they call, fire the whiz.

"It's the stick, shade, and wire. The stick is what you call the stall, the wire's the one who plays the sting, and the shade is the one who blocks his open view. If you're playing a man on his left leg—the money, or the hide, or whatever is on the left front pocket, right? The stick is in front, I'm the wire, the shade's gonna block the inside view from here. So it's the stick, shade, and wire. A three-man team is always the best team.

"It's also called a cannon, or a shot player. They call you a pickpocket if you stay local. Locals are just pickpockets, and once you cross state boundaries, then you enhance your skill—you have to enhance your skill to go in a state where you know no one and you're going to try to survive.

"You go to a laid-back town that don't have no whiz players coming through the town, you can go and warm the town up for at least thirty days. Get you three weeks of work before the investigators come out and put the tip on fire. A tip's a crowd. Then you move on. It's a traveling game. That's what it is. You must travel once you become more than a pickpocket. A pickpocket is considered local. Once you become playing the cannon, or a whiz, you must travel.

"In Chicago, they come up playing pappies [men]. In the South, they play nannies [women]. So you learn how to pick a purse better than you learn how to pick a pocket down South. In the west, up north, in New York, you learn how to pick a pocket better than you learn how to pick a purse. For many years, I just played purses. So I could get in a purse, take a wallet out, take the credit cards out of the purse, she's still asleep, put the purse back in, zip it back up, and let her go. If she's standing in line at the bus or whatever.

"Then I found out that men carry the most money. Nine out of ten men, you can see where men have their poke at, or their hide. Some guys weigh three hundred pounds, you can look right in their pockets and see everything they got.

"I don't really prefer any one pocket, but sometimes upstairs is better than downstairs. Sometimes, on the butt is better than off the leg. When I go upstairs, usually I play a guy that's already sitting down on the bus.

"First you fan him—you feel your vic up to see where the money is. You use a very light touch, like the wind. When I fan, I'm gonna come across you. I want to do it myself, if I'm going to play the sting. I want to feel the size of the sting, how it feels, everything.

"When it's like that [the wallet sideways in the pocket], we say it's in the bed. You stand it up first, then you take it out from that position. I say, 'Pappy got a sting laying in the bed,' if I'm working with someone else. What you'd call a stall, or what we call stick, would know that I may need an extra second or so.

"Every sting or hide or poke we play is always played differently. If you commit yourself to this life, you have to go heartedly. What we call heart is nerve. It's all about the victim putting himself in a vulnerable position, because a vulnerable position for a vic may not be vulnerable for the whiz player.

"I'm never nervous. You can't play nerves. If you play nerves it's time for you to forget it. It's time for you to get out of the game. That's the number one thing I explained to you. You got to have nerve, then you acquire your skill. If you don't have the nerve, you can't acquire the skill. Nerve is number one—what they call heart. Your heart got to be into it. You got to love this. It's got to be the biggest turn-on you ever could think about."

Impact

Thieves who operate with stealth, motion, and impedence strive to minimize contact with their victim. Zero face time is their preference. Minimal body contact, zero notice, zero recognition. Others, though, cause contact and use it to their advantage.

We met one of these physical-types years ago in Tangier, Morocco. He claimed to be retired and agreed to talk about his former career, though he was reluctant to demonstrate his moves. However, at the end of our interview, without explanation, he sort-of hugged Bob, bounced around on his toes a bit, and swiped Bob's prop wallet, an empty one he carries around for occasions like these.

A year or so later, we met up with another practitioner.

We had been watching a couple of clumsy pickpockets as they snuck a wallet from a German tourist's backpack. But before the thief could move away, he fumbled and dropped the wallet.

The victim wheeled around. Instantly, the pickpocket bent and picked up the wallet, politely offering it to his unwitting mark, who thanked him. They shook hands. The thieves drifted away, back on the prowl. First we asked the German: your backpack was zipped—how do you think your wallet fell out? "I have no idea," he replied, unwilling to dwell on the incident.

We left him with his perplexity and caught up with the rogue pair, asking if they spoke a little English. Very little. French? *Oui,* they were Algerian.

"We are not police," Bob began in French, "but we saw you take the man's wallet."

"Oh, no, *monsieur* dropped it!"

"We want to know your specialty, what kind of stealing you're best at. For research!"

"*Oui,* research!" The men laughed nervously, but made no move to leave us. They glanced at each other, then, suddenly, the taller of the two—the one who'd done the stealing—slung his arm around Bob's shoulders. Taking quick, tiny steps in place, he twisted his body left and right.

"Play soccer? Football?" He moved his legs against Bob's as if to trip him.

Bob stiffened, aware of this maneuver, this playful sports trick. But he had a real wallet in his back pocket, containing real money. He couldn't allow the tactic to play out. He slapped his hand over his back pocket, trapping the thief's hand in his grip.

"Enough!" Bob said.

"No football, eh? No research." The thief transferred his embrace to his partner, and the two ambled off.

Later that same afternoon, Bob and I both zeroed in on a well-dressed gentleman in a beige sport jacket. We tracked him at a distance. When he stopped, we bent to smell a nearby flower display, moved closer and considered a postcard rack, closer yet and studied a tabletop menu.

He took off again in a hurry and Bob aimed the video. Suddenly he was doubling back toward us and past us, disappearing in a crowd. We ran to catch up, sensing this was the moment. We burst into the moving crowd a moment too late. Our suspect was down on one knee, brushing and shaking the lower pant leg of his startled victim. He rose and apologized, as if he'd been trying to help.

The victim thanked him, but didn't know what for. He was dazed and befuddled when I accosted him, asking brusquely if he still had his money. He felt his front pants pocket. No! It was gone! Two thousand dollars! His head swiveled wildly. Bob was filming. There he goes, I yelled, but the thief was gone.

"He wanted to play football!" the victim said. "Right there in the crowd!"

Our multi-talented pickpocket acquaintance Kharem later demonstrated the soccer swipe for us, a friendly male-on-male distraction technique. Side-to-side shoulder hug, a little leg-play, a little shake of the pant leg, and the wallet is gone, all in good fun.

In St. Petersburg, Russia, the preferred impact is shoulder-to-shoulder, straight on from the front. The klutz apologizes, explained a heroin-addicted thief we interviewed there, while a colleague lifts the wallet from the other side. Vladimir (not our Russian friend and interpreter of the same name) works a particular stretch of Nevsky Prospekt, a privilege for which he pays in cash. (We couldn't get any more information out of him: does he pay the police? A mafia?)

Interview in an Opium Den

In a dim, smoky opium den, we faced the backlit profile of the Moroccan pickpocket. He barely looked at us, concentrating instead on our interpreter. Steaming glasses of sweet mint tea sat before us, packed with fresh leaves of brilliant green. Bob waited to sip his tea until I was half finished with mine—to see if I keeled over, I imagined.

We had come to the *medina* in Tangier in search of a pickpocket, and our hired guide had found him. Al'alla was hunched over a newspaper at the front table of the cave-like café, the only spot within that was bright enough for reading. After ushering us into chairs and ordering our tea, our guide and translator, Ma'halla, spoke in rapid Arabic to Al'alla: "Don't say a word of English, my friend. Let me do all the talking. Just answer my questions in Arabic and we'll both have money for the smoke tonight." Well, he *could* have said that, but it soon became clear that Al'alla had been a skilled pickpocket in his day.

Questions tumbled eagerly from Bob, but Al'alla was no easy subject. Perhaps embarrassed by his miscreant days, he skittered and skirted the core of his story. Bob prodded, encouraged, and teased until he finally found the appropriate tool for extraction. With the glibness of a talk show host and the sincerity of a confidence man, he proffered the camaraderie and respect of a colleague. Bob's disingenuous smile and elegant canards came effortlessly, as if from a spurious rogue. Al'alla relaxed and perhaps followed suit.

Al'alla had honed his talent as a child in Tangier, then traveled to Barcelona for the big time. It was the sixties, and while Tangier revelled in flower power and hippie freedom, its drugs were routed to Europe through Spain. Al'alla found picking pockets far more lucrative and infinitely safer than drug trafficking. People carried cash then, not plastic, and naiveté in travelers was more prevalent than sophistication.

On La Rambla, Barcelona's broad and proud promenade, people strolled like clots through an artery. Kiosks of birds, flowers, and newspapers crowded the avenue. Parrots squawked, pigeons cooed, fragrances of cut lilies and hot paella wafted in the air—it's still like that today. No one suspected the darting figure of a well-dressed gentleman, so obviously in a hurry, as he ricocheted off the moving mob.

Even in his fifties, Al'alla had a handsome face, though its several scars suggested a rough past. He was small and wiry with delicate hands. His soft-spoken manner and gentle composure alluded to the pretender's persona he got away with in his furtive past. Today he worked as an electrician, and his handful of tools lay on the table as we spoke.

I'd been more than a little worried when Ma'halla first led us through the bewildering high-walled alleys of the old city. It wasn't long before I realized we'd never find our way out alone. Was the *medina* really this big, or was Ma'halla confusing us with tricky detours? We lost all sense of direction.

The busy *souk*, with its colorful stalls of spices, brass pots, and rugs, gave way to vegetable sellers who sat on the ground shelling peas, defeathering hens, and stripping mint leaves. Then there were only blind alleys, closed doors, and the occasional Arab hurrying past in his long, sweeping *djellabah*.

Ma'halla was not particularly savory: his face, too, was scarred, and the few teeth he possessed were red with rot. Big and muscular, he wore a cap pulled low over his bloodshot eyes. But his English was good, and he exuded a wary confidence that suited his mission.

The unnamed café was a hangout for small-time crooks and drug addicts. A few strung-out characters packed their pipes behind us as the proprietor boiled water in a

(continued)

Al'alla, a former Moroccan pickpocket, back-lit in a Tangier opium den.

kitchen smaller than a tollbooth. We could have been on the set of Midnight Express, but for the frightening reality of a potentially drugged drink.

As our chat segued into demonstration, a few of the other patrons emerged from their stupors and shuffled near. Bob did a little close-up magic to lighten the mood, and it had an unexpectedly huge effect. Magic as entertainment had not been overdone in Morocco. The men watched one crumpled napkin become two, then a bit of ash moved mysteriously from one man's hand to his other. Everyone's eyes were wide. Bob burned a cigarette right through the front of a man's robe, and it left no hole. The men looked at each other, then chuckled uncomfortably. Bob stepped back, indicating the floor was open for someone else's demonstration.

Finally, Al'alla showed his old hip pocket technique, remarking how very much like riding a camel it was—one never forgets how. His light-fingered lift was a new one to us, a sort-of two-step process accomplished in the blink of an eye. With two fingers outside the pocket the wallet was raised; the thumb and forefinger immediately plucked its exposed edge. Praise was offered all around.

Now another man became involved, also named Ma'halla. He emerged from the depths of the den with an unassuming assurance, as if he felt it his duty to show how things are really done. The two Ma'hallas and Bob and I adjourned to a narrow alley, where I was permitted to videotape Ma'halla #2 as he performed his interpretation of the wallet-steal on Bob.

I'm looking through the viewfinder filming Bob's back as he walks away from me. All our gear hangs on my shoulder. Scary translator Ma'halla is behind me so as not to block my view. I'm all ears. I'm trying to focus, to follow take two. Was that the sound of a switchblade? A shadow flits over me and I flinch, ruining the take. Looking up, I see it's just a thin man in a *djellabah* dragging a little boy. "No photos," he says gruffly, hurrying past.

Finally, we're finished. We returned to the café to thank Al'alla, who was bent over his newspaper again. He rose, as if to shake hands.

Suddenly, Al'alla gave a little hop and collided into Bob with a gentle force. He began to laugh idiotically, raising and lowering his head while he threw one arm around Bob's back and clamped his shoulder in a friendly manner. His feet were dancing and shuffling, knocking into Bob's foot and wrapping around his calf.

Bob had braced himself at the first instant of Al'alla's "attack," but he didn't resist the peculiar, intimate behavior. Al'alla continued his rollicking moves for a few seconds, then gave a great forward kick in the air as a final flourish, and stepped away from Bob.

Was that a Moroccan farewell?

(continued)

Bob fearlessly swigged the last of his mint tea and waved good-bye. Half a dozen hands were raised in return, pale reflections of light in the depths of the dark opium den.

I was definitely ready to get out of the *medina* and lose our unsavory company. We followed our guide through an unfamiliar maze. This was not the way we'd come in. We trudged on in single file, first Ma'halla, then Bob; I followed, recalculating the risks. My shoulders were tense with the perception of continuous threat. Would he lead us into a desolate corner and rob us now? Abruptly turn and brandish a jeweled dagger like those in the shop windows? How did we end up lost and alone with this bulky, menacing Moroccan?

When we finally emerged, blinking, into the sunny square beyond the city walls, we slumped a bit with relief. We still had our cameras, not to mention our skins, intact. Ma'halla grinned, but it looked like a leer.

"This from Al'alla," he said, holding out Bob's prop wallet. "He named that dance 'rugby-steal'."

The perils of Ma'halla, I realized, were all in my head. This rotten-toothed, shifty-eyed, nonviolent thug had fulfilled our eccentric request and protected us from the raging dangers that lurk in the nooks and crannies of my own mind.

We paid Ma'halla double the agreed fee.

Vladimir's limited specialty is back pocket men's wallets. He targets foreigners. As soon as he gets a credit card, he passes it off to his partner. The partner rushes it to a colleague, who goes straight to the airport and flies to Moscow. In Moscow, the credit card is tested with a small purchase at a shop where an associate works; if it works without alerting the merchant/associate, it's maxed out. Due to the expense of flying, one can presume this colleague travels with many credit cards. It's a lucrative business, as you'll learn in chapter 9.

Kharem, too, admitted using credit cards. "I take the train to small towns where they sit waiting for business. They want to make a sale, so they don't ask for identification."

Assumption

A thief needs only a few seconds to assume ownership of unattended riches. Those few seconds are easily found when a woman leaves her handbag in a shopping cart or baby stroller. In the time it takes to select a ripe avocado, the bag is gone and out the door.

Joyce Lerner of Miami Beach had her wallet filched from her bag while shopping in her neighborhood supermarket. It was half an hour before she got to the check-out line and realized it—an obvious window of opportunity for the thief to use her credit cards. When she reported the

Russian pickpocket Vladimir, in St. Petersburg, talks to Bob through our friend and interpreter, also named Vladimir.

incident, police told her they were well aware of gangs that came to Miami Beach every winter and worked many different supermarkets.

Shoe stores in strip malls along the Las Vegas Strip are prime locales for larcenists looking for ignored bags. In fact, shoe shops everywhere beckon to the opportunist. Shoe shopping is serious business, I know, and requires intense focus. Selecting, fitting, walking across the shop, admiring, and—where's your purse?

And, victims tell me that beauty and nail salons are targeted by thieves. Some women become relaxed and distracted and neglect their belongings inside, or leave their purses in their cars so they won't ruin their newly done nails. Leave it to an opportunist to exploit a loophole.

London is struggling with increasing street crime at all its top tourist attractions. Police are peeved about people who supply the opportunities by ignoring their property, even momentarily. The city has a huge problem with theft of personal items inside shops, as well as on the streets. To slow the skyrocketing trend, Oxford Street has been covered with closed-circuit television (CCTV) cameras. Inspector Allan Thompson, of the Marylebone Police Station in London, manages the CCTV program. Describing his frustration, he pointed out an offender caught in the act on videotape: a child under ten years of age.

"You may find it incredible that so many offenses are committed by gangs of young children, but this is happening throughout central

London. There are quite a number of groups—who are controlled, presumably, by their families, but there is no direct evidence of that—who come to central London on a daily basis just to steal people's wallets." Under age ten is significant, Inspector Thompson explained, because "that means they are below the age of criminal responsibility and cannot be taken before a court, and cannot be convicted for offenses that—you can see on this tape—they clearly commit."

Not all of these children are simple assumption thieves, but almost all are opportunists. They're brought to the police station over and over again. When their parents eventually come to collect them, the children are scolded and sometimes slapped—but the police know it's for getting busted, not for stealing.

The assumption thief has the easiest job of all: quietly assuming possession of someone else's property while no one is watching. As I wander through airports across America and around the world, as I stroll through malls, as I do my grocery shopping in my own town, I'm astonished at the number of opportunities I see on offer for the assumption thief. It's just not appropriate behavior in today's world.

I hate to mention the utterly obvious, but what I see in the real world tells me I must. Ladies, in public restrooms, do not leave your purse on the floor at the stall door. Gentlemen, don't do the same with your bags or briefcases.

Las Vegas and other casino towns have a unique version of assumption thieves. They're called bucket bandits and they operate with little or no strategy. Casinos offer enough distractions that a bucket bandit need not bother creating his own. He (or she) simply wanders up and down the aisles of slot machines until he spies a coin pail without eyes attached to it. He snags it and walks away, only hoping he can get off the floor before security nabs him. The cleverer thieves wear hats with brims to shield their faces from the eye in the sky but, basically, this is not a clever thief's game. Casino video cameras are state-of-the-art, cover almost every square inch of their public spaces, and are monitored by skilled security staff. Strangely, bucket bandits go for it anyway, and some succeed.

Yes, some of these guys use crude little distractions—usually by placing some money on the floor and pointing it out to the mark while a colleague swipes her coin pail. But more often, they'll just sit and wait, sometimes at the slot machine that is back-to-back with the one the mark is playing. In some casinos, they're able to reach alongside the back-to-back machines, from one row to another, so the victim never even sees the thief or how it could have happened.

Bob spotted a bucket bandit on the prowl in a Detroit casino when the Motor City was new in the gaming business. We were in town to teach a class for the gaming division of the police department and the casinos' security staffs. Before the conference, Sergeant James Lightfoot gave us a

Vamping on Victims

American whiz player Johnnie Downs worked the San Diego Super Bowl:

"They had a trolley leaving from downtown to the stadium. We played it for a couple of tickets, played for some raw scratch, which is money. When we got on the trolley, the trolley was on fire from other whiz players. We only got one ticket, so we sold it for $1,500.

"Usually, for play-off football games, we try to get in. If you can't get in, you can always get in at halftime, for some apparent reason, so you just work the halftime. If you think you caught a couple of blows, what I mean is victims have woken up on you, that's what you call a blow. When you're playing a victim, the vic wake up on you, kick him his sting back, or kick her her sting back. If you think that you caught too many blows, you just leave the premises. You wait till the fourth quarter, you go back in, and you walk them back out."

Johnnie Downs on Las Vegas:

"When people come to Vegas, they're not really concerned. They know the cameras are here so they're more relaxed and at ease than anything. As long as you're dressed the part and you have a little intellect, you can get next to the man with the biggest money.

"The right mark is gonna come to you in Las Vegas. People are very careless with their money. See, it's not just the whiz coming to vamp on the victims here. Victims come here and get relaxed. That's the main reason Vegas is so good. People come here and they have their guard down. They think the highest security in the world is here in Las Vegas. 'Oh, nothing's going to happen to me, I'm in Las Vegas.' And especially when there's alcohol involved, and, I don't drink, so, that makes them more vulnerable."

mini-tour of one of the casinos, where Bob almost immediately locked on to a suspect. We trailed him around the casino's several floors for ten minutes or so, then called the security camera operators. They weren't on him. We had to leave, so Lightfoot suggested that security officers keep an eye on the guy.

"Thanks to your tip he was arrested and identified as working with a pickpocket team," Sergeant Lightfoot later wrote us. "Casino security was amazed and definitely learned something about pre-incident behavior."

CCTV surveillance has become the norm in private, as well as public, spaces. Many people spot the conspicuous little cameras, vaguely register mild unease, then go about their business. Others worry about privacy issues and, as some call the watchful eyes, "little brothers." September 11 seems to have eased the acceptance of video surveillance, and cameras are proliferating across America and elsewhere.

Johannesburg, South Africa, got a jump start on cameras as a desperate measure after crime virtually shut down its entire central business district. Now, downtown is covered with hundreds of cameras and monitored by a joint concern between private business and the city. Cameras are operated remotely by pampered technicians with police supervision, and can zoom in to read a business card in the hand of a pedestrian in motion.

The German public was aghast at the wholesale infringement of civil liberties and invasion of privacy, and a television news crew went to interview the outraged man-in-the-street. To the crew's utter amazement, they couldn't elicit a single negative comment.

Pretense

Upon arrival in Mumbai, the only thing that begins before photo opportunities is the demand for *baksheesh*. In the few short paces between terminal and taxi, I was mobbed by beggars young and old who, with fingers to lips, all cried for *chapati* or one rupee, about two cents. Without a moment to get his bearings, a traveler is cruelly confronted with the realities of India. Even before my cab coughed to life, I felt the weight of poverty, congestion, filth, and despair.

At stoplights, taxis are mauled by beggars, mostly small children and women with infants. A man extends his hand for a coin. He has no fingers. Another is so thin his backbone is almost visible through the tight skin of his stomach.

A little girl attached herself to me one day as I walked in the Colaba Market area. She couldn't have been more than six. Barefoot, she took giant steps to keep up with me, as I do to keep up with Bob. Over the rocky roadside, in the dusty gutter, avoiding cow shit and dog shit and sleeping people and every other obstacle, she kept up a running monologue as she tagged along for several blocks.

"Hello Madam, how are you? Is this your first visit to Mumbai? You like Mumbai? Where are you from? Something to give, Madam?" She spoke like a little adult, with perfect pronunciation and inflection. I wondered if she really knew English, or if she was just parroting rehearsed sentences taught to her.

"Very hungry, Madam. Something to give, Madam? Just one rupee, Madam, not a lot." Her hair was flying as her dusty legs skipped along. "Very very hungry, Madam. What is your name, Madam?" She went on and on. She was so cute, and trying so hard. I would have loved to give her a few coins, but I knew from experience what that would lead to. I'd be surrounded in an instant by fifty pathetic little children, all cute and all deserving. There's some inaudible sound the lucky one sends out, like a dog whistle, that makes children emerge out of thin air.

Finally, after she'd followed me to our hotel, I said, "Where's your mother? Run back to your mother now!"

"I don't have a mother, Madam. My mother's dead, Madam. Very hungry. One rupee, Madam?"

Begging in the Borscht Belt

St. Petersburg's Palace Square, in front of the Hermitage in Russia, looks like a highway rest stop when forty or more tour buses park en masse. As each bus arrives and disgorges its fifty or so passengers, paupers appear out of nowhere to approach the foreigners, hands out, faces beseeching.

We watched a troupe of about thirty individuals work in shifting pairs and small groups. They were clearly, pitifully poor. Most were dressed in gaudy-colored layers, shawls over skirts over pants; a boy of eleven or twelve wore a girls' dress over baggy shorts with bare legs. They were small people, so tiny; all of the women were under five feet tall.

Every female over the age of about ten carried a child, either tied to her back or slung in a shawl on her chest. It was cold and raining, yet more than half the group was barefoot. They were extremely dirty, both skin and clothes, and many of the babies' faces were badly scabbed. Little boys ran and played happily between attempts at begging: "Rubles? Dollar? Deutsch mark? Pleeeece," and they were off again. But the sad-faced girls and women lugged their babies pathetically from bus to bus, looking for handouts.

A few women and girls made attempts to board buses, but they were invariably scolded when they woke the sleeping drivers. We spoke with a few tour guides who claimed that the group stole, if they could, anything passengers left in the buses. "And when they appear to be begging," we were told, "it is only a distraction." The guides said that these poor people live on the edge of the city, in the forests, and that they are made to give most of their day's bounty to tyrant bosses, who lived in gaudy mansions in considerable wealth.

Although my Russian researcher, Vladimir, trekked out to the forest on the eastern edge of the city, he failed to find the tyrant boss or the gaudy mansion. He did find and speak with the troupe's "baron," but his investigation failed to support any claims of regular payments to the baron. "As several women said to me and it also seemed to me," Vladimir said, "all the bits of money, food, or whatsoever the women manage to get on the city street go right into their houses, where normally five to eight children and a husband expect to have something for dinner."

According to Captain Yury Vasil'ev, chief of the anti-pickpocketing department of the St. Petersburg police, there are three to five official reports per day of tricking, extortion, or stealing committed by these so-called beggars. He claims that the number of unreported cases would be five to ten times higher.

Groups of twelve to twenty at a time tend to work the squares, major tourist spots, and city streets, the chief said. Usually they appear to be begging for money. "One or two women will offer to read your palm, or just beg for your cash, while their mercurial kid or another woman quietly cleans out your bag," said Vasil'ev.

Three or four women of the group are always assigned to make sure that the place is totally "police free". Occasionally, a policeman manages to determine who from the group is hiding a stolen item. "Then, a pass-the-parcel game begins," Vasil'ev said, "leaving the lawkeeper with just an easy-to-solve puzzle of why this little kid has run away from here so quickly." A favorite technique of the beggar-thieves, the policeman said, is for a unit of two or three individuals to work at the overcrowded bus stops all around the city. "While rarely actually boarding the buses, they operate in those hectic seconds

(continued)

while some seventy to one hundred passengers are mercilessly squashing themselves through one bus's doors.

"Almost 90 percent of regular Russian pickpockets are drug addicts," continued Vasil'ev, "which is the factor that negatively influences their performance. On the other hand, these beggar-pickpockets always operate with a sober head—determined, knowing that it's up to them how much food they will bring to their families in the evening." That makes them far more difficult to arrest than their other Russian colleagues, he added. "Even caught red-handed, they always have excuses. Almost all women can show valid certificates which verify that they have some five to eight children—which makes them untouchable under Russian law."

I emptied my pocket for the little girl and ducked into the hotel as she scampered off.

Other children and a few mothers carrying babies begged for milk powder, inviting me to buy it in a nearby shop for them. I heard some visitors snidely remark that this was just a ploy, that the beggars would just sell the milk powder. Why? They're desperately poor and truly need it. It's obvious they need food, not drug money.

In chapter 1, I described how Maritza and Ravenna, children in Rome, pretend to beg under a sheet of newspaper. In Barcelona, Nezira and Gemila carry big slabs of cardboard, roughly torn from a carton. On it, scrawled in Spanish, is "No work. No money. No eat. Thank you for some money." The women, thirty-one and twenty-eight years old, shove the cardboard horizontally into the waist area of their target and look up with enormous eyes. Under the cardboard their nimble fingers open fanny packs and rummage through pockets, unseen by owners.

"These two are this city's most prolific pickpocket pair," police officer Giorgio Pontetti told us when he sat in on our interview of them.

Gemila, from Bosnia, is one of Barcelona's most prolific pickpockets.

Gemila and her partner, Nezira, discuss the pros and cons of stealing from a man's inside jacket pocket.

Two young pickpockets use newspaper to shield double steals: from the victim's shirt pocket and pants pocket.

How is one to know desperation from deception, mendicants from impostors? One begs to eat, another begs to steal. The impostors, those who steal under the pretense of begging, can be found all across southern Europe. Some attempt to tug at heartstrings with scribbled claims of being refugees, and perhaps they are refugees. Others have given up pretense altogether, keeping the cardboard but omitting the written request for money. For them, any prop will do: a map, a section of old newspaper, an infant.

Yes, even an infant. A sleepy baby in a sling on the chest poignantly communicates hunger and need. And if the woman with the baby comes close enough, the baby will act as a shield for her hands. It's not uncommon for these babies to be in the midst of nursing at their mothers' bare breast: all the more distracting to the victim. Irreverent? Perhaps. Deceitful? Absolutely.

Finally, it is frequently claimed that these women will sometimes toss their babies at their victims, which distracts the victims to an extreme and occupies their hands at the same time. Although we've heard it said many times, we cannot substantiate the assertion.

Beggar-thieves Nezira and Gamila had it all figured out. They had plopped their slender bodies into childlike positions on the ground, cross-legged, and dropped their jackets into a heap beside them. They were both pretty, with long dark hair and teenage faces. They squirmed, fidgeted, and repeatedly glanced up to Officer Pontetti for encouragement and approval.

Two thieves (right), shove cardboard into the waist of their victim (left), allowing them to steal from pockets or a fanny pack beneath the cardboard, unseen.

"I go up to people," Gemila explained. "If they say go away because they know I am going to steal from them, we just go away." She shook her bangs out of her eyes. "But if they seem to be innocent, then I will go for them. They have no idea that I'm a bad person and want to steal money."

Gemila grinned, hideously transforming her pretty face into a week-old jack-o'lantern's as she revealed her rotten teeth. She lit a cigarette.

"Japanese are hardest to steal from because they always throw up their hands and step aside," Nezira said. "They don't want to have anything to do with us, so it's hard to get close. They don't want to get involved."

"Germans are so-so. Americans are difficult, but they have so many dollars!" Gemila laughed with embarrassment at her own daring, dipped her head, and looked at Nezira. Nezira giggled, then both fell apart, as if they couldn't maintain seriousness for more than a few minutes at a time.

They're serious on the job, though. Bob used a lipstick camera, which, as its name implies, is the size of a lipstick, to film a similar duo. We put money-sized cut paper into an envelope, put the envelope in a fanny pack, and zipped the pouch closed. Bob wore it. Soon enough, a pair of women approached us making kissing faces, an odd combination of worried eyebrows, pursed lips, and pleading eyes. One's cupped, begging hand steadied the cardboard balanced on her other arm. Bob held his little wide-angle lens at hip height. Under the cardboard, the film showed, the beggar-thief opened the fanny pack, removed the envelope, and closed the zipper. With a final mimed kiss and the envelope hidden beneath their cardboard, the pair wandered away.

Rich man, poor man, beggarman, thief. Was this M.O. used in the mid-1700s when the Mother Goose rhyme was written? Perhaps it was originally "beggarman-thief."

When the two women saw us again half an hour later, they gave us the finger.

Other Techniques and Tools

Back to our jack-of-all-trades, Kharem. We accidentally caught him in the act a year after we first met him. Neither of us recognized the other. All I noticed was a suspect—someone whose behavior caused me to observe intensely. As I watched him from the back, Kharem showed me something new.

He was working the throng around a lively three-shell scam. (I'll discuss the three-shell scam in chapter 8.) The pickpocket, whom I still had not recognized, wedged himself into the spectators and then gave me a perfect view of a move I'd never seen before. With his right elbow held high, a jacket draped over it, he snuck his left hand across his chest and into the shirt pocket of a man standing on his right. I saw a heavy wallet in the man's shirt pocket, and the thief's fingers feeling for it, wiggling like a hand-shadow spider.

But he missed it. The mob surged forward a bit and the mark moved out of position. The pickpocket wasn't fazed. With sinewy grace, he pirouetted once around me and around the person to my left, then twirled smack into an elderly couple, separating them. He reached for the woman's chest area, but I couldn't tell what he was after: her purse, which she clutched to her chest, or the chunky gold chain that hung to the same point. He didn't get anything as far as I could see, and the husband of the woman shouted at him. He departed quickly, but immediately crept back to get a better look at me, then grinned with recognition. It amused me that he remembered me first, despite the fact that I'd been analyzing, editing, and showing video of him for a year. Then again, I'd been focused on his hands—and he has eyes in the back of his head.

Kharem has a few other tricks up his sleeve that I feel are just diabolical enough to elevate them into the strategical styles of chapter 7. He's an unusual character. Most thieves we speak with specialize in a narrow range of techniques. Kharem's broad expertise spans many disciplines of theft, as well as poetry. More on him later.

How to nick a wallet, let me count the ways. I've given examples of methods that depend on speed, stealth, seizure, motion, impedence, impact, assumption, and pretense. But I haven't said much about the intricate details of technique. Every pickpocket develops a unique style, as distinctive as the way a man shakes hands on a deal or kisses a lover. The movements become a part of him and he cannot betray them.

Finesse is not always required, particularly when a thief operates on speed, seizure, or assumption. Combined with stealth, motion, impedence, impact, or pretense, however, finesse is devastating.

"Oh, I'd feel it," most people say about the lifting of a wallet. Would you? Several cunning techniques are designed to prevent that. "Fingers that can tickle the back of a fly," said a London pickpocket describing the finesse he uses. With some techniques, the thief's hand barely enters the subject's pocket.

In Naples, the pickpocket capital of the world, Luciano floored us with his casual revelation when Bob asked him about his specialty.

"The front pants pocket. Especially when I think there's loose money. I am good at that, maybe better than anyone." He was looking at all our pockets.

"Can you show us?" Bob boldly requested.

Two plainclothes police escorts had accompanied Luciano to his interview. The junior officer's Levis were biker-tight. Our interpreter, Andrina, and I wore skirts. It was obvious that Inspector Borgomeo, head of the undercover *Falchi Squad,* would have to be the volunteer victim. Luciano glanced at him nervously. Borgomeo hesitated only for an instant. He opened his wallet gamely and put a few folded bills deep into his front pocket.

Luciano wiped his mouth with the back of his hand. I could hear the rasp of his whiskers. He rose reluctantly and positioned himself close to Borgomeo.

He gingerly inserted his first and middle fingertips about half an inch into the officer's tight front pocket, the nails against Borgomeo. With his thumb remaining fixed on the outside, he let his two fingers do an imperceptible stationary walk against the fabric, delicately pulling up and crimping the thin lining of the pocket, bunching it invisibly inside. The folded bills rose like an ace from a deck, right out of the pocket.

I felt like applauding.

Luciano palmed the cash, but immediately returned it to Borgomeo.

The inspector, who had stood awkwardly with his hands held unnaturally away from his body, grinned with disbelief and admiration, despite his cross-purpose. It was just a small smile, which he quickly suppressed.

"It's even easier when the pocket has no topstitching," Luciano explained. Leave it to an Italian to know the shortcomings of topstitching.

As Luciano resettled in his seat, the inspector surreptitiously thumbed his money before replacing it in his pocket.

Meanwhile, Bob sat back astounded. He had wondered for more than thirty years if there was any truth to the rumors he had heard whispered by police as early as 1965. There had been talk of a mythical method,

A Close Shave, or, Honey, There's a Hole in My Handbag

Archil Zantaradze keeps a razor blade in his mouth the way someone else might store a tired wad of gum. Gently curved against his upper palate, he can dislodge the blade with a bit of tongue suction and discreetly arm himself in an instant.

Of course, pickpockets, by our definition, are nonviolent. The razor—actually half a blade—is meant to slice a pocket or a purse, never human flesh. The technique is a specialty of Zantaradze, St. Petersburg's most notorious Georgian pickpocket, and peculiar to his compatriots.

Zantaradze perfected this dangerous practice while just a teenager. (I can imagine the manipulation easily: as a kid, I removed my retainer the same way. But I never worried about drawing blood!) He was taught by his own father, as all his brothers were. And before he ever even scraped a razor against his first soft whiskers, he could shoot the blade with awesome skill from its wet storage place to his soft palm. His dexterous tongue snaps as quickly as a frog's and he catches the razor in his hand as neatly as a magician palms a card.

Zantaradze's sleight of tongue is not unique among the criminal population of Russian Georgians. Those who aren't taught at home learn in jail, where the razor blade is a vital commodity. Desperately creative, inmates find inconceivable functions for the simple object. Indeed, when attached to a short length of wire and pushed into a power outlet, the lowly blade miraculously becomes both a little heater and a water-boiler. And, "a skillful cut of veins may lead a tired prisoner, if not to death, then into the relative comfort of a prison's hospital bed," my Russian journalist friend Vladimir explained. "Life accounts in prisons are also known to be settled with this small metal device. Not to mention the ordinary functions of the razor blade, like shaving or paper cutting."

Vasily Zhiglov, our St. Petersburg police informant, arrested Zantaradze some months before my questions to him, and thereafter had ample opportunity to interview him. Lounging in prison, Zantaradze was unembarrassed but surprised that he had failed to bribe his way out. Officer Zhiglov acknowledged that not all policemen can resist this "easy-sounding temptation," as the sum represents full, or at least half, of a policeman's monthly wage. (The bargaining usually starts at five hundred rubles—twenty-five dollars at the time of this research.)

It was not without a certain pride that Zantaradze admitted to Zhiglov that he, along with at least four other Georgians, spent the summer of 1998 in France "working" the streets and stadiums of cities hosting matches of the World Cup. Zantaradze maintained that a skilled thief could easily make three to five thousand U.S. dollars per day by extracting cash from the pockets and bags of the hordes of often-drunk soccer fans cruising the streets and shops of every hosting city. The French towns, unaccustomed to such crowds and crime, were unprepared and understaffed for the deluge.

Officer Zhiglov estimated that there were about seventy Russians, mostly from Moscow and St. Petersburg, who combined the pleasure of watching World Cup matches with the labor of cleaning out other fans' bags and pockets. He said that before heading to "work" in a foreign country, a pickpocket would thoroughly study the criminal code of that country. "And one would certainly prefer to work in France or another

(continued)

European nation where the law is much softer on this particular crime than, say, in Arabic countries," Zhiglov said. Each year Russia receives about a dozen of its returned citizens caught stealing abroad.

Igor Kudelya, senior lieutenant of the St. Petersburg pickpocket squad, said that on frosty winter days, when other pickpockets' fingers "have frozen senseless," the Georgian can be spotted warming up his fingers by exercising them with two or three small metal balls before entering a chosen work spot.

almost sleight of hand, they'd said, that would empty a man's front pocket as gently as a feather blown from a robin's nest. No one had ever seen it done, but victims swore they never felt a thing. Like a magician's closely guarded secret, the technique was shrouded in mystery, if it ever actually existed at all. And Luciano had innocently revealed it without fanfare or formality.

"I think I'm particularly good at this technique because I have light fingers," he volunteered, rubbing his thumb against his first two fingertips like a safecracker about to spin a dial. Or a rat fink suggesting a bribe.

Hardly anyone who hears about this miraculous method can resist giving it a little try, just to see if it works. Unless you're a contortionist, you can't try it on yourself. Fingernails must be against the body, thumbtip pointed straight, perpendicular to the body.

Another technique we saw but didn't see. We were riding the green line in sweltering Athens. A woman in a yellow shirt and her male pal were already on the train when Bob and I boarded. They moved aside, making it easier for us to get on, then sandwiched Bob, separating me away. The man pressed a flaccid shoulder bag against Bob's pants pocket while his partner tried to get Bob's prop wallet.

"That was good," Bob said to me in Swedish, our code-speak, because we assume few people understand it. "She tried but didn't get it." Probably because Bob's pocket was pretty deep. We don't want to make it too easy for them.

Giving up, the man hung his bag on his shoulder and inched away innocently, riding in sweaty silence. As the train approached Omonia station, he readied himself for another attempt.

A Greek gentleman boarded. The couple, still on the train, blocked his way.

"Excuse me," the Greek man said. "Let me get by."

The couple slid around behind him. The woman flashed a flat parcel down low. Amid the confusion, I saw a hand briefly grip a pocket. In the swirl of people, I couldn't identify whose hand it was, or even whose pocket. I was holding a camera low, blindly aiming at the known thief's hands. Bob held his camera near the ceiling, pointing down.

The train hadn't left yet. The thief pushed himself through the crowd with his partner close behind. He stepped off the train, but the Greek man was quick. He grabbed the perp's wrist, pulling him back onto the train. The woman walked.

"Come here!" the victim said in Greek.

"What do you want, mister?"

"You took my wallet!"

"What did I take?" he asked. "You're out of your mind. Search me! Look, look!"

The victim groped desperately in his empty pocket and released his assailant. The thief left, the doors slammed shut, and the train departed.

"Did he get your wallet?" we asked. "*Portofoli?*"

"Yes, he got it. I wasn't sure if it was him or not, not 100 percent."

We asked the victim if he'd like us to go to the police with him, that we thought we might have the steal on film, and we certainly had the faces of the thieves. But no, he didn't want to.

"He didn't get a lot of money. I had 10,500 drachmas." (Approximately twenty-seven dollars.)

A victim on a train in Athens grabs a thief by the arm. The thief's partner had already slipped off the train and gotten away with the victim's wallet.

"What did he say?"

"He said he didn't do it." The Greek threw up his hands.

Sweaty and spent, we retreated to a shady streetside café in the Plaka to have a light lunch and review our footage. Over *tzadziki* and flat bread and cold fried eggplant, we unwound, cooled off, and rewound our cameras. Hunched over our tiny screens, we scrutinized the film.

The whole story was there: the thief, his accomplice, and the Greek victim boarding. You can't take for granted that everything will be on film when shooting from the hip. And we make plenty of camera mistakes in moments of high tension or excitement. We pressed play on the other camera. Sipping *retsina,* we held our breath through shaky minutes of feet, unidentifiable body parts, then noisy confusion.

And there it was, clear and close up. It took exactly a second and a half. While his accomplice positioned a flat parcel as a shield, the thief had used both hands on the right front pants pocket of the Greek. His right hand pushed the wallet up from the outside of the fabric while his left reached only an inch into the pocket. This is a technique dips call "kicking the poke." They raise it from the depths, or turn it into a better position for lifting. The pickpocket neatly clipped the raised wallet between two fingers and let the Greek simply walk away from it. It happened so fast we didn't see it, but our camera did.

What we can't see, but most certainly happened, is the thief's pass to his partner. He pulled up his shirt and invited a search because he was clean: he'd given the wallet to his cohort, who escaped.

Like Luciano's accordion pleat, we call this finesse. Thieves who use it have an edge, but they can be bested. They're still opportunists. We don't have to give them the opportunity. We just have to be aware that they have tricks and techniques most of us wouldn't dream of. You think you'd feel it, but you could be wrong.

Lastly, there are tool users. Luciano told us about using scissors. A snip along the side of a tight back pocket will let a wallet plop into a waiting paw. Remember, Luciano works on trams, where people are packed close together and physical contact is the norm; it's noisy, bumpy, and swaying all over the place.

Although he doesn't use one, Luciano also told us about long tweezers that are slipped into back pockets to fish out wallets. A known or accused pickpocket caught with tweezers on him goes to jail. Officers of Naples' *Falchi Squad,* those powerful plainclothes police, showed us a couple of tweezers used this way.

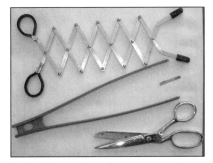

Tools of the trade: catclaw, tweezers, scissors, and a strip of razor blade.

Another tool is used in dark or quiet places. We call it the catclaw for its sneaky grabbing ability. It's uncommon, but still useful when the thief can clearly see the object of his desire just within reach. It has a scissors' handle that, when squeezed, extends a sort of rubber-tipped pincer. The function of this utensil is not so much to extend the thief's reach, but, rather, to make his reach invisible; to make it inconspicuous and unobtrusive.

We're all surrounded by an invisible membrane defining our personal space. When someone gets too close, we sense it immediately. If it's a stranger, we not only feel uncomfortable, but we become guarded.

A pickpocket must get close to you in order to do his stealing. If he doesn't have a reason to enter your personal space, if he can't logically create an excuse for the trespass, he might use the catclaw. With it, he can silently penetrate the invisible barrier of the unsuspecting mark. He can enter forbidden territory without setting off a danger alarm. He can get in, get out, and disappear—without ever being noticed.

A movie theater is the perfect setting for this sort of steal: it's dark and still, and the victim's attention is elsewhere. Perhaps a catclaw was used in the theft at Prince Edward Theatre during the musical, *Mamma Mia*. Perhaps it was used to reach the Hanson's bag at the sidewalk café. With this tool, a thief can slip in, grab the goods, and he's gone.

Razor blades are a more delicate and more brutal. Sihle, a twenty-four-year-old pickpocket in Johannesburg, is a razor blade specialist. He described how he uses it to cut back pants pockets. He slices just under a

Bob and two Johannesburg thieves, Sihle (left) and Mondli (right), who is reformed.

Railway Raj

With a firm grip on the patient's big toe, the hospital orderly entered the police inspector's office. He carried the full weight of the patient's plastered leg, which extended from the wheelchair without any other support. As he was pushed from behind and pulled by the toe, the patient hunched awkwardly in the rusty iron wheelchair. A male nurse had the ancient chair tipped precariously back, which thrust the broken leg to a painful height.

As he was wheeled in, the patient gripped the armrest of the chair with one hand and clutched his broken ribs with the other. A procession of plainclothes police and hospital staff followed. The patient was a pickpocket, brutally beaten by his most recent victim.

Mumbai police inspector Ashok Desai had not required much prodding to produce a pickpocket. He sat behind the desk in his lilac-colored office at Victoria Terminus and chatted amiably with us, shoes and socks off, cap off, smooth bald head reflecting the slow revolutions of a ceiling fan. Curiously eager to cooperate, he buzzed his peon and ordered him in Hindi when we asked to interview a thief. Shortly thereafter, his office doors were thrown open and the broken criminal wheeled in.

"Now let me explain something," Bob said, leaning forward. "If he lies to me, I will know. I want only the truth."

Without waiting for translation, the pickpocket replied in Hindi. "I speak only the truth to you," he said, Inspector Desai translating. "I swear to you." He raised his open right hand and placed it stiffly against his nose and forehead, thumbtip to nosetip, like a vertical salute.

Before the battered thief was brought in, the inspector wanted to be certain that he wouldn't be glorified in the press, nor made fun of by us. The man had received the beating he deserved, Desai said. His huge curled mustache held the shadow of a smile. While we waited, he dictated a memo to an assistant and sent another running for *masala chai,* spiced milky tea. Pigeon feathers swirled on the floor in a mini-whirlwind.

Rahul was wheeled in and parked beside Bob. A posse of police and medical staff stood behind his rusty throne like male ladies-in-waiting. After promising truth, Rahul looked back and forth between Bob and the inspector with alert eyes, and answered without hesitation.

He steals only on trains at the passengers' moments of boarding or alighting, he explained. Never on buses. His only victims are wealthy businessmen, easily identifiable by the size of their bellies and grooming of their mustaches. He tapped his own thin mustache and sunken belly, indicating the local signifiers of affluence. All the police recognize Rahul and his gang. For that reason, they usually commit their thefts a station or two away from Central Station. He was caught this time because he'd been drinking a little and his reflexes were slow. He was sloppy. It was a bad mistake. He pressed his broken ribs and grimaced.

Rahul works with a sliver of razor blade, which he hides in his mouth between his cheek and lower gum. Using a broken matchstick, he demonstrated how quickly he could manipulate the blade. With it, he slices open the satchels of affluent businessmen on trains while a partner holds a newspaper or canvas bag at the chest or neck of the victim, preventing him from seeing.

(continued)

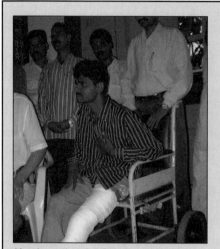

Mumbai pickpocket Rahul was badly beaten by his most recent victim. Standing behind him are hospital orderlies and plainclothes police officers.

"Show me," Bob said, coming around Rahul and squatting beside him. Rahul was handed a newspaper and then demonstrated how quickly he could open a bag beneath the shield of the paper.

This is done while boarding or exiting trains that are so crowded that people can barely turn their heads, Rahul and the inspector explained.

"Do you ever cut pockets with the blade?" Bob asked.

"No, only bags. But I know others who cut pockets. Two brothers, they always work together."

"I want to talk to them. Where can I find them?" Desai asked.

"I don't know," Rahul said. He seemed afraid for a moment.

"Last question," Bob said. "What will you do when you're fifty?"

"I have a taxi medallion and badge. If I get the chance, I would like to ply the taxi on the road." He paused. "But I do not think I will get the chance."

It's possible that Rahul works under an Indian mafia. Neither he nor the inspector suggested this, but other Indians who analyzed portions of this interview on video thought it was likely.

"Where there is big money there is mafia," an Indian working in the security business told me. "Your pickpocket, he was afraid to talk about other thieves he knows. He didn't want to tell the police inspector. And as to driving a taxi, probably the mafia will never let him quit the steal business. Your pickpocket will continue his work on the trains, I believe."

bulging wallet or cell phone, and the thing just drops into his hand. He prefers to work in bookstores, while people are bent over looking at magazines. Sihle stores his razor blade in the cuff of his long-sleeved shirt, where he's made a small slit in the edge.

For an older model cell phone, he can get 200 rand (about US$17 at the time of this research), and for the latest Nokia he can get 1000 rand (US$87). When he gets credit cards, sometimes he uses them, but most of the time he sells them to local gangsters who use them to create new cards, a first step in identity theft.

Almost all of the opportunist's dirty work is preventable. I agree, it's not practical to live in preparation for the worst at any moment. Bob and I say, practice safety as a habit. Stash your valuables wisely, and try not to send signals that you're worth a thief's while. Other, easier targets will always be there to tempt the opportunist. Don't make him even glance at you. We say, forget the flashy jewelry when you're out and about.

"But this is a fake Rolex," some say smugly. "I paid twenty dollars for it in Miami." No comment on the purchase of counterfeit goods, but do you really want to be mugged for a fake Rolex? Do you believe a criminal can tell the difference? Not even in Naples, where Rolex robbing is as common as running red lights, can a thief tell before he's got it.

"These are CZs," women tell me, tugging on glittery boulders in their earlobes. "It won't break me if I lose them." Listen: losing the earrings is not the point. You're sending a signal to anyone who cares to pay attention: "Look at me! Notice my wealth!" The one who tunes in may or may not want those CZs; he may decide to linger and observe and find your Achilles' heel, the chink in your armor. It's not coincidence when a bag is snatched in the one moment you look away. You've been stalked. Why? You are an attractive target. You are wealth.

If you are a tourist, chances are you look like one. That's not a put-down. We can't possibly look like a local wherever we are. We don't dress, act, or sound like the natives, even within regions of the United States. I'll never forget the time Bob and I came back to America after six months in Sweden.

We flew straight to Orwigsburg, Pennsylvania, to do a private show. I had never felt like such an alien as I did in that town. That thought had solidified long before a roadside breakfast at the Family 3Cs diner, where the perky little waitress asked, "Where are you guys *from?*" with the unsaid ending: "space?" Was it because I asked for the definition of a "dippie," a menu item with no description?

The big boss had described his employees, his "boys," as backward and painfully shy. He said we'd think they seemed dumb, ignorant, but that they're highly skilled at their individual jobs, and they were loyal, good workers. At the party, Bob and I looked at all these beefy boys with their hefty wives, trying to figure out their lives and values. They didn't look dumb; they looked innocent and close to the earth and less worldly than anyone we'd encountered in many years.

The event was held in a dismal lounge at a Quality Hotel. The pitiful effort at decorating (helium balloons rubbing against the low ceiling) matched the pathetic catering (macaroni salad and barbeque chicken). And this was the big party of their year! To be fair, I must add that the boss's warmth and generosity toward them (and us) was impressive.

Culturally speaking, this was as fascinating an experience as any other exotic destination we'd visited. And on the positive side, we spoke the language. Somewhat, anyway. As always, I tried to pick up a little of the lingo—I now know that I can order a "dippie" and expect an egg. But what would the Orwigsburgers think about being considered exotic, and a fascinating study? I suspect we and the natives examined each other with the same dubious skepticism and sideways looks, like two isolated cats meeting for the first time.

Anyway, there we were in our own America and no doubt we stuck out like two city slickers in a dairy barn, similar to the time I showed up in Boyd, Texas, for a show wearing New York black instead of dirty denim. Who knew? We didn't mean to stand out—we just did.

The point is, most travelers can be seen as travelers, and a traveler is at a disadvantage. When we travel, *we're* the foreigners. We're outsiders, even if we don't realize it. We don't have street smarts, even if we do at home.

Bob and I say, prepare yourself in advance. Travel light in order to travel confidently. Leave your shiny sparklers at home. On the road, lock up what you love. On your body, tuck them in. The idea is to enjoy your journey without worry.

So the big question is . . . where should I keep my money? What's the safe way to carry my things?

And the ambiguous answer is . . . it depends on who you are and where you're going.

First analyze yourself. Are you a worrier? Overconfident? Carefree? Forgetful? Only you can choose the level of security for you. Will you be trekking in the highlands of Peru? Walking with elephants in East Africa? Or going to museums and the opera in London? What's the tone of your trip, elegant? grungy? in between? What's the weather? Summer clothes, especially women's, have fewer pockets and far less security. No one is likely to get into the pockets of your jeans if you have a heavy coat over them.

We say keep your wallet in your tightest pocket, but in many situations that isn't enough. A wallet in a visible pocket is an invitation. Awareness helps. But maybe you don't need to carry a wallet. Slim down your necessities, if you can.

Wrapping a wide rubber band around the wallet is a popular technique. "It helps us," said Johnnie Downs, who's been picking pockets for twenty-seven years. "A rubber band makes it stick to our fingers better, and it compresses the wallet so the corners don't catch."

Excellent products are readily available for the safekeeping of your stuff. Under-shirt pouches are pretty good, but they can usually be detected and demanded in a mugging. For all but the most dangerous streets, they're a good option. Better yet is the type of pouch that hangs inside the pants, attached to your belt by a loop. These come in a full range of materials, from nylon to cotton to leather. We love these.

Another kind of pouch fastens around your waist and is worn beneath your clothes. These come in infinite styles, sizes, and varieties and are excellent for men and women. It's a little more difficult to get to your money or credit card when you need it, but it's worth the extra effort. Sometimes these are referred to as money belts, but they're not. A money belt is a regular leather belt worn outside trousers; it has a zippered compartment on the inside. You can fold in a few large bills or travelers' checks, but it won't hold much.

What about the ubiquitous fanny pack, a.k.a. waist pouch, a.k.a. bum bag? Well, it's good and it's bad. On one hand, all your goodies are right in front, on your body, in sight. On the other hand, the fanny pack shouts out, "Here's my stuff!" For the most part, Bob and I recommend them for security, if you don't mind the fashion statement they make. We have never seen, and rarely heard of, their straps being cut. *However:* in some locales, particularly in southern Europe, pickpockets are extremely adept at opening fanny packs and stealing their contents while you're wearing it. I recommend a simple preventative: fasten the zipper with a safety pin or with a paper clip and rubber band. Anything to frustrate wandering fingers. For the fanatic, a fanny pack made by DayMakers of Santa Barbara incorporates numerous safety features, including steel cable through the strap, a concealed buckle, a hidden key clip, and built-in zipper locks.

A new English company called KarrySafe has a line of wonderful products, including a Velcroed roll-top knapsack and a laptop case with a breakaway strap and alarm. One KarrySafe product we like is called the Stealth Belt. Made of sexy, stretchy lingerie fabric, it's a sheer black accessory for women meant to be worn under the clothes but, possibly, revealed. The belt has four tiny pouches that stretch to accommodate credit cards, cash, keys, and even a small cell phone. When Bob and I go out among the lowlifes and I don't want to worry about my things, I wear a Stealth Belt. The company is developing a masculine version of it.

 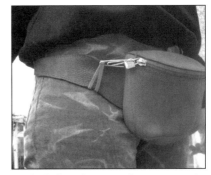

These two techniques—a paper clip through the zipper tabs (left) and a paper clip connecting the zipper tab to a rubber band (right)—are usually enough to foil most fanny pack trespassers.

Lastly, there are several companies that make clothes for travelers with zippered, Velcroed, and hidden pockets. The Canadian company Tilley is an option if you care for the somewhat dowdy styles they offer.

No solution is perfect. None is invincible. But if you carry only what you need, and secure those things wisely, you'll avoid anxiety and better enjoy your travels. So dress down, stow your stuff, raise your antennas, swallow three spoonfuls of skepticism, and have a great time.

Theft Thwarters #4:
How to Foil the Opportunist

Everyday Travel-Safe Habits

- Don't make it easy for a thief.
- Admit it: you might not feel it.
- Travel light. If you don't need it, don't bring it.
- Don't send signals that you're worth the thief's effort. Forget the flashy jewelry when you're out and about. Knock-off watches and costume jewelry are no better; the thief can't tell they're fake.
- Never flash your money. Try not to reveal where you keep it.
- Don't get lulled into a false sense of security. A shop is not an insular haven. Potted trees lining a sidewalk café are not a protective wall.
- If someone penetrates your personal sphere and gets closer than necessary or makes you feel uneasy, look at the person. That is often enough to make a thief move on.
- Be suspicious of bumps or jostles. They could be a distraction.
- Beware the sheet of cardboard or newspaper pushed against you.
- Be wary of hoards of friendly children with inquisitive hands.
- Beware aggressive beggars.

Where to Carry Cash and Valuables

- Men: Keep your wallet in your tightest pocket; button the pocket if it has a button.
  - ☐ Turning your wallet sideways may make it more difficult for a thief to remove.
  - ☐ Loose or gaping front pants pockets are invitations to a thief. So is a wallet that protrudes from a back pocket.
  - ☐ Velcro and zippers are deterrents, but no pocket is pick-proof.
- Women: If you carry a purse, try to give it nerve endings: hold it snug against your body, never let it stick out behind you, and especially never let it stick out behind you *open*.
  - ☐ Use a wide-strapped bag and wear the strap diagonally across your chest, or a short-strapped one with the purse tucked under your arm.
  - ☐ Keep your bag closed properly. If it has a flap, wear the flap against your body.
  - ☐ Keep your wallet at the bottom of your purse.

- ☐ Never hang your purse on the back of a chair in a public place. Keep it on your lap. If you must put it on the floor, tuck the strap under your thigh, or put the chair leg through it.
- ☐ Be sure your purse is in front of you as you enter revolving doors, board trains, etc.
- ☐ Never leave your purse in a shopping cart or baby stroller.
- ☐ Never set your purse down in a shop so you can turn your attention elsewhere.
- ☐ To prevent a drive-by bag snatch, walk far from the curb, on the side of the street toward traffic.
- ☐ If your bag *is* snatched, let it go. It may be impossible to fight the instinct to hold on, but try to ingrain that thought. You can get seriously hurt in a bag snatch.

- If you must carry a large amount of cash, use a money belt or wear a thin pouch under your clothes (some excellent models hang from your belt inside your pants).

- Fanny packs may not be the height of fashion, but they are safe *if you secure the zippers,* which are easily opened by practiced thieves. Use a safety pin, a paper clip fastened to a rubber band around the belt strap, or string. Anything to make opening the zipper more difficult.

- Consider some of the travel safety products on the market.
  - ☐ See the Stealth Belt featured at *www.bobarno.com.*
  - ☐ See the "Silo" fannypack at *www.daymakers.com.*
  - ☐ See travel clothes with special pockets at *www.tilley.com.*

Public Transportation —Talk About Risky . . . 6

On a recent August day, Bob and I counted at least forty pickpockets in Rome's subway, just in *one station,* on *one platform!* What must be lurking in the rest of the system? And police seemed to be *friendly* with the thieves! With a cheap wallet planted on Bob, we tested our theories that (a) we look like complete suckers, and (b) the subway in Rome is absolutely infested. We had a new, low-light micro-camera, which we'd hidden in a sunglass case. Bob held it and pointed it freely. *Every* time we got on a train, our wallet was taken. Despite our years of prowling, we were dumbfounded. I can hardly express our amazement at the sheer number of repetitions we experienced. Our conclusion: an unprepared tourist on Rome's public transportation hasn't got a chance.

Supplicants in the Subway

As we rode the steep escalator to the depths of Rome's Termini Station, we marveled at the swirling, pushing, roiling crowd of passengers. Before we reached the bottom, we could see several uniformed officers on the platform. Bob groaned.

"Bad luck for us. There won't be any pickpockets with the police around."

It was nearly noon. We thought we'd have a quick look anyway, then surface for a lunch of Roman-fried artichokes and zucchini flowers. But as we were funneled off the escalator, we immediately recognized the abused-looking face of a pregnant pickpocket we'd filmed years earlier. Again, she was big with child. The woman, perhaps twenty years old now, swayed on her feet and smiled as she kidded with the officers.

What was going on?

Had it not been for that familiar face, we wouldn't have looked twice at a trendy teenager nearby. The girl wore cute, tight pants rolled up at

Two female pickpockets in Rome's subway. The one wearing a cap later stole Bob's wallet.

the cuffs, a clingy, low-cut top, and the latest in designer eyeglasses. She wore a gaudy choker and makeup, her lips darkly outlined with pencil.

In no way did she fit our previous pickpocket profile. Her dark hair was short and straight, neatly cut at shoulder length, sticking out beneath a black baseball cap. Slung across her chest, she carried the latest style shoulder bag, the body-hugging, wide-strapped leather pouch with extra cell phone, eyeglass case, and coin compartments attached to the broad strap. Smart and sassy, she did not at all resemble her dowdy, pregnant friend. The girl was suspect by association.

The two girls conversed together, and with the uniformed officers as well. At first we assumed the girls had been arrested and were awaiting police escort to the station. How silly of us. After five or six minutes of chat, the girls and officers wandered from the bottom of the escalator to the train platform, which was momentarily quiet. Their joking and laughing continued, and there was even a little friendly physical contact initiated by one officer.

A new crowd soon built up on the platform, and our attention turned to a perfect suspect, a pudgy male. We watched his eyes, and the way they locked on to another passenger. He moved to his chosen one and stood close.

The train swooshed in and stopped abruptly. Its doors slid open and clotted streams of human beings gushed forth, flowing, somehow, into the mass of bodies waiting on the platform, coalescing into a solid, writhing, determined organism. The new being contracted, then broke into bits, dispersing like grains from a punctured sack of rice.

She has just returned Bob's wallet and is now nervous and uncomfortable, trapped on a moving train with her victim.

Three pickpockets in Rome. The one standing center stole Bob's wallet, but dropped it on the floor after persistent demands for its return.

The pudgy male followed his mark onto the train, shuffling in tiny steps so close, so close. He wouldn't allow anyone to separate them. Bob and I followed, intending to film him, but we were roughly shunted to the right by a last-second surge of passengers as the train doors tried to shut. There was no way we could filter our narrow bodies through the dense pack to get closer to Pudgy.

Before we had time for disappointment, Bob turned to me.

"All around us," he said under his breath.

Yes, four young men, on three sides of Bob and one behind me. They were eyeing each other. The tallest, in front of Bob, already had Bob's wallet.

"Give it back," Bob said, firmly but quietly. "Give me the wallet."

No response. Four pairs of wild eyes now flicked everywhere but at each other, everywhere but at their victim.

"Give me the wallet." Bob hardened his voice and stared at the tall one.

Plunk. The wallet hit the floor and the men stepped aside.

I picked it up as the train reached a station. Bob was still glaring at the four. He intended to follow them onto the platform.

The foursome got off and we were right behind them. But there, on the platform, was the pudgy male we'd followed earlier. We dropped the four and snuck up on Pudgy, who was now behind a crowd waiting to board while a stream of others disembarked.

Bob's camera was still rolling.

"Pudgy" stole from a subway passenger's cargo pocket.

Behind the waiting passengers, Pudgy did a slow lunge, reaching his hands as far forward as possible. Bob leaned dangerously against the train, straining to see, angling his camera. Pudgy stretched toward a man who shuffled slowly toward the train door. With both hands, he opened the Velcro flap, then put one hand right into the cargo pocket low on the man's thigh, and came out with a wallet. He turned and rushed away down the platform, suddenly followed by a cluster of children like the Pied Piper. We followed him to an escalator where a security guard, watching our pursuit, shouted, "Kick him! Kick him!" over and over. Obviously, Pudgy was well known in the area, and frustrated guards have little authority over crimes they do not witness.

Where were we? I gave Bob the recovered wallet and he replaced it in his fanny pack. We turned to look for a station name and there, standing in a just-arrived train, was the trendy teenager in the black cap.

We dashed on before the doors slammed shut. The train lurched and gathered speed. Squashed against the door, we scrutinized the passengers. Now I noticed that the teen girl wore the small crude tattoos often associated with criminal tribes: two on her upper arm and at least one more on her hand.

"Give me back the wallet," Bob said quietly. I didn't even know she'd taken it. She tossed her hair and looked away, inching closer to the door.

"Give it back." Bob pointed his sunglass case directly at her. He'd already filmed her hand in his fanny pack. Now he focused on her face.

She licked her made-up lips and blinked nervously, trapped beside her victim. Finally, she unzipped her shoulder bag and removed Bob's wallet. She handed it to him meekly.

The train came to a stop and the stealthy opportunist made a quick escape. Bob and I returned to Termini, ready for lunch. We'd only been three stations away.

Back at Termini, as we shuffled along with the mob toward the escalator, we saw the uniformed officers again and, with them, the pregnant pickpocket, the trendy teenager, and at least a dozen others.

Instead of surfacing for lunch, we lingered on the platform, watching the interaction. The area had cleared of passengers. Six or eight police officers sauntered around among the fifteen or so in the pickpocket gang. There were women with babies on their chests, women without babies, and many children. All of them, pickpockets and police, loitered comfortably together in a loose and shifting association. Passengers began to arrive again, but the platform was still pretty empty. A clutch of women formed a huddle nearby, bending inward. Soon they straightened, a knot opening like the petals of a daisy, or a fist opening to reveal a treasure. As the women moved away, each counted a wad of bills and stuffed them into a pocket or backpack. They made no effort to hide their swag.

The Making of ABC *20/20*: Subway Steals

"How much money do we have, Arnold? Show me," I said. "Good. Now turn a little toward me. We want them to see where you put your wallet."

Arnold Diaz, ABC *20/20*'s investigative reporter, flashed his money obediently and stuffed it into his back pocket. He was rather unattractive wearing the black spectacles that contained the latest high-tech hidden camera, and a bit bulky around his normally slim middle, padded, as he was, with transmitters and recording packs.

"They're directly behind you now," I whispered to Arnold, "two white-haired grandfathers."

I knew my voice would be transmitted through Arnold's wire to our nearby producer and hidden camera photographer, who stood nearby. Then they'd know who Bob and I suspected of being pickpockets, and where to direct their cameras.

The elderly gentlemen shuffled and fidgeted, eyed each other, and stuck close to Arnold. One carried a section of the morning paper. At midmorning, this did not raise anyone's suspicion.

Since I was facing Arnold and the suspects were behind him, I could keep a surreptitious eye on them. Bob and I had pegged them only minutes after entering the Rome metro, as they milled in the track-side crowd. Bob also wore hidden camera eyeglasses, and he carried a digital video camera as well.

A train blasted into the station and Rome's late-morning rush hour scrum crashed face-to-face on the platform, opposing teams fighting to get on and off the train. Amidst the confusion, Arnold and I pushed ourselves on, an ordinary tourist couple, we seemed, with Bob nearby. We didn't know where the train was going and didn't care. But we were pleased to notice the grandfathers had followed us on. The other two of our small and maneuverable team slipped into the car's other door, where they could watch us from a short distance.

Arnold Diaz wore a backpack stuffed with foam to make it stick out, and rigged with a hidden camera pointed down toward his hip pocket. If his wallet was picked, we hoped we'd get a clear shot of the picker's hand and the extraction.

"The deed is done," Arnold said in an undertone, not thirty seconds later. The three of us grinned. The train screeched to a halt at the next station, the doors slid open, and we burst out, team and perps, splattered onto the mostly empty platform of an unimportant station somewhere under the Eternal City.

"Hey! You have my wallet!" Arnold went directly after the grandfathers, looking for a confrontation. Bob, the producer, the photographer, and I fanned out on the platform, surrounding them. "Where's my wallet?"

Later, Arnold commented on the thieves' meek manner, their total lack of self-defense, and their obvious understanding of his accusation in English.

I summoned station security, police were called, and the whole group of us moved upstairs to a security booth.

"Get us a flashlight," Bob requested. "He may have thrown the wallet onto the track." In the commotion, one of the Italian geezers had slipped away and the other had dodged over to the opposite track and pointed down with his rolled newspaper, possibly dumping Arnold's wallet there. In any case, a flashlight never materialized and neither did the wallet.

(continued)

We emerged from the Spagna station into the swirling tourist mobs at the Spanish Steps. We were a giddy procession high on success: a news-crew-cum-victimized-visitor following a pair of police and half of a pickpocket duo. We wound our way to the police station while the producer used a cell phone to call our driver, still back at Termini Station. By the time we'd made our official report, the van was waiting for us outside the police station.

The five of us dove into the van, laughing and full of excited anticipation. Jill Goldstein, our hidden camera expert, took charge, unrigging Arnold, Bob, and herself, popping out cassettes, and hur-

ABC 20/20's investigative reporter Arnold Diaz confronts an elderly pickpocket in Rome's subway.

riedly labeling them. She put the tapes into players, one by one, rewinding while the rest of us craned to see the monitor.

"Here's Arnold's glasses-cam," she said, showing us the confrontation with the pickpocket on the platform.

"This one's Bob's." Obviously. Taken from above the heads of the crowd on the platform, when our thief was only a suspect. The grandfatherly gentleman looks up and around, around, around, then his eyes dart quickly and sharply downward, toward Arnold's back pocket. Repeat. Eyes meet those of grandfatherly colleague. The two are together, but not too close. Innocent until proven guilty. Bob turns away. He can't stare at them. When his camera returns to the elderly pair, they're moving slightly side to side. They seem to be creating and preserving an airspace behind Arnold, positioning themselves to prevent anyone from intruding, yet maintaining that innocent distance.

The train comes and Bob gets it in his camera. Pan to Arnold, Bambi, and two suspects, who all press into the crowd at the train entrance.

Interior, train. Jerky. View of swaying crowd from just above their heads.

"Here's Arnold's backpack camera," Jill said. We watched the dark frames of indistinguishable motion. Then:

"There it is. His hand! Going into Arnold's pocket! Don't worry, we can lighten it in editing." The thief's fingers slid into Arnold's pocket and stayed there.

"That's 'kicking the poke,'" Bob explained. "He's positioning the wallet for easier extraction."

"Yeah, I could feel his hand in there forever," Arnold said.

"But only because you were concentrating on it," Bob said. "Ordinarily, you wouldn't have felt it at all, or you wouldn't have thought anything of it."

"No, I would have just thought I'd been bumped in the crowd."

Finally, the hand comes out with the wallet. It appears to go into the thief's own front pocket.

"The wallet's too dark," the producer said. "I shouldn't have gotten brown. You can't see it well enough in the low light."

Jill suggested marking the next wallet with green tape. A great idea.

Later, analyzing the footage of our subway exploits, we were aston-ished to see the trendy teenager lift another wallet before she took ours. Her victim was a woman who clutched her handbag to her chest. Beneath it she wore a fanny pack. Bob's camera, held low as we entered the train, recorded what our eyes had missed: the trendy teenager's tattooed hand unzipping the fanny pack, removing a wallet, and rezipping the bag. Then she brought the stolen goods up to her own bag, and out of the camera's range. Two wallets in two minutes! That could add up to serious money, depending on how many palms had to be greased.

In Paris, there's a new trend. Pickpockets are putting on smart business suits and blending in with groggy morning commuters whose laptops are unguarded. Or perhaps it isn't a new trend, but a resurrection of the style portrayed in the 1959 movie *Pickpocket,* written and directed by Robert Bresson. No one gives the well-dressed thieves a second look, flummox-ing police and infuriating travelers.

Though the French are fed up with pickpockets on their trains, they can't seem to do much about it. Headlines like "Pickpockets saw business drop" after terrorist bombings closed the subway show the city seems almost resigned to a class with a license to steal. Conductors repeatedly go on strike against growing crime, calling for more security and better communications. Their summer of 2001 strike was prompted when a group of pickpockets tried to throw a conductor out of a train window. French conductors' unions shut down 75 percent of train service for twenty-four hours, then life was back to normal for commuters and thieves alike, with nothing changed. Sounds more like the Wild West than the *haute Paris* we might imagine.

"Petty crime is rife in Mumbai, too," said Goolshan Hathiram, an Indian university professor, "not unlike that found in any other major metropolis. Crowded trains and marketplaces are the areas favored by our scoundrels." Pickpocketing, bag snatching, and chain ripping are all com-mon, she explained, and commuters on the overstuffed lines into and out of Mumbai Central are particularly at risk. "Handbags are easily snuck into," Professor Hathiram said, "and married women, who must wear gold chains around their necks, are especially vulnerable."

I thought of Smriti Shah, who lost so much on a train to Mumbai. "We think the robber marked us back in Kanpur," Smriti said, "and bought a ticket on the same train. They saw the mark on my forehead and my jew-elry, and could see that I was going to a wedding. They knew I'd have jew-elry in my bag."

"Thieves often attack passengers without even boarding the trains," Goolshan said. "A hand will reach in through a window as a train pulls into another mobbed station, a gold chain will be grabbed and snapped off a woman's neck, and the culprit disappears into the masses."

In Mumbai, three young women boarded a train during off-peak hours. They had an entire car to themselves. A boy joined them at a later stop and, as the train was pulling into the next station, he grabbed the purse of one of the women. Although the purse contained less than two dollars' worth of rupees, the woman resisted, holding tight to her bag. Her two companions were petrified, and shrank back against the opposite end of the car. When the compartment doors slid open at the station, the boy gave a mighty yank and the woman tripped out of the car after him, still holding onto her purse. As the desperate boy finally twisted his prize from her grip, the woman fell onto the tracks across the platform, where she was immediately run over by an oncoming train.

"If her misery could have ended there," our informer told us, "it would have been better. But the woman lives. She lost both her legs."

Just another petty crime?

The state of the subways in America has loosened, rather than tightened, since September 11, with many police officers reassigned to other, more vital, positions. But trains are still a favorite venue for pickpockets, especially now that credit cards are such valuable plunder.

"Here's what they do," a New York pickpocket cop told me. "They steal from someone they know is going on a long ride. Like they steal from someone at Penn Station who's going to New Jersey, say. That's about forty-five minutes. Then they sell the credit cards to a buyer right away, who tests it by making a small purchase. The thief gets $500 for each card that tests good."

"We ride the trains every day," said Sergeant Randy Stoever, head of the NYPD Transit Bureau's Manhattan pickpocket unit. "We know who they are. I keep a book, called *325 Pickpockets,* and I keep it updated." The book contains mug shots of known thieves and Stoever's officers study it. He keeps another for "lush workers," those who roll and rob drunks. "We go undercover," he said, "and I've taught my guys how to look without making eye contact. We ride the subway, and we go where the money is. That's where we find them."

When we rode the New York City trains with Detective Lothel Crawford, he pointed out the same suspicious behavior obvious to Bob and me, but he commented on the suspects' attire. Baggy pants might indicate a pervert, not a pickpocket, though the behavior at first seems similar and noticeably odd. Los Angeles Metropolitan Transportation Authority undercover officers recently discovered the same phenomenon when they went looking for pickpockets in the mass-transit system. Now they're arresting more perverts than pickpockets.

Bus, train, and subway stations are magnets for lowlife opportunists. Risks to the unwary traveler begin as he enters the building or before, if the surroundings are seedy. To an unemployed alcoholic, or drug addict, or general scoundrel, the wallet nestled in a tourist's purse or back pocket contains ten or a hundred or a thousand times what he needs for his next drink or fix or smoke. City spokesmen may insist that their thieves don't target tourists, but the fact remains that tourists make up the bulk of victims. Tourists are easily recognized as such; they're presumed to have money; they're distracted by new surroundings; they are not aware of local risks. Thieves simply go for the best bet.

In Las Vegas, Bus 301, which travels Las Vegas Boulevard (a.k.a "the Strip"), attracts its share of tourists and thieves along with locals. While the bus company claims to get few reports of theft, Las Vegas Metro Police know better. Still, the number of incidents doesn't come close to overseas proportions. When Bob and I went bus riding with the Vegas pickpocket squad, we found the buses spacious, and not nearly crowded enough for major mischief. Boarding, a thief's prime moment, is only allowed at the front door, which is not as conducive to lightfinger work as the back doors are, away from the driver. The only opportunists we found were fare-jumpers.

Public transportation systems are a ripe mélange of locals, tourists, and thieves. Many stations have little or no security. Ticket lines, waiting areas, platforms, shops, and restaurants all require extra vigilance

Pickpocket warning signs provoke passersby to pat their pockets, revealing to a lurking thief where their goods are kept.

against the lurking threat of theft. The problem is, we never know who to suspect. Sure we can pick out the obvious skulks, but who would have recognized the ancient fellows we filmed stealing for *20/20?* Turns out that grandfather gangs are not unheard of in Rome. A few years back, police in Rome described the doings of eighty-one-year-old Domenica Panella and his two accomplices, sixty-eight and sixty-three years old, who worked over luggage-burdened tourists at Tiburtina train station.

Officials are caught in the usual publicity trap. Do they warn the public at the risk of scaring them off the system altogether? Or keep mum, and risk anger, negative press, and potential liability? Most stations with significant problems post warnings to passengers. But these work to the clever thieves' advantage. What do you do when you see a sign that says *watch your wallet* or *pickpockets work here?* If you're like most people, you instinctively touch it. You pat your pocket. You show the lurking thief exactly where you keep it.

Nerves of Steal

Luciano's morning hit was tense. He had ridden the trams during what should have been rush hour, but for the relative desertion of the business world. The city was shut, shop fronts literally shuttered and padlocked for the summer holidays. Luciano had tried and failed four times that first hour, backing off each attempt at the last second. Once the tram lurched and he bumped clumsily into his mark, and once he thought he was noticed by someone sitting nearby. The other two efforts just weren't right—he couldn't get the right angle.

Finally, he got close to a businessman in a sport coat. It was one of the last crowded trams of the morning. The mark was hanging onto a ceiling strap with one hand and trying to read a folded newspaper in his other. His jacket was hanging open. Luciano, hating face-to-face work, broke into a sweat. He used a floppy leather portfolio to shield his hand as he slid it against the breast pocket, where he'd seen the weight of a wallet.

His partner Stefano was so close Luciano could smell the espresso on the blocker's breath. Yet, they never looked at one another. Luciano willed his hand to be steady and light. He willed the mark to keep reading. He hoped the leather wouldn't snag on a fold of fabric.

Pinching the wallet between his middle fingertip and the nail of his first finger, he slipped it out. It was a smooth move—textbook. He slid it down to thigh level along with his brown portfolio, and Stefano's hand was ready, as if by instinct. Stefano then plunged the wallet into his own deep pants pocket, and covered the bulge with a plastic grocery bag. At the next corner he stepped off the tram, before it even stopped. Luciano stayed on two blocks longer, heart pounding, then got off and met Stefano midway, as usual.

Stefano had already dumped the leather. They split the proceeds equally.

"Why should the blocker get an equal share?" we had asked Luciano. "The skill is yours. The pressure is on you."

"The risk is the same," he answered.

Coffee with Thieves

An August Sunday in Naples, 2001. Summer holiday for all of Europe and most shops were closed. We bought bus tickets at a kiosk with our last coins, dodged the wild traffic, and crossed to the narrow center strip to wait for a crowded bus. I carried a small video camera in my hand and wore a fanny pack containing my digital camera. Bob had a hidden camera, its guts stowed in a shoulder bag he wore across his chest.

A number one bus arrived, jammed. I didn't think we'd be able to get on. The doors jerked open and a few passengers tumbled out like crickets escaping from a child's jar. Bob and I shuffled forward with the mob as the people onboard compacted. We would never voluntarily join such a scene were it not for the call of research. This was highly unpleasant: beyond funny.

"No way. Let's wait for another," I said to Bob.

Two clean-cut middle-aged men who'd gotten off the bus were now behind us, corralling the doubtful like sheepdogs. Somehow, with their encouragement, we all got on, filling spaces we hadn't known existed. The good Samaritans kept us from bursting off the bus in the pressure while one yelled, *"Chiude a porta, chiude a porta."* Close the door!

My chest was pressed against a vertical pole. A wiry man in front of me had his back to the same pole. Glancing down, I saw his hand behind his back, blindly trying to make sense of the zipper tabs on my fanny pack,

A crowded tram or bus is a perfect milieu for pickpockets.

which I'd paper clipped together. I watched, half amused, half outraged at his audaciousness.

We'd already made half a dozen or so tram trips that morning and had been pickpocketed on most of them. We hadn't yet seen the same thieves twice. By now it seemed a certainty: riding a crowded bus or tram in Naples meant intimacy with a thief. Well, let me qualify that to specify buses and trams on lines that tourists might travel; specifically those stopping at the ship and ferry terminal, the archeological museum, and the train stations. Looking at the protective behavior of local passengers, bus bandits seemed to be an accepted fact of life, as if there's one in every crowd.

The disembodied hand couldn't solve the puzzle in its fingertips. It dropped, or crawled away of its own accord. No success, no accusation.

Bob suddenly reached for my camera and held it high above the compressed mob, pointing down.

"Give back the wallet," he said quietly. "There's no money in it."

"Okay, okay," said one of the good Samaritans. He handed it back with a sheepish grin below ultra-cool wraparound reflective sunglasses. In the video, you can see him lower the wallet to his thigh and check its contents.

"Come talk to us," Bob said in French as the doors popped open. "Just talk—and coffee."

"*Caffé? Caffé?*" The thief raised an invisible little cup to his lips, pinkie outstretched. "Okay." But when the doors opened there was a cat-and-mouse game as all four of us hopped off and on the bus with opposing motives. They were trying to ditch us. Finally Bob and I were on the ground with one of the pair while the other hung in the doorway of the bus, reluctant. "C'mon," we all yelled to the last guy, and he finally joined us.

The men led us into a bar across the street and, as we entered, I realized we had no money with us. Horrified, I pulled the last note from my pocket, not even enough for an inexpensive Italian espresso.

"No problem, you are my guests," said the Italian who spoke French, with the hospitality of a Neapolitan. He ushered us in with the same warmth and efficiency he'd used to herd us onto the bus. He ordered three coffees, four glasses of water, and one almond milk.

"Bambi and Bob," we introduced ourselves.

"Mario," said the one who spoke French. He studied us quizzically, as if he'd never been invited for coffee by a man whose wallet he'd just swiped.

"Tony," said the reluctant other, and we all shook hands.

Mario was trim, fifty-ish, with smooth skin, curly salt-and-pepper hair, and a receding hairline. He wore a crisp white T-shirt tucked into blue shorts secured with a leather belt. With a watch, gold ring, cell phone, and snazzy shades, this was no lowlife, drugged-up desperado. Mario looked respectable, like anybody's brother.

Mario works on trams and buses in Naples, but more lucratively on long-distance trains to Monte Carlo and Paris. He steals credit cards and uses them to buy Rolex watches, which he then sells for cash.

Tony was a little rounder, and clearly the junior partner. He squinted under a blue baseball cap. Have you ever wanted to know where a pickpocket keeps his wallet? His was in the pocket of his blue button-down shirt. It was Tony who'd first tried to take Bob's wallet on the bus, but Mario who succeeded and slipped it to Tony.

Unlike most of the other cities we've visited, Naples' thieves and con men are homegrown. They're not immigrants, handy to take the rap, or despised illegals doing what they can for their very survival. These are Neapolitans practicing an age-old profession without, as far as we can tell, a shred of shame.

Over coffee we chided and joked, conversing easily in French. Having accidentally established ourselves as professional colleagues, we rode the misconception to our advantage, encouraging Mario to tell us about his world. As Mario spoke, I recorded him with a visible, hip-held video camera, which I tossed around casually. I was worried about being caught with the camera running. Bob and I were jolly and friendly, belying our nerves and disapproval. Tony was reserved, possibly due to his lack of French. Mario was enthusiastic and embracing, but was he feigning? We thought not.

Naples has a history steeped in crime and a people sincerely warm and jovial. It just might be the thievery capital of the world. I'm not sure, though; there are so many contenders. Myth and history tell us that it is the birthplace of pizza, but today this gritty, passionate, mob-infested city is better known for its pickpocketing. Who's involved? Who lives in the underworld? Who's on the fringes? It's impossible for an outsider to know.

"Do you have any books on the Camorra crime family?" Bob asked later in a bookshop.

"Camorra! The Camorra is a fantasy," the shop owner replied dismissively. He was smiling though. In Naples, one only *whispers* about the Camorra.

Although a crowded bus or train is Christmas for a pickpocket and a minefield for a passenger, our most vulnerable moment is as we board. All the action, distraction, and swirl of people creates a perfect milieu. When a pickpocket succeeds during boarding, he won't get on at all. Bob and I

A Misunderstanding and a Proposition

"First let me explain," Bob said. "I work in casinos. I do big operations. I also do theaters. I am an *artiste.*" He looked around for someone wearing a watch. "Let me show you."

Bob reached a long arm out to a newcomer in the bar and lifted his watch, his customary proof of comradeship.

"Oh, bravo!" Mario and Tony laughed. "He took the bus driver's watch! Good job, well done." The driver got his watch back and faded into the background. Is it logical, or odd, that pickpockets and bus drivers hang out at the same bar?

"Me, I steal credit cards," said Mario. "Visa—wait, wait, listen to this! You speak all these languages. If you work with me we'll make so much money. I know all the cities. Florence, Venice, Viareggio. . . . We can work in Rome, Naples . . ."

Mario was convinced that Bob worked at casinos and theaters as a thief—a real *artiste.* It was only later that we realized the ambiguity of Bob's earnest attempt at a job description.

"But there's no money in Naples!" Bob scoffed.

"No, no, here is good! Here I steal credit cards. Then I go to a shop and buy Rolexes. Rolex! You understand? Then I sell them, get money, and I share with my friends."

Unintentionally reinforcing the concept that Bob did this for a living, Bob laughed, bumped into Mario, and lifted the wallet from Mario's back pocket.

"Oh, I see what you do! *Multi-bravo!*" Mario said, and, in Neapolitan, explained to the bartender what had happened. "He took my wallet, he's pretty smart! We came in here to have coffee together." Mario didn't mention the other part, that he'd taken Bob's wallet first. But the bartender probably knew that.

"I have some friends at shops who help with these things. We'd make a good team, you and me. If you work with me, I can give you each two million lire every day." That's a thousand dollars a day, each! "Have you been to Ischia? To Capri?"

Mario's cell phone rang. *"Bueno.* I'm by the Vesuviana. Okay, I'm coming over there. *Ciao.*"

Mario and Tony spoke to each other for a moment in Neapolitan, trying to figure out why Bob does this. He does it as a hobby, they concluded, just for fun.

"Madam, you want to try?" Tony offered me a taste of his almond milk, which looked intriguing, but I wasn't about to drink from a stranger's—even better, a known thief's—glass. Bob and I were concurrently on the trail of the "yellow bomb," in which patient thieves in Turkey spike drinks with Nembitol or benzodiazepine, then rob the knocked-out victim.

"No, *grazie.*" Looking at Tony, I pointed to the T-shirt he had draped over his shoulder satchel. I pointed to the T-shirt and smiled, tapped my head like "I know," then waggled my finger and shook my head. The international pantomime worked, and Tony laughed. "No good," he agreed, and stuffed the shirt into the satchel. I hadn't noticed the hanging shirt when we were on the tram together but, if I had, it would have signaled "pickpocket" in a big way.

"Tomorrow I go to my family," Mario said. "My wife is in Calabria with the children. I am driving to Calabria this evening to be with them, and I'm coming back tomorrow."

I tried to picture this bus-working wallet-thief heading off to a seaside vacation.

"Here is my mobile phone number," Mario said, handing Bob a piece of paper. "Call me. Any day is good."

"But we're leaving Napoli," Bob began.

(continued)

Mario interrupted. "Listen to me properly. The eighteenth and nineteenth of this month I will be in Florence. Florence is very, very good. I know everything about it. I can find out right away if the credit cards are good or not. And you would be a perfect partner because you speak French, English—"

"And I speak German, as well," Bob said. Wait—was he buying into this?

"So you come with your wife and we're going to take credit cards only for Rolex. We'll work on the train that goes from Florence to Monaco to Paris." Mario made a stealthy swiping motion. "There's a lot of good stuff we can do together."

"That's difficult for me."

"Listen. I get on the train that goes to these places, Vienna, Florence, Monaco, Paris. I go all day long and I take only credit cards. We make fifteen to twenty million lire in one day. If you want, tomorrow, call me."

Wow. That's seven to ten thousand dollars. Now I pictured Mario roaring down the highway in a Ferrari, adoring family eagerly awaiting the hard-working dad at their private summer villa.

"I can't call you tomorrow, but maybe the day after. We'll be in Venice for three days."

"You work in Venice?" Mario looked surprised. "Okay, but you pay attention. Be careful there."

"Yes, I know," Bob said. By now it was too much to explain.

"If you do it properly, this is a fabulous job. Especially in Venice."

"But there's a vigilante group there."

"I know, I've been there for *Carnivale*. I know the place."

We said our good-byes and thanked Mario for the coffee.

"This is Napoli! You are my guest," he said. Right, the same guest he'd tried to rip off half an hour ago. We ambled back to the buses, the four of us, splitting to opposite ends of the waiting passengers.

Bob and I, a bit stunned, wanted to get on the first bus that came along. As one pulled up and we moved toward the door, Mario shouted from thirty yards away: not that one, next one. Then he and Tony hopped on another and, presumably, went back to work.

get our best footage as we step onto public transportation, I with camera, following him with wallet.

Nancy Braun, a mad-as-hell American expatriate living in Prague, was had while boarding Prague's infamous tram number twelve.

Nancy, a thirty-eight-year-old baker, rode the tram to and from her shop every day. She hadn't paid much attention to the thieves on board until the day her own bag was stolen. Her arms were full of groceries, she explained, and the thief spun her around on the tram as she entered and he exited, just as the tram was starting to move on. When she came out of her involuntary pirouette, Nancy found her pocketbook gone and one bag of groceries stuck in the closed door of the tram, the bag outside as she held onto it from the inside. She was flustered and furious, and cried as she watched her assailant skip away. Nancy was incensed because she saw what was coming from the beginning yet was powerless to stop it.

From that day, Nancy became somewhat of a vigilante. She continued her daily rides on tram number twelve, but scrutinized the riders. When she saw suspicious behavior, she shouted to warn fellow passengers. If the police wouldn't do anything about the problem, Nancy would take it upon herself. And as a one-person prevention force, she was highly effective.

On the Trail of a Train Robber

Luigi Panella is a composite of several thieves we've watched and interviewed. He made his career on public transportation, particularly enjoying trains.

While neither a pickpocket nor exactly a bag snatcher, Luigi had an effective method of separating valuables from their owners. He was simply a bag taker. He chose unattended luggage of the appropriate size that was stowed in the luggage racks, overhead shelves, under seats, or in the aisles on trains.

Luigi began each workday with a quick scan of the station's posted departure schedule. He was not against taking a bag left on the platform by an arriving passenger, but stealing from departing trains was far less complicated. He could be guaranteed instant separation from his victim, miles within minutes.

Luigi kept a handy stash of empty bags from previous thefts. His favorites were canvas duffel bags stiff enough to hold a nice shape even when empty. He'd patiently hang around his hidden stockpile until the platform was deserted, then open his hiding place and select a container. With the bag convincingly fluffed into shape, he'd head for the platform of the next departing train.

It was simple to board the train, as tickets were never checked until the journey got under way. Then it was just a matter of passing through the cars, loitering a little, and waiting for the right moment. Finding an unattended bag was never difficult. The hard part was choosing which to take. That was the crapshoot. A computer or bag full of other electronic items was always better than ending up with a sack of dirty laundry or, worse, somebody's cake or casserole. That had happened too many times to count.

Luigi lingered at the ends of the railway cars, where people stowed their luggage on racks just inside the doors. That was the easiest place. But he found from experience that the most valuable items were kept close to their owners, overhead or on the floor near their seats. And, he found, most people didn't keep a close eye on their belongings. They'd even leave their seats, presuming their things were safe.

When Luigi took a bag, it was always with the aura of utter confidence. He picked it up as if it were his own. He tried to be sure no one could see him, but if someone did, he would not look guiltily around, giving away the game. No one on the train knew which bag belonged to whom, anyway.

A moment or two later, Luigi would cover the stolen bag with his empty duffel. It was then that he felt most cocksure. He could saunter all the way through a carriage if he wanted to, through the entire train, even. Who would know? Who would stop him?

If he was lucky, the train would still be in the station and he could hop off immediately. If not, he'd stroll through the cars, careful to avoid the conductor, and get off at the first stop.

Once off the train, Luigi had to consider how to get rid of incriminating evidence most quickly. He could do it in the men's room, at a Dumpster behind the station, sometimes even in the bathroom on the train. He always stripped away identifying papers. Luggage tags, business cards, mail. But he'd keep most everything else. The bag itself would be added to his collection. Everything else would be kept, sold, or traded with flea market vendors.

Luigi's lucrative career came to an abrupt end when Italy's railway police set up a sting operation. Luigi was only one of many criminals put out of action, at least temporarily.

The railway police keep their own offices in Italy's major train stations. As well as railway offenses, they also take reports of city crimes. Not only are their stations highly visible to incoming visitors, but they're also open twenty-four hours a day. In Milan, when tourists are directed to *Centrale* police station to report thefts, they often mistakenly go to *Centrale* railway station. The railway police accommodate them.

Inspector D'Amore Vincenzo of the Milan railway police bought his own personal computer, and has developed a complex database of personal theft crimes. With enthusiasm, Inspector Vincenzo can break down incidents by week, month, year, type of crime, location, nationality of perpetrator, and victim. He can display reports in text, lines, graphs, and in brightly colored pie charts.

Inspector Vincenzo explained the deceptively innocent system criminal pairs commonly use on trains. Timing is everything for this ruse. It's usually practiced just as a train is pulling out of a station. Partner A will board a train and move through the cars, looking for a potential victim. Partner B will remain on the platform, following A's progress along the train. When A finds a likely passenger, he throws a signal through the window to B on the platform. B waits for the train to begin moving, then knocks urgently on the window to get the passenger's attention. As he obediently turns to open the window, the traveler becomes a victim: A grabs his bag and jumps expertly off the moving train.

Even if he has noticed the theft, the victim will never jump off a moving train, which would have gained speed by the time he could get to the

How Laws Tie Hands, and Cut Them Off

Sharif spat a mouthful of blood as he laid his right arm across a wide tree stump. He had chewed the inside of his cheeks to shreds in the days since he'd been caught picking pockets in the Grand Mosque at Mecca. As an Egyptian man in Saudi Arabia, he was not entitled to extradition for his crime. He was to be punished swiftly, and in public.

Meanwhile, in Spain, Kharem dusted himself off after a police beating, gave a fleeting wistful thought to the cash he surrendered, and went back to work.

"I *never* hear of pickpockets," said Dina, an Egyptian woman who works as a tour guide with Abercrombie and Kent in Cairo. "I have never had a tourist in my charge complain of theft. Neither have my colleagues. If someone were to try to steal, the people around would beat him black and blue. They would knock him down and kick him, even burn his fingertips. It just does not happen here. Cairo is such a crowded city, we must live like brothers and sisters."

Contrast Egypt with Italy, where there are just too many thieves for the police to deal with. Without exception, every police officer we interviewed throughout Italy (and much of Europe), threw up his hands at our first mention of pickpockets.

And while each officer showed a thorough knowledge of the perpetrators and their methods, we found a serious lack of record keeping. No information is shared among countries, among agencies, even among stations in the same city. In fact, most officers do not even have computers in which to feed the data.

In Venice, the Municipale Police told us they are only interested in Venice, not in Italy or Europe. Because they never see the actual crime, the squad can't arrest or jail; they "just open the door to the next city" so the problem becomes someone else's.

Still, what's the value of numbers, patterns, and percentages? Italy's laws work against pickpocket police, and this is typical across Europe. Almost every European official we interviewed (with the notable exceptions of those in Naples and St. Petersburg) blamed the preponderance of pickpocketing and bag snatching on illegal immigrants. But the countries simply cannot get rid of their illegal aliens.

In Italy, the first problem is administrative. When immigrants are caught without papers, they are politely given fifteen days to pack up and leave the country. They are released. And that's the end of it. The immigrants often do not leave. They do not choose to return to the hell holes from which they came.

Secondly, many of the foreigners have no passports or identification. And without documentation, the north African countries from which many of these people come refuse to accept their repatriation. We cannot expect to see a reduction in street crime without giving law enforcement officials the laws to back them. Their hands are tied.

In Egypt, where people live "like brothers and sisters," Cairenes live side by side in rivalry and harmony; it's common to see men strolling arm in arm or holding hands. Across Egypt, a quasi-vigilantism controls low-level crimes. Misdemeanors and serious offenses are dealt with according to criminal code.

Egypt's judicial system is based on British and Italian models, but modified to suit the country's Islamic heritage and influenced by its ancient laws. Most of Egypt's laws are consistent with, or at least derived from, Islamic law, the *sharia*.

If Egyptian pickpocket Sharif Ali Ibrahim had committed his crime in Egypt and had been caught by alert citizens, he would have been severely beaten. If he had been caught

(continued)

by the police, he'd serve a significant prison term. And if he'd been found guilty of steal-ing from one of Egypt's precious tourists, his sentence would have been trebled.

But Sharif committed his crime in Saudi Arabia—in fact, at Islam's holiest place. He had picked the pockets of worshippers praying in the Grand Mosque at Mecca. Therefore, following strict Islamic *sharia,* Sharif Ali Ibrahim's right hand was chopped off with a sword, in public.

door, and would probably have even left the platform area. The baffled victim is left powerless at the scene of the crime, quickly gathering speed on his journey to elsewhere.

It must be our warped sense of fun, but Bob and I love hanging out at Rome's Termini station. It's busy, but not uncomfortably crowded, and the ambiance is constantly changing and is different on each platform depending on where trains are going or coming from. Underground, Termini subway station is Rome's most concentrated pickpocket terrain, and outside is where the infamous Bus 64 begins its route.

We were loitering on the platform one day, observing as trains arrived and others departed. Suspects were everywhere and shifty behavior so prevalent it was almost the norm. The massive schedule board clattered as it was updated, old-fashioned letters falling into place. A train would be leaving soon for Florence. We wandered over.

So much to look at. Elegant Italians boarded, some foreigners, families with children. Bob and I studied the men on the platform, especially those in pairs. We walked slowly among them, getting a sense of the mood.

Departure time came and went and the platform traffic thinned. Most passengers had boarded; a few ran to make the delayed train, no doubt glad, for once, for the unreliable timetable. All the windows of the second-class cars were open for air and jammed with arms and heads hanging out, cigarettes dangling from fingers and lips. The train doors were con-gested, too. Second-class cars are notoriously hot and stuffy when trains aren't moving.

A squat man with messy hair walked along the train, straining his neck to look into its windows. He didn't exactly fit our profile of a suspect, but who were we looking for? And what is a profile, anyway? We followed. Could we have found one of the bag-snatch scammers Inspector Vincenzo had told us about? Don't get too close, we told ourselves; don't get too excited. Let it play out.

We followed him along the almost-empty platform.

I heard a gritty, grating sound behind me: something heavy. Nothing would make us take our eyes off the squat man as he scanned windows. It was a long train. We'd follow as long as he'd walk. The train was bound to leave any minute.

"Emilio! Emilio!" A businessman was leaning out a window, waving his arm and shouting. The squat man turned sharply, looked, and bolted back two cars to the shouting man. The train whistle blew. On his toes, the squat man handed something up to the businessman. A cell phone. The train lurched into movement and began its slow glide out of the station. The businessman smiled and tried to shake hands with the cell phone-bearer, but they couldn't connect.

There was that gritty, grating sound again. We turned to see a twenty-ish man adjusting the marble seat of a bench. He gave it a final shove with his knee and, with something in his hand, sauntered casually to the moving train and pulled himself up.

It had looked like a crumbled nylon bag in his hand.

"I don't believe it!" I was swimming in adrenaline. Drowning in it.

"Did you see his face?"

"No. Maybe he'll jump off the train."

"We'll wait and see."

"What do you think he was doing with the bench?" I asked.

"Either he put something in or took something out," Bob guessed.

We plopped down on the cool marble and watched the train disappear. No one jumped off. No one came slinking back to the platform. Another train pulled in on the opposite side of the platform. Its passengers streamed out and cut off our view of the tracks.

We decided to go visit Maresciallo Pinna, chief of the train station *Carabinieri,* whom we'd met on a previous visit, and his officer, Commissario Santacroce, who spoke decent English.

"Why don't we go have a look at the bench?" Santacroce suggested. "My colleague will take you." In Italian, he instructed a female uniformed officer. "Go there, she will meet you," he added to us.

Bob and I went back to the bench. It was between two pillars on the platform, a marble top on a stone base. There were several like it on each platform. We circled the bench, looking for anything odd. I reached to feel the weight of the top surface but Bob stopped me.

The policewoman drove up on a little three-wheeled car. She got off and pointed to the bench with a question on her face. She didn't speak English. We nodded. Without a plan or a forethought, the officer tilted up the heavy marble slab, which immediately crashed down and broke into three pieces. She wrung her hand and looked away for a moment while blood oozed from a long cut. From a first aid kit on the little car the policewoman took bandages and ointment. We waited silently. The platform was empty.

After tending to her injured hand, the officer removed the broken marble sections, which had landed inside the bench. Though they must have weighed almost a hundred pounds each, she refused our offer to help lift them. She placed them on the ground. As she removed each slab, Bob and

I peered into the hollow of the bench. It was filled with trash: dirty plastic bags, empty soda cans, empty whiskey bottles. The officer removed it all with a grimace instead of gloves.

Finally, deep within the stone cavern, she found a bag-snatcher's booty: a crumpled collection of twenty or so carry-all-type bags. Made of canvas, plastic, vinyl, and leather, with zippers, buckles, and drawstrings, they were all colors, all qualities, all empty.

The officer backed the three-wheeler to the now-empty hideaway and methodically loaded the mound of trash or plunder onto its tiny bed. Handling all of it a second time, she layered first the cache of bags, then the garbage, then the broken marble slabs, faithfully recreating the original *torte*. Without a wave or a *ciao* she drove off, leaving the yawning stone box like a ready sarcophagus.

Some days later, we reserved a couple of seats on the Milan–Venice intercity train. After a long day of fruitless prowling and trailing, we collapsed sweat-sticky onto springy seats in a comfortable compartment where four businessmen were already seated. Departure time passed and the train still sat in the station, unmoving. We slid the glass door of the air-conditioned compartment closed to keep the warm passageway air out. Twenty minutes later the train was still sitting in the station. We looked listlessly out the window at activity on the opposite platform, discouraged by our day's lack of accomplishments.

Suddenly, our compartment door was roughly shoved open. A long, black-sleeved arm reached in and snatched a fine leather briefcase from the luggage rack over the head of the white-haired gentleman across from us. Fast and without warning, the perpetrator barely broke his stride as he reached in, grabbed the bag, and continued down the passage.

How quickly entire concepts can fill the mind! In that fraction of a second, Bob and I both thought we'd found our man, that luck presented him to us on a silver platter.

While we were busy processing those thoughts, the white-haired man across from us leapt to combat. He blasted straight up from his seat like a jack-in-the-box and, with one swiveling step, had the wrist of the bolting fellow in a vice grip.

Bob and I could absolutely not believe our eyes. Here we had tramped up and down the streets of Milan for eight exhausting hours in ninety-degree heat and not found a single incident. Then, relaxing in the air-conditioned comfort of a second-class compartment, the thief comes to us for a private performance!

There was an abrupt exchange in Italian—just a few words—before our neighbor reseated himself with a chuckle, and without the briefcase.

The white-haired man had thought his own bag was being stolen from above his head—we all had thought so. However, the briefcase actually belonged to the "bag snatcher," who had forgotten it when he arrived on the train half an hour before. He had run back to find it, and was concerned about getting off the train before it left the station again.

The next week, refreshed and energized after R&R&R in Venice (we can never resist research), we rode the causeway train to Mestre, the mainland gateway to Venice. There, waiting for an overnight train to Prague, we had plenty of time to slip back into sleuth-mode. We prowled around the station, dragging our luggage.

A long train was being prepared to leave for Budapest. I had time to walk its length and examine its graffiti, an exuberant international mélange. I wondered how many of the turbid designs were begun in Italy, touched up in Austria, revised in Romania, and completed in Poland. I recognized writing in Russian, Greek, Italian, German, and Spanish. Could artists send messages back and forth to one another, a kind of coded shuttle? I watched a little round man in blue overalls run frantically from car to car, hopping on, peeking in, jumping off.

Our train to Prague was on the next track and would be leaving soon. Bob pointed out a lowlife on the graffiti-train, standing in the open doorway of a first class car. The man was unshaven, unkempt, wearing a dirty T-shirt and baggy track pants—not the epitome of a first class passenger. Beside him in the doorway stood a Japanese woman, smartly dressed with a Chanel-type purse on her shoulder. How did this dubious character escape the scrutiny of the overalled official? He must have either hidden in the restroom when he saw the worker coming, or he jumped on just after.

From the platform, the little man in blue overalls shined an official green light toward the conductor, the train gave a little toot, and lurched toward Budapest. The worker swung himself up onto the last car as it trundled by him.

The train began to pick up speed, but just before the last few cars left the platform area, our shabby suspect proved himself. He leapt off the quickening train with a glint of gold chain purse strap trailing behind him. We saw the victim's arm wave briefly out the train door, but there was too much noise to hear if she yelled.

On the platform, the bag snatcher needed only two giant steps to reach the stairs that led down to the tunnel below and out to the freedom of the street.

A Greek Tragedy

Unfamiliar fingers fiddled with the flap of my bag.

I let them. My American Express card was in the purse, along with a small camera and other things I'd hate to lose. Still, out of the corner of my eye, I watched without interfering.

I was wedged like a flimsy pamphlet between big brass bookends, and about as immobile, too. We had just boarded the metro train at Omonia Station in downtown Athens. The train was packed with its usual proportion of locals, tourists, and pickpockets. It was hot, airless, and odoriferous to distraction.

Bob and I had been separated by a force from behind as we boarded the car in a crush of bodies. The power behind the force stood between us: two large men in their thirties. I had one hand on a ceiling strap, the other protectively clutching a cheap-looking canvas bag on my shoulder, which perfectly disguised my laptop. My purse hung low and appeared vulnerable.

The fingers tugged gently, but I knew it was futile. I had tied a small knot in the leather cord of the drawstring bag. I allowed the man to try solely to confirm to myself that he was what we suspected him to be.

Bob and I had watched these two on the platform. They were neatly dressed, clean-cut, and spoke Russian. They stood apart from one another as if they weren't together. Their behavior on the platform made them suspects. When an uncrowded train came and they didn't get on it, they were as good as guilty in our minds. Then again . . . we didn't board that train either.

We squeezed onto the next sardine can and Boris and Igor (as I'll call them) pressed themselves in behind us, then between us. Igor bumped hard against me, spinning me against my will as he orbited around me.

Bambi wedged in a train in Athens. All eyes are on an incident, as Bob accuses a thief and a witness makes a scene.

Just a little self-serving do-si-do accompanied by a fleeting expression of apology as he positioned himself to his secret advantage. Physical contact was unavoidable in the overcrowded car. Against my forearm, I could feel Igor's wrist twitching as his fingers played with my bag.

The two men looked everywhere but at me. As Lothel Crawford taught us, *watch their eyes.* They seemed to be making unnecessary head movements, looking here and there as if they had no idea what was happening down below and were not responsible in the least for any mischief their hands might do.

Igor didn't mess around long. At the next station, he slapped his forehead in a pantomime of "stupid me, I forgot something!" and slipped off the train. Boris followed. Bob and I did not.

Then they surprised us: they reboarded the other end of the same car, enabling us to observe them. Although the Russian-speaking pair towered over the short Greeks and most of the tourists, our line of sight wasn't perfect across the mass of passengers.

Igor looked at Boris and Boris looked away. They had sandwiched a woman tourist and separated her from her husband, just as they had done with us. This was their method of stabilizing the victim, of impeding her movement. The couple took it in stride though, and braced themselves with both hands against the jerking and jostling of the train as it sped to the next station. They were understandably oblivious to the intentions of their neighbors. But they were unacceptably oblivious of their belongings, their situation, and their vulnerability. We were dying to shout out, to yell, "Pickpocket!" It is our deepest urge and instinct to warn others of the danger we're so aware of. However . . .

We didn't. For the reasons we have discussed and will further explain, we let the situation take its course. We reminded ourselves: we are researchers in the field, observing and documenting a specific behavior, and we use the knowledge we gain to educate many. Once again and with twinges of guilt, we refrained from interfering.

Athens' green line is notorious for pickpockets. This convenient route is heavily used by tourists from Piraeus at the southern end, where ferries and cruise ships dock, to Thiseio for the Acropolis, Monastiraki for the Plaka shopping district, and Omonia Square, the city center. When these trains are crowded, and they frequently are, they're pickpocket paradise. Thieves thrive on the forced physical contact, distraction of discomfort, and bodies hiding their dirty work.

Boris and Igor were swiveling their heads with exaggerated nonchalance. The train lurched into darkness for about three seconds. When it emerged, Igor lowered his sunglasses from the top of his head to his eyes. A "got-it" signal, we reflected later.

Still pretending not to know each other, they shoved impolitely through the standing crowd to position themselves against the doors. They were first to exit the train as the doors slid open, and they separated immediately, walking in opposite directions on the platform. The tourist couple was almost last to get off the train, so we jumped off too and caught up with them. We could see right away that the woman's bag had been slit with a razor.

Why hadn't those thug-like thieves sliced my bag? I knew they wanted it. Perhaps they thought the leather was too thick, or they weren't happy with their access or angle. Possibly the knot in my drawstring signaled my awareness of potential danger. Maybe they thought someone could see them, or their getaway would be hindered.

Boris and Igor left me for someone else. It's proof of the tremendous coordination of innumerable aspects required from the perpetrator's perspective. So many factors must be in alignment before a thief will take a chance, so many conditions must be just right. With such a delicate balance necessary, it is not difficult to throw a monkey wrench into the thief's equilibrium. Eliminate one or more of the elements he requires, and he'd just as soon move on to an easier target with a higher likelihood of success.

Such Risk . . . Is a Taxi Better?

With such risks on public transportation, is it safer to take a taxi? Sometimes, for sure. But taxis have their hazards, too. Some cities are known to have an illicit taxi trade of unofficial, unregulated operators who solicit with lowball prices and aggressive touting. There, travelers are warned to use sanctioned cab companies only. This is not always practical, granted, or even easy to discern whether a taxi in a foreign city is official or not.

A traveler's first introduction to a city's cab offerings is often at an airport or train station. The options may bewilder, with trains, buses, shuttles, semi-private limos, official taxis, and cut-rate cars. It's a good idea to head straight for some sort of transportation desk and do not allow yourself to be waylaid by an interloper, even one who seems to be official, or one who catches you inches from the official desk, as if he belonged there. A transportation company's first goal is to get you into its car or van or bus, and some will use any means of deceptive practice to snag you, including claiming to be official.

Every travel guide reminds the visitor to agree on a price before getting into the car, or to agree to use the meter. Try to agree before the driver or tout hefts your luggage into the trunk and you've got one foot into a murky deal that sucks you in like quicksand.

Watch too, that you get the driver you expect. You may be approached by someone who says, "You need a taxi? Where do you want to go?

The Making of ABC *20/20*:
On the Heaven-to-Hell Express

Bob and I took the *20/20* crew on the infamous Bus 64. Its route, between the Vatican and Rome's main train terminal, is ruefully called the heaven-to-hell express. Consistently overcrowded, the line's frequent buses carry an intimate assembly of tourists, locals, and pickpockets.

A typically jam-packed 64 swerved to the stop at Rome's Via del Plebiscito. Its three sets of doors burst open and a few people were disgorged. Half a dozen approached the doors to board, though there didn't seem to be space for them. A suspicious gang also appeared: two women carrying infants and a young girl. They'd gotten off the front of the bus and walked back to reboard at the rear door. Only pickpockets jump off a bus and reboard it, or another on the same route.

"We have to get on!" I said to Arnold Diaz, and we pushed our way up onto the first step. The doors tried to close and bounced back open. Bob jumped on. The bus started moving. The doors tried again to close. Our camera crew stood open-mouthed on the street, unable to board.

We were just a few cigars more than the humidor could hold, crammed like an economy pack of sausages. The sides of the bus must have been bulging. Our suspects pushed forward a little, allowing us to meld into the crowd so the doors could close. Romans groaned and complained. The bus lurched and jolted. It smelled of sweat.

The last time Bob and I rode Bus 64, a middle-aged Italian man had dipped into Bob's pocket. Bob was holding his video camera up near the ceiling, anchored against a pole. He pointed the wide-angle lens down, capturing the whole swipe. In his pocket, Bob had folded a thousand lire note around some cut newspaper and secured the bundle with a rubber band. The Italian man had plucked the wad.

We watched the Italian as he glanced at the roll. The cut newspaper was too obvious. He saw it was a sham, thought it was a sting, and, yet, he was trapped on a bus so crowded the doors wouldn't open. He waited until the bus lurched again, then delicately replaced the money and fake bills, not realizing he'd been made.

"Rolling?" I asked Arnold. He had remotes to turn his cameras on, but it was easy to forget in the sudden action.

"Yep."

One of the babies began to cry. I couldn't blame it, down there at elbow level. One of the suspect women had gotten herself between Arnold and me. Now that the doors were closed, I lowered one foot back down on the step. From that low angle, I could see Arnold's fanny pack and the crying baby that was being used to shield it. And I could see the hand that felt for, then opened, the zipper. I saw a flash of green "X," the tape that marked our prop wallet, then the zipper being closed. I waited a moment, then said "Let's get off." Bob knew what I meant. We had enough years of eye contact to read one another. But Arnold didn't. He felt his fanny pack. *Then* he knew.

The bus stopped and the doors struggled to open. I leaned hard into the women, who also seemed to want to get off, and cleared the doors for opening. A rush of hot, polluted air blew in, but it felt fresh and cool compared to the air on the bus. Bob and I leapt off the bus, followed by Arnold, then the women and children.

(continued)

"You took my wallet!" Arnold stormed after the thieves.
They looked at him quizzically. "You took my wallet! Give it back!"
A flash of green "X." The wallet dropped onto the sidewalk. The women said nothing. Arnold pursued, still rolling.
Hopeless. The thieves kept walking, without shame, without embarrassment, on to another bus, to exchange one working environment for another, and obtain an entirely new set of gulls.

Come, I'll take you." You think he looks okay, he speaks decent enough English so you can communicate, and he puts you in the back of a cab. Then—surprise: a different driver gets in who barely speaks a word of English and may be unpleasant in other ways, too.

An unofficial taxi scam may result in an overcharge of a few bucks, a hefty overcharge, or worse. I met an Indian businessman in Atlanta recently, who had gone to Rio de Janeiro to visit his client, a Brazilian airline. He took an unofficial taxi from the airport to his hotel in Ipanema, where the driver stopped in a deserted lot a bit away from the hotel, claiming he wasn't allowed to park closer.

The businessman shrugged, having already taken the cab ride, and realizing he could easily carry his suitcase to the hotel himself. As he was lifting his luggage from the trunk of the car, a small boy, about eight or nine years old, stuck a gun in his side and demanded cash. The businessman looked at the driver and instantly felt he was in on the stickup, and that was why he had parked so far from the hotel. Unaccustomed to having a gun tickling his ribs, unsure of the capacity of the serious-looking kid, he turned over his entire wallet.

Unofficial taxis are unregulated. Drivers may be uninsured, or even unlicensed. They may drive unsafe cars. They may be ordinary citizens trying to earn a little extra cash, or they may be highway bandits with partners waiting around a corner. You can always find out in advance how to recognize official taxis, or you can have one called.

Once you've chosen your ride and negotiated the charges, you're ready to go. But wait—watch to ensure that all of your luggage is loaded into the trunk. No need to make hasty assumptions. You don't know the driver, and he doesn't know your bags.

In Las Vegas, if you don't request otherwise, taxi drivers will take you through the new tunnel, a direct link to the freeway, and this will certainly add a few bucks and a few minutes to most journeys. That may not be a big deal, but other route deviations can be. It's always wise to ask in advance what the approximate taxi fare to your destination should be. Ask your hotel when you book it, then ask the driver before you get into his cab.

Low-grade taxi scams, I'm sorry to say, are many and varied and take advantage of the naïve and tired visitor. Some cabbies start their meters ticking before you even load your bags, some add on fraudulent extras, some try to charge per passenger. I don't mean to slam the trade—most drivers are trying to make an honest buck. It's the nasty minority who give the profession a bad name.

To make a general statement, it's usually recommended that travelers abroad only take taxis from a major taxi queue or those ordered from a

Breaking All the Rules

The faster he drove, the longer it took. When our Jordanian taxi driver was pulled over for speeding, the delay cost us a precious twenty minutes, maddening after almost three hours of bureaucratic red tape with immigration. Polite patience had resulted in a flat "no" to our attempts to get to Petra, and though we finally acquired official permission, our entire morning had been wasted. It never occurred to us that we might apply the age-old institution of *baksheesh,* and we probably wouldn't have, anyway.

The speeding ticket was not the first of our delays. Five minutes out of Aqaba, the driver flagged down a passing associate and had us transfer cabs. The new driver, upon hearing our remote destination, pulled up to a roadside tent from which he bought a spare tire; a good idea, we thought. Next was a petrol stop, and then a military examination of documents and inspection for contraband. Once on our way, our driver, who spoke no English, attempted to show us that he could make up for lost time. Either he didn't see, or didn't believe, the radar warning.

In America, we drive on the right side of the road; in other parts of the world, they drive on the left. In Jordan, however, they drive smack down the middle of the road, and, at the last instant, when one can see the crazed grin or dazed monotony on the face of the oncoming driver, a quick flick of the wrist rocks the two vehicles into a perfectly timed dodge. The road from Aqaba, is a conveyor belt of lumbering big rigs. Our little taxi felt like a minnow in a stream of sturgeon, and we winced at the shifting slivers of space our driver slipped through. His impeccable judgment often left little more than a gasp and a warm breath of clearance between our car and the eighteen-wheelers on either side. Not to worry though—the taxi was adorned with a full complement of lucky charms, from a larger-than-life-size bunch of grapes suction cupped to the windshield, to the eye-in-the-hand-of-God stickers on the dash. Obviously, then, it was those lacking the lucky trinkets whose cars and tankers littered the roadside in mangled, burned-out wrecks.

Petra is surely the most remote location I've visited, if measured by effort expended as well as distance traveled. We careened off the main highway onto a rolling, twisting road to nowhere; rocky desert as far as the eye could see. A lonely, black-robed nomad or two herding a few sheep and goats were the only signs of life.

Endless desert slid past the taxi window in a monotonous, flesh-tone blur, or were we standing still? We were the only car on the road at least, so our sole panic concerned miles-per-hour and what might be coming over the next hill or around the next bend. And of course we wondered if there really was a Petra at the end of this route. We were at the mercy of a hell-bent Bedouin, with all our eggs in one basket—an officially sanctioned "taxi."

dispatcher. Passengers should not get into a taxi that already has another person in it, and should not allow a driver to pick up another person along the way. Windows should be closed and doors locked. Passengers should note a driver's cab or license number, and possibly even say it out loud to prevent potential games.

That said, let me comment from the perspective of a real-life frequent traveler. The truth is, sometimes we take chances. Sometimes we engage our judgment, consider what we know of a place, the time of day, our location (city or boondocks), our snap impression of the driver and his car, and even how desperate we are for the ride. I hate to use that vague, intangible, nebulous term, "common sense," because so much more comes into play. Sometimes, we just grab a cab.

And I can tell you that taxis can be an excellent deal. Not just getting you from here to there, but showing you around and giving you a sense of a place. Drivers know what visitors want to see, and an astute driver will figure out what *you* want to see. Especially if you have limited time in a city, a driver-guide can be the most efficient, most economical, and most rewarding way to go. If you're lucky, his knowledge and personality will also add to the experience.

One of our best days in Mumbai was spent in one of its yellow-roofed black taxis, bat-like, driven by sense of sound. The driver crammed in all the city's highlights—from the amazing *dhobi ghats*, where all Mumbai's laundry is hand washed, to the "caged girls" in Falkland Marg Street brothels, to the white marble Jain temple, and Chowpatty Beach. We drove with the windows open. Traffic was a swerving, swaying two-step of taxis coming together and repelling like magnets, each cab trailing its own strand of exhaust in an intricate invisible macramé.

Air quality is even worse in Bangkok, where many citizens walk around in surgical masks. Cars creep through gridlock, so the choice transportation is the tiny, three-wheeled duk-duk. The noise and fumes are awful when you're just a body in the middle of such heavy traffic, but the maneuverability can be exhilarating.

In Cairo once, we found ourselves a taxi for a three-hour journey to Port Said in the north of Egypt. We joined Cairo's evening commute, but became somewhat alarmed when the driver seemed to be taking a short cut. We soon recognized the streets of Khan el Khalili Bazaar, where the driver pulled up to a tiny bakery, parking beside an olive cart. From the car window, the driver shouted to his sons that he'd miss dinner. As an afterthought, he had his sons hand in a few breads, one for each of us. Pita-like, covered with sesame seeds on top and stuffed with a thin layer of marzipan, they were a delicious gift. It was all against the hard and fast rules of smart travel, but somehow the calculated risk fell within our indescribable latitude for adventure.

By the time we left the city the sun had gone down. Egyptian-style, we shot recklessly down the dark desert highway toward the Mediterranean Sea: headlights off. As oncoming vehicles came vaguely into view, they and our driver flashed headlights, momentarily blinding one another in greeting.

We've taken unlicensed taxis in Russia, when our local friend Vladimir has flagged them down and instructed them for us. In Lima, a taxi driver made a scary detour to his house "to get some documents," leaving us alone in the locked car. Then he proceeded to our destination, coasting through every red light and stop sign to avoid carjackers and banditos. On an unexpected visit to Lusaka, Zambia (our connecting flight was canceled), we had a taxi driver find us a hotel—that tactic has worked well for us in Cairo, too. We took a taxi on a mountain road in Tanzania with absolutely bald tires. In Kenya, Portugal, and Indonesia, we've ordered drivers to slow down or let us out.

When we travel, we take risks. Not everything is done American-style, and that is presumably why we've left home in the first place. We may ride in a car without seat belts, sail through red lights, and eat proffered food against all advice. We simply have to make balanced judgments. We may be wrong sometimes, and we may suffer for it. But we might also have the time of our lives.

Theft Thwarters #5:
Public Transportation

Buses, Trains, and Subways

- The moments of entering and exiting crowded public transportation are your most vulnerable and a thief's most rewarding.

- Suspect the motive of anyone eager to help you into a crowded bus or train.

- Be aware of your surroundings. Don't permit a stranger to move into your personal space.

- If you're in a crowd, be particularly aware of your valuables. Suspect bumps or jostles: they may be a distraction technique.

- Don't make it easy for thieves. Let them choose someone else.

- On a crowded bus or train, take your wallet out of your pocket and carry it (and all your valuables) in your hands against your chest, where you have full control and awareness of it. Or place your hand in or over the pocket where it's kept. (Even though this does reveal where you keep it.)

- Do not leave your bag unattended on a train. Do not leave it on luggage racks at the end of the carriage. Be aware of it if you place it on an overhead rack.

- Thieves on public transportation can be men or women, grandfathers, mothers with infants, trendy teenagers, or small children. You will probably never finger the thief, but he or she will recognize you as a mark.

- The presence of security guards does not mean you can let your own guard down.

- Beware who's outside a train window. Stay out of grabbing range.

- If you're pickpocketed in a crowd, try demanding the return of your item. It might mysteriously hit the floor. Shout out, too, on the off chance an undercover police officer is nearby.

- If your bag is grabbed, let go. Nothing in it is worth the physical risk to you.

Taxis

- Before finding a taxi, determine approximately what the fare should be to your destination.

- Go to a transportation desk in an airport or train station when you arrive, and don't get waylaid by an interloper.

- Take only official taxis. If you can't tell by it's markings, use a taxi stand or have one ordered from a dispatcher.

- Negotiate with your driver before getting in his cab, and before loading your bags in. Agree on a price, or on using the meter. Ask what the extra charges are, if any.

- Check that all your luggage has been loaded into the trunk.

- Tell the driver you want the most direct route.

- Don't get into a taxi that someone else is already in. Don't allow your driver to pick up an additional person en route.

- Note the driver's cab or license number.

- Keep taxi safety in perspective; combine these suggestions with your specific situation and your good judgment.

- Definitely consider using a taxi to make your own tour.

- Travel does involve risk. Use balanced caution.

Scams—by the Devious Strategist

7

Flower Gift Lift

She looks like your grandmother—possibly even your great-grandmother. With a gap-toothed smile, she offers you a single red carnation. Wordlessly, she pokes its short stem through your buttonhole. Is the old woman an unofficial ambassador of this island resort town?

"One peseta," she pleads, or "one cent."

Her black skirt and apron make you think of "the old country," wherever it was your family began. Her simple cardigan sweater, dingy and pilled, gives her plump body a cozy look, a familiar look. Wisps of gray hair have escaped from the babushka tied tight beneath her chins. She is the image of trust.

The foreign coin she asks for is less than nothing to a tourist. Why not? You smile. You open your wallet, and extract a small note.

Grandmother springs to action. "No, no, no," she says urgently, as if you're giving too much. Is the flower a gift, then? Or does she want a donation? What is she trying to communicate with such concern creasing her forehead?

She reaches for your wallet, points to your money, touches it. Whatever language you speak, she doesn't. The international symbol for "this one" must do. Sign language and monosyllabic utterances.

Without words, grandmother is trying to convey something. Her hands are fluttering around yours, pointing, tapping, hovering. A small bunch of red carnations is in her left fist and their spicy fragrance is intoxicating as she waves them around.

You're focused on your wallet, your money, the old woman's hands. What is she trying to tell you? If you'd look at grandmother's pallid face, you'd be surprised to see such fierce concentration, such tension and determination. But you don't look. She's pointing, tapping. What is she trying to say?

She gives the bill back to you and you put it away. "*Altra,*" she insists. Finally, she taps a bill half exposed in your wallet. It's the same one you offered in the first place! Her eyes flick up to yours for an instant. Permission sought and granted. With thumb and forefinger, the old woman removes the bill, nods her thanks, and pushes on the wallet with the bouquet. Put the wallet away now, is her implication. We're finished.

Her last glance lacks grace, lacks the kindness you would expect from a welcome-woman. Oh well . . . it was a small donation.

Or was it? It may be hours before you realize the old woman's expertise.

With incredible skill and speed, she has dipped into your cash, snagged most of the bills, and folded them into her hand. She never takes all the notes—you'd notice. But most of them have been hooked around her third or fourth finger, expertly manipulated under the flowers, and hidden in her fleshy palm.

She's a one-trick magician, a walk-around performer who needs an audience of one. And her audience participation act leaves many a disbelieving assistant in her wake. She may as well have asked for a volunteer. "Hold out your wallet and I'll show you a trick." She needs no applause; her reward goes into her apron pocket.

Thirty to forty women practice this form of filching every day in Palma de Mallorca, Spain. They linger where the tourists are: around Palacio Almudiana in particular, and in the small cobblestone streets around Plaza Mayor. The women perform one-on-one, but they work in groups. We see them walk "to work" in gangs of six or seven, gossiping merrily along the way. As they approach their territory, they don their "uniforms," tying dark aprons around their waists, and scarves on their heads. Many are

Two claveleras *stick their fingers into tourists' wallets.*

younger women, in their thirties, forties, and fifties. The youngest eschew the scarves and, instead of aprons, tie jackets around their waists, keeping the pockets available.

At Palacio Almudiana, we planted ourselves at the end of an elevated walkway to the Moorish fortress. We had a JVC professional video camera on a tripod that day—a huge, heavy thing—and with its long, fine lens, we could film close-ups unnoticed at a distance.

From around a corner at the far end of the stone walkway appeared a group of six men—German tourists, we later learned. Happily oblivious, they had just toured the fortress. As they turned into the otherwise empty walkway, five women from the morning babushka brigade rushed after them, literally running, with heavy, effortful steps. The eldest woman found a victim first, grabbing the arm of one of the men and roughly poking a flower into his shirt. As she began her swindle, all four of her colleagues attached themselves to four others of the men. In a jolly, holiday mood, the men allowed the women's aggressive physical appeal without suspicion.

It only took about two minutes. One by one the men broke free, some wearing red carnations, some not. As they sauntered toward us on the walkway, folding and replacing their wallets, the five women regrouped behind them and disappeared around the far corner. Bob stopped three of the Germans.

"Did you lose any money?" he asked, without explaining what we'd just witnessed.

"And why would we?" one of the men challenged.

"I saw you with some thieves," Bob said. "Count your money."

All three brought forth their wallets and checked their contents.

"Fifteen thousand pesetas—gone!" one of them shouted. That was about US$85 at the time.

"They got twenty-five thousand from me," said another, "and now I realize how. She said she wanted a peseta and I tried to give it to her. But she returned it and now my money is gone."

"I was pinching the wallet like so," the third man explained smugly. "She wanted to get into the wallet, but I didn't let go. I have all my money."

We filmed numerous encounters by this gang and by others, in this location and around the town, on this day and over the course of ten years. Without speaking to each victim, it's impossible to state the percentage of these thieves' success. Even the victims aren't always certain whether or not a few bills have been taken, or how much money they started with. Only the thieves know for sure. Clearly, it's a worthwhile game for them.

In one brilliant piece of footage, several women can be seen earnestly engaged in their one-on-one scams. We pan from one encounter to another, close up. One of the women is seen "closing her deal," pushing her left

The tourist has accepted a carnation from the clavelera, who now aggressively digs in the tourist's wallet, using a newspaper and bunch of leaves to cover her extraction.

fistful of flowers against her opponent's wallet. As she steps back, apparently satisfied, she loses her grip and money flutters to the ground. The victim and thief both notice, one puzzled, the other disgusted.

In another scene, an Asian visitor smiles delightedly when a bright red carnation is tucked into his shirt pocket. The old woman, dressed in black from head to toe, raises one finger. One peseta, she requests. The tourist withdraws his wallet and offers a bill, still smiling. Taking the money, the woman raises her finger again, then returns the bill. As the Asian tourist replaces his money, the thief moves in on his wallet and a subtle battle ensues. The man's expression begins to shift from pleasure to perplexity, then consternation. The woman, defeated, snatches back the flower and moves on.

Palma de Mallorca has long been a favorite holiday destination for Germans and Swedes, and for Europeans in general. Many British retire to Mallorca, or have second homes there. Ferries bring day-trippers from mainland Spain, and cruise ships regularly dump sightseers by the thousands to bask in this balmy Spanish paradise. Its beaches and nightclubs are a perennial draw, and have been long before the spotlight hit Ibiza. Low-lying criminals, too, are attracted to Palma's easy-going lifestyle and laid-back law enforcement.

"*Claveleras,* that's all we do!" one of Palma's police officers told us in exasperation. *Clavel* means carnation; *claveleras* are the thieves who use

A clavelera *offers a carnation, intending to get her sticky fingers into the tourist's wallet.*

them. The police officer had stopped us from filming an incident at the *claveleras'* request.

"Why do you protect them?" I asked the cop. "They've been here for years!"

"It's not possible to arrest them," the officer said. "They only took two hundred euros. It's not enough. They must take three hundred."

"But they've been doing this for years! It's ruining Palma's reputation."

"Yes. I know all of them. Their names, their addresses."

"Then why don't you let a tourist, like me, put four hundred euros in his pocket, let them take it, and then you can arrest them," Bob said.

The conversation circled unsatisfactorily, revealing firewalls between politicians, law enforcement, journalists, tourist bureau, and the unfortunate tourists. We, like the police, threw up our hands.

We met Douglas and Evelyn Massie outside the fortress, yet another pair of British victims. Their nemesis was a young woman, perhaps in her thirties, who wore track pants and a jacket—an updated wardrobe.

"Would you like to go to the police station?" we asked them. "You won't get your money back, but a police report might help you with a claim to your insurance company and we'll translate for you."

At the police station we were perfunctorily handed a poorly photocopied theft report form in English. Heading the list of common M.O.s was "woman with carnation". The Massies duly checked the box while Bob and I marveled at a system that could officially acknowledge and

The Offer of a Flower Is a Foil for Filching

Bob and I trailed a trio of young women through Palma's shopping district. Working separately but near each other, they halfheartedly approached a seemingly random selection of meandering tourists. Most ignored the women's overtures, but one amiable couple paused with interest.

Bob filmed the scene and I alternated between watching the scam and watching Bob's back. He was balancing a huge camera on his shoulder and I carried the ponderous tripod and brick-like battery. Neither of us could hear the exchange, if there was one, but the con artist must have made her desires clear. The male tourist had his wallet out, then replaced it in his front shorts pocket. Bob and I could see the pocket from where we stood, behind him. As we watched (and filmed), the con woman reached across the man and put *her* hand into *his* pocket! She made no particular effort to disguise her move, and the man did not react at all. How brazen she was, and how trusting was he. How well she read him.

Suddenly, I was roughly pushed. I had failed to notice that one of the thief's partners had observed our camera focused on her teammate. She raised her hand to push away the camera and I blocked her with my arm. Her fist crashed down on my wrist, breaking my stainless-steel watchband.

"No photo!" she shouted.

Now Bob swung around and looked at the woman through his lens.

"No photo!" she yelled again, and ineffectively waved a tissue at the camera. Then she swiveled, bent, and rose in one fluid motion, and hefted a massive rock. In a classic pitcher's posture, she aimed for the camera lens. A frame captured from the video makes a lovely portrait of her, rock poised in one hand, dainty bouquet of carnations in the other.

Wound up and ready to smash our camera, she bared her teeth and raised one foot.

"Hey, hey, hey!" commanded a male voice behind us, or something to that effect in the woman's language. A cloud of dust rose and the earth shook as her boulder plunked to the ground.

With a sneer, the would-be destroyer turned and rejoined her companions, who had just finished their scam. Bob and I caught up with the victims.

"First they pretended to give us the flower," the woman said cheerily, "but then they asked for one peseta." She and her husband were both smiling, amused by the bold stunt and pleased to be interviewed.

"When I gave her some money, she gave it back," the husband cut in. "She said no, no, no. And she put her hand in my pocket and the hand came out. I only lost 400 pesetas."

That explained their jovial mood.

A clavelera *ready to smash our camera with a rock.*

simultaneously condone such activities. After all, we'd observed this swindle for ten years: same women, same technique, same locations.

A tattered photo album was put before the Massies without comment. Page after page of female mug shots stared up from under plastic. There was the grandmother gang, and there was a pair of tall sisters we'd watched. There was the Massies' snaggle-toothed tormentor and there, grinning wryly, was our infamous rock thrower.

The Massies huddled judiciously over their theft report and laboriously printed out in block letters a story that would likely never be read.

But their tale will be told—by the Massies and by thousands of people who have had the good fortune to visit Palma. The story begins: "There was an old woman, who gave me a flower . . ."

Low-Caste Strategist or Glorified Opportunist?

A strategist thief is one who creates his own opportunity, one who operates on a specific plan, one who steals with malice aforethought. The lowest strata of these are not much more than glorified opportunists. To me, though, (and these are my definitions) an opportunist with a clever enough scheme gets a strategist rating.

Take Yacine, a north African illegal immigrant thief who works in Athens, Greece.

"I have a favorite technique to use in restaurants," he told us, "but it only works in winter, when men hang their jackets on the backs of their chairs. I could show you, but I don't have a jacket, and you don't have a jacket. No one has a jacket in Athens in the summer." He hunched his shoulders, raised his palms.

"We'll go buy one," Bob said, and we had Yacine lead us to a men's shop. There followed a hilarious scene in which a pickpocket selects a sport coat based on an analysis of its array of pockets. When a suitable jacket was purchased, Yacine chose a quiet café for our demonstration. Two of his colleagues joined us for lunch first, during which a cell phone rang.

Harik, twenty-eight, illegally visiting from Albania, pulled a phone out of his pocket and put it on the table. Then another, and another. He had half a dozen cell phones on the table before he found the ringing one. It had been a lucrative morning for Harik. He opened the back of the phone and pulled out its SIM card. The ringing stopped. Harik tore the tiny chip into shreds.

(An aside: want to buy a cell phone in Athens? Hundreds of men stand packed in a pedestrian shopping lane in the Plaka area, each displaying a phone or two. If you show interest in a man's wares, he'll pull from his pockets his other offerings, up to a dozen phones.)

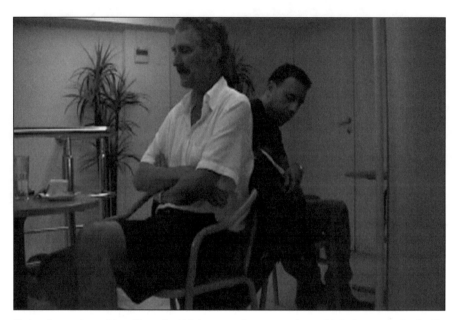

Yacine demonstrates his café steal, which he uses when a man hangs his jacket on the back of a chair. Sitting back to back, he slips his hand between his jacket and his mark's.

"The new jacket is yours, but I need a jacket, also, for this method," Yacine said as he set the scene. "I'll use a shirt for the demonstration."

He arranged Bob and me in bentwood chairs at a café table and ordered Greek coffee for us. He settled himself at the next table. Then, back to back with Bob, hand behind his back but hidden between the jackets, he snagged the wallet. I was facing him and saw nothing suspicious.

Yacine is an opportunist because he needs a fool for a mark, someone who's left himself open. But he works with a strategy that gives him an advantage over the ordinary opportunist, so he has a wider field of potential victims. He's more dangerous than his lesser fellows because he succeeds within the perceived shelter of upscale commercial establishments. He also has grander conceits. Yacine's ultimate goal is America.

Our meeting with Yacine took place only three weeks before September 11.

"I will soon be going to Canada," he told us. "All the plans are made. My past doesn't matter, I will have false papers. A new name, you understand? No problem, I will slip in. I will fly from Paris to Montreal first. Montreal is easy for me. I speak French. I have many friends there. I will apply for asylum, as an Algerian. Which I am. And from Montreal, it is not difficult to slip into America."

Yacine's Café Special

"You be the victim, Bob. Here's the jacket. Put some euros in your wallet, empty is no good. Now put it in the new jacket. I don't care which pocket! That is never something I decide. Now hang the jacket on the back of your chair. Perfect. Now, please. Have a seat. Drink your coffee.

"I will take the seat behind you so we are back to back. I have this shirt in my backpack, which I can use to simulate a jacket. I'll hang it on the back of my chair. Now Bob, here is the secret: I will readjust the chairs so they are not exactly back to back. I'll slide mine a little left or a little right. It doesn't matter which way.

"Look now. I'm sitting right behind you. Our jackets are back to back on our chairs. I just slip my hand behind me and into your jacket. I don't turn around. I can feel the pockets and quickly remove the wallet. See?

"You think that's good? Thank you. Put the wallet back and I'll show you something better. This is my best take. I will get the money only. I will not take the wallet. Just the money from it. It's the same technique, but it takes a few seconds longer. Look now, I've got it!

"When I do this, the man never even knows. He thinks he spent the money somewhere. Very good, no?"

One month later, Yacine called us in America. He was in Paris, following his plan. It was four o'clock in the morning when our phone rang. We imagined him using a stolen cell phone.

"I just wanted to tell you, I'm very sorry about what happened. You know, the planes. I am sorry."

I mention this to establish a link: pickpockets are terrorists' lowest-level enablers. It is partly their efforts that make possible the financial fraud that funds terrorism. Credit cards and identity documents reap thousands of dollars apiece in the wrong hands. Unsophisticated thieves are paid up to several hundred dollars per card by organized gangs who know that the criminal bottom-dwellers are easily recruited. More on this later.

Kharem is another opportunist who doubles as a minor-league strategist. When we first met him, he was prowling the perimeter of a breakdance performance near the top of La Rambla. He carried a black plastic bag to cover his hand as he unzipped the duffel bags of spectators.

"My job is pickpocket. I have this job seventeen years," he said in English, over coffee in a little restaurant, then launched into French, telling us that he worked in Paris for twelve years until he was expelled from France.

Kharem raised the plastic bag from his lap and put it on the table. He had a "unique technique," he explained, his own method, something he invented and believes he is alone in using. He opened his plastic bag to show a handful of Barcelona postcards. He fanned the postcards and extended them to me across the table, as if offering them for sale. Then he withdrew them, leaned back in his chair with satisfaction, and tipped up the cards. Beneath them, he'd swiped my empty coffee cup.

He does this on La Rambla, Kharem told us with pride, where he approaches diners at outdoor cafés. When he removes the proferred fan of postcards, he takes a wallet or camera with it.

Thieves love the anonymity of large Internet cafés.

Small valuables are snatchable when Internet users' attention is on the monitor.

The Heart of a Thief

Does a pickpocket keep his appointments? Bob and I loitered on a corner with our interpreter. We were a unanimously doubtful trio already considering alternative plans for the day.

We'd found Kharem a week ago, almost a year after we first met him.

"Kharem!" I'd said, and his jaw dropped.

"Nice lady. You remember my name. I am honored." He swept his thumbtip against his forehead, fingers fisted, in a quick, subtle gesture.

Absolutely punctual, Kharem approached now with a smile and the thumb thing, that curious salute of his. He was immaculately dressed in a short-sleeved button-down shirt, white pants, suede loafers, and the inevitable tool over his arm: the jacket. We introduced him to our friend Ana, our interpreter for the day, and teased him about his punctuality.

"I wasn't working today; I came straight from home. That's why."

We settled around the same table we used the week before and reminded ourselves and Ana to keep our voices down.

"What happens when you're caught, Kharem?"

"When I'm caught, the police usually beat me up and take my money. It's not bad because I won't have to go to jail. Jail is like death. One hour of being there and I feel dead." He signaled for a waiter.

"How long have you spent in jail?"

"Many times."

"But how much time altogether?"

Kharem smiled with his mouth but not his eyes. He raised both index fingers and gestured as if conducting an orchestra.

"He won't say," said Ana. "I think he means let's move on to something else."

"Do you think the police recognize your face?"

"Yes, they do. But they know I never hurt anyone. My crime is small. I'm not getting millions of euros. I'm not rich. I don't have a drug habit to support . . ." He went on in Arabic-tinged Spanish.

"He seems to feel almost justified in what he's doing," Ana said, amazed. "He's talking about the police who take his money, the politicians who get away with so much and never go to jail. And other financial . . . what do you call it?"

"White collar crime?"

"Yes, and that he never hurts people."

Our drinks arrived: espresso for Bob and me, a beer for Kharem, a soda for Ana. Kharem passed the sugar and distributed napkins to each of us from an overpacked dispenser.

"How are you treated in jail?"

"It's not pleasant. Look at my finger." Kharem showed the mangled third finger of his right hand. "A guard did this to me. He handed me some papers and when I reached for them, he slammed shut the cell door. It was clearly intentional."

He brightened. "Last Sunday, after we parted, I got a wallet with one thousand euros. I used the postcards to do it."

"Ah, no wonder you're not working today. You took the whole week off!" I joked.

"No, I used that money to pay some fines. When I've paid them all, my record will be clear."

(continued)

"Do you save any money?"

"No. When I get enough, I pay my fines."

"How will you ever get ahead?" Bob asked. "What about your future? What will you do when you're old?"

"Who knows about the future. No one knows what will be tomorrow, anything could happen." He reached to move a strand of windblown hair from my face, a gesture I found overly familiar, almost forward. "I live only for today. I live like a bird." Thumb salute. "I am free."

"What is this thing you do with your thumb?" I asked, copying the move.

"It means 'good.'"

"I've never seen it before. Is it Algerian? Or Lebanese?"

"Combination," he said dismissively, so I gave up.

"Did you go to school?"

"I can read and I can write. What more do I need of education?"

"What do you do when you're not working?" I asked. "Do you have a passion for something?"

"I write poetry."

"What about?"

"Freedom. Love. Family. Living like a bird."

"Will you recite one for us?"

"They are in Arabic. I cannot."

"Do you have family here in Barcelona?"

"No, I have no one. I have no friends. I am not allowed in France, where my daughter is. I haven't seen my mother and father in seventeen years and my brothers are dead. These are the people I love. If I cannot see my family, why should I see anyone? They are my friends. They are the ones I love."

He did the thumb thing and smiled with his mouth but not his eyes.

Kharem with Bambi in Barcelona. "You are like a sister to me," he repeatedly said to Bambi.

Apparently, Kharem doesn't realize that this is a fairly common technique used in Internet cafés. Web surfers, intent on their e-mail or gaming, often set a wallet, credit card, or cell phone on the desk in front of them, beside the keyboard. Perhaps Kharem did invent the postcard trick, but he's not alone in using it. This "unique technique" vanishes so many valuables from right under noses that many Internet cafés flash warnings on screen.

That's how Jennifer Faust, of Canada, lost her wallet. She had it next to her keyboard at Easy Everything Internet point on La Rambla. Jennifer, though, had filled out our Theft First Aid form, and therefore easily canceled her credit card accounts. Still, in the hour that passed while she fetched her Theft First Aid sheet, approximately one hundred dollars had been charged to one of her cards. This particular Internet point, now called Easy Internet, has more than 350 terminals in long rows and is open to anyone who cares to wander in. On our visits there, we spotted several teams, at different times, carrying packs of dog-eared postcards.

Another low-level strategist practices the Pile-up-Pick, a.k.a. the Sandwich Steal. This is an opportunistic theft based on impedence, but its tight choreography elevates it, in my classification, to a strategical one. Again, an opportunity must present itself, but around it a mini-drama is played out. The script calls for three players: a victim, a dip, and a stall. The setting: an escalator, up or down; interior or exterior; day or night.

The victim is sandwiched on the moving stairs by the other two. Just as the escalator ends, the stall drops keys or coins, bends to pick them up and causes a pile-up. As the threesome compress in the crash, the dip picks the pocket. Las Vegas, with all its pedestrian overpasses on the Strip, has a problem with this, but it's common everywhere in malls and department stores. Foreign variants of this production are sometimes rewritten: in Hong Kong, they substitute bag slashing for pocket picking; in Los Angeles, they drop contact lenses.

Maria, an American who's lived in Barcelona for seven years, works as a translator. She and her visiting parents were coming up on a subway escalator when a woman dropped her keys at the top, in front of Maria's father, causing a pile-up. Her father felt his wallet go and, with quick reflexes, caught the pickpocket. By luck, there happened to be a policeman nearby, who demanded the wallet. The thief returned it, but the cash had already been removed. "Where's the money?" Maria's father asked the thief. The pickpocket just shrugged but the policeman knew: it was in his mouth.

Excuse me as we descend to cesspool level, just for a moment, where we find the scatological strategist. This lowlife hangs out in public restrooms, waiting for the mark's most inopportune moment, at which time she may drop a handful of coins from the next stall. In this believable scenario, you're asked to help push the scattered money back over, while a toilet teammate reaches over the top of your stall door and takes your bag off the hook. I think it was at Los Angeles International Airport, where these thefts became so prevalent that officials removed the hooks from inside stalls. Loathe to see their lucrative scam scuttled, the nasty bottom-dwellers took matters into their own hands and reattached their own hooks.

The Duplicitous Strategist

The strategist elite are those who make participants of their victims. Like the Palma *claveleras,* they're in your face with a story. Their only goal is to walk away with your wallet. Consummate con artists, they're the slipperiest, wiliest, and most difficult to detect. Garbed in a counterfeit persona designed to gain your confidence, they lay bait and entrap their prey: usually the unsuspecting traveler.

Pseudo Cops

These strategists concoct ingenious schemes. Who could avoid falling for what happened to Glinda and Greg? They were walking in a foreign park in—well, it could have been anywhere, this is so common—when a gentleman approached them with a camera. He asked if one of them would mind taking his picture, and the three huddled while he showed them how to zoom and where to press. Suddenly, two other men arrived and flashed badges. The man with the camera slipped away while the two "officials" demanded to know if the couple had "made any transaction" with him. Had they changed money with him illegally? They would have to search Glinda's bag, and they did so, without waiting for permission.

"It all happened so fast," Glinda told me a few days later. "I knew something wasn't right, but I didn't have time to think." The "officials" absconded with Glinda's wallet, having taken it right under her nose. In variations on this theme, the pseudo cops only take cash, saying it must be examined; sometimes they even offer a receipt. Needless to say, they never return and the receipt is bogus.

On first impression, the pseudo cops' scam is believable. Their trick requires surprise, efficiency, and confusion. They don't allow time for second thoughts. Theirs is a cheap trick, really. They depend on a fake police shield to gain trust; they can't be bothered to build confidence with an act. Authority is blinding, and that's enough if they're fast. It's a thin swindle, but it works.

The Pigeon Poop Practitioner

A more leisurely ploy is perpetrated by the "clean-you-off-clean-you-out" good Samaritan impostor. Bob and I met many of his victims before we finally found him—or rather, he found us.

We'd been staking out a suspicious trio at Temple de la Sagrada Familia, Antoni Gaudi's spectacular cathedral and Barcelona's number one tourist attraction. The building has been under continuous construction since 1882, despite the architect's death in 1931. For a small fee, one can wander through the site and climb its three-hundred-foot spires.

It was a long amble back to La Rambla, so we zigzagged south and west, block by block, with no particular pattern. It was a pleasant route we invented, strolling past fabulous architecture, under lush green trees, while a cool wind blew and pigeons cooed.

At the corner of Consell de Cent and Girona we saw a beautifully ornate pastry shop façade that reminded us of one in Palma de Mallorca. We decided to peek in and see if they served coffee. We were still debating and postulating about the team at La Sagrada Familia as we crossed the street in front of the *pasticeria*.

As I stepped up onto the curb, I felt a slight wetness on the back of my knee below the hem of my skirt, as if I had splashed in a puddle. Not impossible because it had rained recently.

Reflex made me glance into the street for the source puddle, but in that same instant I knew there was no puddle. I asked Bob to look at my back but I *knew* what it was. I was horrified and exalted simultaneously. We were about to meet a charlatan, a gentleman thief with a fiction, an ersatz Samaritan, and the most elusive of pickpockets.

Bob confirmed my disgusted suspicion: I had thick blobs of brown yuck on the back of my clothes, and so did Bob.

In that instant of offended confusion, while we admired each other's backsides and laughed and grimaced, before we could organize our thoughts in those few seconds, a man in shorts swept up to us, map in hand, sunglassed and baseball capped.

"Iy, look," he pointed out. We swung around. "Bird, bird."

Where did *he* come from? Out of the blue, it seemed. Still, we knew who he was. We knew *what* he was.

"Come, I help," he offered with compassion and authority, ushering us into the pastry shop we'd been headed for. He already had a neat pack of Kleenex tissues in one hand, a small bottle of Evian in the other. He was more prepared than we had expected. Bob began recording with his video camera.

Employees didn't seem surprised in the pastry shop. They observed our intrusion with the vague interest of ranch hands regarding mating dogs. The man in shorts pressed a tissue into Bob's hand and turned me around by the arm.

"You clean," he said to Bob politely but insistently, indicating my back. He didn't want to appear unseemly. You clean her and I'll clean you—out. That was the idea. We'd heard the story many times from victims. While the husband cleans the wife, the man in shorts cleans the husband. Rather,

The infamous Pigeon Poop Perpetrator, known by Barcelona police and too many visitors only as a "man in shorts". Here, inside the pastry shop with Bob and Bambi, he offers a ready pack of Kleenex tissues to clean up the imitation pigeon droppings he has surreptitiously applied.

he pretends to clean the husband. What he cleans is his pockets. And disappears before you know it.

Neither of us were good researchers this time: I didn't cooperate fully, out of repulsion. And Bob was too busy filming to do his part. He was supposed to clean me off. But every time the impostor coached Bob in his role, Bob just said okay, fussed with his new camera, and failed to come to the aid of his wife. How could he videotape the scam if he were a participant? But how could the game continue without all the players?

Our man in shorts got frustrated and tried to slip away. We managed to waylay him though, outside the shop. We tried to get him to talk to us, to show us his squirt contraption, to tell us where he's from. He was insistent about no video, no camera, but he didn't rush off too obviously. He backed away slowly, trying not to look suspicious. Finally, he broke into a little trot and dashed into the handy metro stairway. Was its proximity coincidental? We think not.

Barcelona police, it turned out, had been looking for the man in shorts for years. They knew his M.O., his territory, and that he was Peruvian. And they knew he always wore shorts. That was it. They now had his scam and his face on video.

We walked back toward La Rambla looking over our shoulders, hyper observant. Bob and I disagree on the participation of the pastry shop people.

I say they were in on it. I say the man in shorts buys his bread there and always leaves a hefty tip. I say they were awfully quick to bring out a roll of paper towels and laundry detergent when the man in shorts left. I say everyone's a suspect. Bob says it's impossible, they couldn't be in on it. It just happened to be the corner where opportunity struck for the man in shorts. He couldn't do his thing on only one corner in all the city.

J. S. Brody, an advertising executive in New York City, was a victim of the man in shorts. He remembers being astonished at the amount of

A victim of the Pigeon Poop Ploy shows off his dirtied pants.

bird droppings on his backside and his mother's. "What do you have here, eagles?" he'd asked. The incident took place several blocks away from the *pasticeria*. For the clean-up operation, the pigeon-poop practitioner had drawn them into the lobby of an apartment house. So much for my theory on location.

Gender Exploiters

A New York strategist chose another tactic. Instead of gaining the confidence of his victim, he used bystanders as his unintentional allies. My informers witnessed a furious, high-volume argument on the street between a man and a woman. The man was pulling off the woman's mink coat. The woman was screaming for help. The man explained to all nearby that he said she couldn't buy it, and he needed to return it right away. The woman shouted that she didn't know the man, he was stealing her coat. The man said she was his wife. The woman said he was lying. Was it a brazen theft or a domestic dispute?

Ego-stroking sex-based scams target vulnerable loners, or those who appear to be single. In a bar scene or come-on, some people suck up flirtation as if it were a windfall. Flattery becomes a white noise that all but drowns out warning bells. Bob and I watched in Barcelona, while a working girl latched onto a man strolling along La Rambla. She pulled him into a shallow alcove and he couldn't, or didn't, resist her handiwork. Both parties appeared to be into it until the woman's groping fingers became light fingers. Coincidentally, the man's wife and daughter caught up with him just then, too, as he and his intimate thief were not two steps off the sidewalk. We have no idea how he explained the scenario and evidence of his willing participation to his family.

Indian Shit Trick

"We were about to cross the street in Delhi," a British traveler told me. "It was very crowded, people pushing and going in every direction. We stepped off the curb between some parked cars that were very close together. I was just concentrating on getting through them and across the street. A man bumped into my husband as we were squeezing between the cars. He followed as we crossed the street, and as we reached the other side, he pointed to my husband's shoe. 'Shit,' he said. We looked down and saw it. It was shit on my husband's shoe. The man offered to help us clean it off, but we thought we knew what he was up to. We thought it was a scam. We'd heard that they do that, then demand huge sums of money in payment, and they don't let you go until you pay. So we said no, and walked away with shit on the shoe."

Of course Kharem has a version of this one. He had led us into a seedy alley, long, dim, and deserted, eager to demonstrate, at Bob's request, his expertise on inside jacket pockets.

"I don't want to go much further in this direction," I said, chicken as usual.

"Don't worry," our interpreter soothed me. "I know where we are." That was Terry Jones, our Barcelona-based friend and bag-snatch authority.

Kharem stopped at a graffitied niche where a stone water fountain was the sole feature.

The only jacket among the four of us on this warm spring afternoon was Kharem's prop, the "tool" he used over his arm. He put the jacket on Terry and took a fat brown wallet from his own pocket.

"Whose is that?" I asked him.

"Mine!" he laughed, and put it in Terry's inside breast pocket. I should have asked whose *was* it.

"Wait till these people pass." A couple ambled toward us, oblivious to all but themselves.

"Shall I do it on those tourists?" Kharem asked.

"Noooo, we'll wait," Bob said, and the rest of us laughed nervously.

"It takes two people," Kharem explained. "One spits into his hand, then applies the spit onto the victim's right shoulder." Standing behind Terry, he showed how to "help" the victim by pointing out the mess. After indicating the shoulder to Terry, who couldn't see that far behind him, Kharem grasped the upper right sleeve with his right hand and Terry's left lapel with his left. With both hands, he twisted the jacket slightly around to the right. This accomplished two necessities. It successfully turned Terry's attention far to his right, and it intentionally made vulnerable Terry's left inside breast pocket. With perfect timing, the "pick" of the pair, approaching from the front, would then have free access to the wallet.

Kharem suggested I be the spitting Samaritan and, as Bob filmed and Terry cooperated, we easily stole the wallet. Kharem high-fived his new partner.

"Eeew," I said, pulling my hand away. His was wet.

"It's not spit!" he said. "It's from the water fountain!" I hadn't noticed that he'd gotten a quick drink.

Spit, shit, what's the difference? The object is to apply a substance that the victim wants off *now*. Something disgusting, something staining, something smelly. In New York, they use mustard. In London, ice cream. Mix and match. The strategist has created his opportunity, complete with an excuse to get up close and personal, to touch, to take.

A female pickpocket on La Rambla uses sex as a distraction.

Women are the most frequent victims in bars and nightclubs, where drink drugging is on the rise. Coasters that test for certain drugs have recently been developed, but are criticized as ineffective because they only detect gamma hydroxybutyrate (GHB) and ketamine, two common date-rape drugs. Thirty-four other drugs that accomplish the same end go undetected; that leaves a lot of options for drink druggers. A woman doesn't necessarily have to pass out to be victimized. Diminished judgment is enough to compromise defenses, and that can happen even with undrugged drinks. In Sao Paulo, Brazil, women do the drink drugging. They're known as "Mickey Finn Girls," and they rob their knocked-out men of everything. Food- and drink-drugging is a widespread problem now, both in the United States and abroad. I mention it here because the perpetrators often befriend their victims, as do the other duplicitous thieves in this section.

Shoulder Surfers

The vital bit of information the shoulder surfer needs from you is your ATM PIN. As his moniker implies, he somehow peeks over or around you

How to Lure a Young Man Using the Momentum of His Own Ego

"Make sex with me, baby."

The girl was suggestively dressed and appeared drunk. George Rawson, only a recent resident of Costa Rica and infrequent visitor to San José, didn't quite know what to make of her. The girl was hugging him, her hands everywhere, fondling, feeling. Before George could decide how to respond to the groping curiosity nuzzling his chest and holding his hips, the girl appeared to change her mind. Abruptly, she turned away and stumbled off, into the arms of several girlfriends.

George had never encountered this behavior in Wyoming, his home state. The girl had startled him, but not unpleasantly. Flattery had certainly been one of the many feelings flitting though his jumbled mind when the girl's hands slipped below his belt.

As he resumed his walk across the city trying to make sense of this odd assault, he instinctively put his hand on his back pocket. Obvious—his wallet was gone. The girl had been a pickpocket.

When I met George on a muggy November day in Puntarenas, Costa Rica, he'd been living and working in the area for a year. Three of his visiting male friends had been accosted in exactly this manner, he said, despite his warnings. Often, the girls come on in groups. As soon as they get a wallet, it's passed to one of the girls who swiftly departs. Moments later, they all move on.

"They're professionals," he said with a sort of admiration. "It's happening right now." He waved his arm toward the mixed crowd of locals and tourists. "Right here, someone is losing something, I guarantee it."

as you enter your code. He may pretend to dial his cell phone when, in fact, he's storing your numbers in it as you tap them in. With his team around him, he may pretend to videotape his pals when, in fact, he's zoomed in on your fingers. Another method relies on a substance applied to the number pad itself. Once you've left the machine, the scammer can at least determine which keys you've pressed, if not their order.

That done, the shoulder surfer must complete step two: acquire possession of your bank card. Some morph into pickpockets at this point, watching closely where the card is put, then following the moneybags until an opportunity is presented or created. Others, those who best fit into this section, have devised devious methods of getting that bank card without the time or effort spent following its owner. One is simple distraction. As the machine spits out your cash, surfer A points to money on the ground (his) as if it's yours, while surfer B snags your card as it pops out. You assume the machine ate your card, slap the machine, and leave without it. Now the surfers have everything they need.

ATM Scam

Debbie Tinsley, from the United Kingdom, described the following method that occurs in Spain and England, among other places:

"A slim plastic pocket is placed in the slot of an ATM. When a person puts in her card, it doesn't work and can't be ejected from the slot. She thinks it's been swallowed.

"A helpful Spanish-speaking person is on hand with a mobile phone. He kindly phones the helpline number on the ATM for you (but of course it's not really the helpline, it's his friend around the corner).

"He gives you the phone so that you can talk to the 'ATM helpline.' They then ask you for all your details, including your PIN code, and when your helpful Spanish friend goes with you to report the incident to the Spanish police, his accomplice comes and fishes out the plastic pocket, containing your cash card.

"How clever is that? It happened to a friend of mine in Sitges, Spain. My friend's account was emptied in a matter of hours."

Trickier surfers put wax or gum in the card slot so your card doesn't come out. They are able to retrieve it, though, and, again, have everything they need to empty your bank account through another ATM.

Express kidnappings are the latest terrifying trend. Victims are threatened with weapons as in a mugging, but are taken to ATM cashpoints and made to empty their accounts, or withdraw their limits. Bob and I don't proclaim expertise in muggings or other violent crimes. Avoidance would rely on the usual advice: don't flash your cash, dress down, stay away from isolated areas, and move with purpose.

In Argentina, where the drastic economic situation has bred creativity, express kidnappers are dressing up as market researchers, complete with clipboards, and interviewing people in line at cinemas. In this simple way, they manage to get the names and addresses of people going in to the movie. They then contact the subjects' families, claim the relative has been kidnapped, and extract ransom money—all while the supposedly kidnapped person is just watching a movie. The lesson here points to the importance of privacy and power of greed. Why do those movie-goers provide their personal information to strangers? Undoubtedly, they're promised a "free gift" will be sent.

The obvious protection against ATM scams is to closely guard your PIN and preserve the space around you during your transaction. Cup your hand over the keypad as you enter your code—observers have been reported using binoculars from a distance. Always use well-lit ATMs, avoid those in isolated areas, and avoid those with loiterers. *Never* give your PIN to anyone. A bank employee will never need it and never ask for it. Value your own privacy: release your personal details only to those who require it.

Protect Your Sphere

In chapter 5, I referred to Plaid as a gentleman thief, but let's face it: compared to the practitioners in this chapter, he's a lowly opportunist. I meant gentleman in its most literal sense: he's gentle in manner, as far as thieves go. The gentleman thief of the strategist variety, however, is a consummate con man and more dangerous than Plaid by far. By design, he thwarts suspicion and earns his intended victim's confidence by his dress and demeanor. He puts on respectability and trustworthiness as if they were a jacket and tie, then garnishes the look with manners and decorum, like cufflinks and a spit shine. But his garments are mere costumes, uniforms donned for gainful occupation, flimsy façades contrived to trick us into allowing him access to our spheres.

How can one beware the wolf in sheep's clothing? It's our nature to trust first, suspect later, and it's darn difficult to overcome our nature. We almost always give the benefit of the doubt, assuming one is innocent until proven guilty. Especially in a foreign country, where we're unfamiliar with local customs, we hesitate to doubt a motive for fear of offending. So how can we be alert to this insidious impostor?

Bob and I hate to imply that strangers cannot be trusted—most can. Yet, for every crook and scoundrel we meet, for every victim's story we hear, we feel ourselves harden. Our antennas get longer, our trust diminishes. We say: protect your sphere. Don't let a stranger penetrate your personal space. Question the unknown person who suddenly wants to be your friend—the stranger who wants your confidence.

Theft Thwarters #6:
Stymie the Strategist

■ This one should be obvious. Do not ever let anyone touch your wallet.

■ Remove valuables from the pockets of a jacket before hanging it on the back of a chair.

■ Do not leave a wallet or credit card sitting exposed in a restaurant, Internet café, etc.

■ If you're questioned by a policeman, ask to see his ID. A bona fide law enforcement officer won't be offended. An impostor will usually scram.

■ If you are going to allow yourself to be groped by a stranger on the street, first stash your wallet with a buddy.

■ Carefully guard your PIN code at ATM cashpoints. Don't let anyone "assist" you with transactions. If loiterers are present, you may want to use another ATM.

■ Value your own privacy: release your personal details only to those who require it.

■ Be kind to strangers, but keep a good grip on your valuables at the same time. Strategist thieves create devious scenarios to divert your attention or gain your confidence (hence: "con artist").

■ If you don't know the customs in foreign cities, be on guard if you are approached by a stranger. Even the innocent gift of a flower on the street can become a pickpocketing incident. Dilute your friendliness with a dose of caution.

■ **Escalators:** Recognize the pile-up pick. The person in front of you drops something just as the escalator ends, bends to pick it up and causes a pile-up. As people compress in the crash, the person behind you picks your pocket or purse.

■ **Public restrooms:** Rude, but true: you may or may not notice a hand reach over the door and snag your bag off the hook at the most inopportune moment. Loop the strap around the hook and keep your eye on it. Dropped coins in the stall next to you could be a distraction ruse.

■ **Helpful cleaners:** Heads up if you hear "something dirty got on you—let me help you clean it off." He'll clean you out.

- Strategist thieves can be men or women, children or grandmothers, pairs, gangs, or solo. They can be well dressed, or dressed like a tourist (carrying map and water bottle). You will probably never recognize a pickpocket, but he or she will recognize you as a mark.

- Tune in to your own alarm bells. If you're suspicious of someone's motive, observe carefully.

- Suspect the unknown person who suddenly wants to be your friend—the stranger who wants your confidence.

Con Artists and Their Games of No Chance

8

Buy-a-Brick

"Pssssst. Come 'ere. A brand new Sony video with flip-out color screen. In the box. $250. Here, have a look, try it out. Look, here's the box, and all the accessories. Battery, a/c adapter, microphone. Only $225? *Mama mia!* Okay, it's yours! Here, we'll put it in the box for you, see? And a bag so you can carry it easily. Okay, thank you very much. Here's your bag."

You *saw* him put the camera in the box. You *saw* him put the box in the bag. So how did you end up with a sack of salt?

A better question: What were you doing trying to buy a thousand-dollar video camera on a street corner? What were you *thinking*?

Yes, the seller looked like a decent man; he seemed okay. But that was not his son with him, it was his partner; and their performance together is as precise as a tango. Not only that, there are four or five teams per corner in the hottest areas, competing with such subtlety you'd never suspect they're running a scam. After all, if they let on, you're not likely to buy from any of them.

As usual, observation tells the story. The swindler approaches you with the camera and, once you take it in your hands, he summons his partner, who brings a plastic shopping bag through which you can see a box. The box is opened for you and you see that it contains the promised accessories.

How can you go wrong? You'll take it! You place the camera in the box *yourself,* and tuck in the flap. You dig for your cash, which you cleverly placed in a pouch beneath your shirt, or in a money belt, or in your sock. You offer the money and take the bag. You even shake hands. What a deal. What a steal!

What you never noticed was the critical switch. You were intentionally distracted for half a second, while the "son" passed by with an identical box in an identical bag. The bags were swapped. It's the classic bait-and-switch.

You might think it difficult to fall for a scam like this one, but it happens many times a day on a certain corner in Naples. Ship officers and crewmen are primary targets because the con men know their ships depart shortly after the purchase and it's unlikely they'll return. Ordinary tourists are also easily tempted.

Bob and I first observed this trick in 1994, and have watched it develop over the years to include cell phones. In the beginning we were afraid to film it. From pickpocketing and bag snatching by motor scooter to extortion and murder, all crime in Naples is said to be mob-related. The Camorra, Naples' mafia, is made up of some eighty clans and thousands of members who operate in the city. Not that Bob and I knew that when we began our audacious stakeout of these grandfatherly crooks. But the vague knowledge we had was intimidating enough for a couple of lightweights. If you want to infiltrate the bad guys, you better know what you're doing.

Eventually we began to film from across the street, and then to acquire bits and pieces up close with an exposed camera held casually. After all, tourists carry cameras and shoot the sights, so ours wouldn't be incongruous. The following year we were more brazen, and carried a small digital video camera hidden in a shopping bag with a hole cut for its lens. This worked fairly well, though we were as nervous as a thief in the act. It was this setup that got us our first clear footage of what we'd seen with our eyes so many times: the switch.

The move is simplicity itself; its timing perfection. The salesman tries to back up to a corner of a building, usually a magazine kiosk or a phone booth, anything to shield the substitution. That allows him to lower his hand and the bag while his unseen partner does the swap.

In the bait-and-switch scam, a man swaps packages out of the buyer's sight. The original package contains a video camera in a box. The replacement contains a sack of salt in a similar box.

Our first clear capture of the actual swap occurred on a sidewalk. The partners were running after their customer, afraid they'd lost the sale. They did the switch behind him, right out in the open. It's beautiful in slow motion, like world-class magic. You see the "magician's assistant" hand over one sack, turn, and tuck an identical one under his jacket.

When the sale had been concluded, Bob told the victim he'd just been swindled. The man didn't think twice. He turned and bolted down the street, caught the con men, and got his money back, no questions asked.

In later visits to Naples, as our equipment improved, we used tiny hidden cameras with remote controls. This allowed us to get the ultimate exposés, including the scenes we helped capture for ABC's *20/20*.

Eventually, we were introduced to a trio of swap-thieves. I was waiting on a corner with Luciano, the tram thief, while Bob fetched a translator. He was gone forever, it seemed. Meanwhile, it was my job to entertain Luciano and keep him from disappearing, from going back to work. We tried talking, but both of us were frustrated by the language barrier.

"Pacco," Luciano said, pointing toward bait-and-switch Central, where a few men offered video cameras and cell phones to innocent, but greedy, foreigners. He waved them over. I tensed, wondering if they'd recognize me, worried about what Luciano was telling them about us. These were mobsters, intimidating men impervious to laws. *"Pacco,"* Luciano said again, indicating the three men who each had an electronic item in his hand, and I understood that *pacco,* Italian for package, was the slang term for their swindle. Also, that they all spoke rudimentary English.

"I am Davide," one of the *pacchi* said, "and my friend is Guiddo and he is Giandamo." I was obliged to shake their hands.

"Amigos, four years," I told them, patting Luciano's arm. Luciano said something in Napolitano and they all nodded. The *pacchi* told me that they "change" packages. I said I know, they sell water, or salt. They laughed. I was dizzy with conflicting emotions: high on being "inside" this fraternity of impermeable criminals, and full of fear and revulsion at the same time. With a jovial façade, I took a camera bag from one of them and made a show of tugging a zipper on it, as if it couldn't be opened. They laughed again, knowing I was referring to the trick of gluing or melting zippers to delay the discovery of the scam.

We struggled with conversation until a few tourists wandered over and the *pacchi* pounced, pitching their wares. I got instant sweat in my armpits and a heartbeat in my throat. They caught my eye and I gave a barely perceptible nod. Inside, I was petrified. They carried on, eyes flicking back to see that I wouldn't interfere with their scam. I couldn't believe they let me stay in the vicinity. One piercing look and I would have fled.

Their quarry eventually decided against the purchase and walked away. The *pacchi* waited an instant, then ran after the mark making the switch without cover, in front of my watching eyes, and calling behind the mark: "Papa, papa," hoping now to make the sale at any ridiculous price.

Bob returned just then with an aura of urgency that dominated my attention; the *pacchi* scene faded out like a movie transition. Officially introduced now, it's unlikely we'll be able to film the Naples switcheroo again.

What astounds us most about Naples' bait-and-switch game is not the fact that it occurs right out in the open in full view of surrounding residents and businesses. Nor is it the perpetuation, the reliability of finding these guys on the same corner, year after year. Nor is it the fact that they haven't been bashed up by a returning pack of angry victims.

No, it's that the crime is committed smack under the noses of Naples' law enforcement agencies. It is tolerated, to say the least.

The primary location of bait-and-switch activity is directly across the street from the city's maritime terminal. Visiting cruise ship passengers congregate in the area, and must traverse the corner to walk anywhere. They usually pause there, either gathering the nerve to cross the wild traffic, or recovering from just having done so. Other people are in the area to catch ferries to Capri, Sorrento, or Ischia. There on Via Cristoforo Colombo, tourists and, presumably, others, are scrutinized by Marine Police sentries. Naples' City Police patrol by car and, in packs of five, on foot. There is also the Falchi Squad, the civilian-dressed motorcycle cops who look for "micro-crime". All these, and the republic's military force, are usually present on this intersection.

Yet, with all but a nod and a wink, the fearless mobsters carry on.

Lest you think only the most exploitable tourists fall victim to this scam, let me tell you about Ian. An officer on a premium cruise ship, he's spent years traveling the world. He knew about the bait-and-switch scam. He knew that streetside video camera sales in Naples ended with rip-offs.

It was a hot summer day in 2001. Ian was walking on Via Toledo, a fashionable shopping street half a mile or more from his ship. A young man on a scooter approached him and offered a video camera for three hundred dollars. Ian said no. The man offered him a lift on the scooter. Sweaty and tired, Ian hopped on. When they reached the ship terminal, the man showed Ian the camera. Ian held it. He tried it out. He was impressed.

"My greed got the better of me," Ian said. "I told him to wait, and I'd be back in ten minutes. I thought when I came back I could bargain for an even better price."

Ian returned with cash.

"On the way out, I passed another officer on the gangway and told her I was going off to buy a video camera. She said 'Oh Ian, don't, you'll come back with a brick.' But I told her I knew what I was doing, I'd be careful.

"The guy was still waiting on his scooter. He seemed nervous and in a hurry. He agreed to $250, so I bought it. I saw him put it in this bag."

Ian showed us a vinyl camera bag.

The Making of ABC's *20/20*: Bait-and-Switch

The lawlessness of Naples stunned us all. Even Bob and I, who have been there many, many times, were newly amazed at the reckless race of vehicles.

"They say the traffic lights are merely a suggestion," our Roman driver laughed as he pulled to an abrupt halt. "Here we are."

We had only a morning to shoot the scene and, as we hadn't made an appointment with the con men, we'd need luck as well as efficiency. Would they be working? Would we find them on the corners we were familiar with? Would there be any ships in port, full of potential suckers? Bob and I felt the pressure. We'd brought a network news crew all the way to Naples with no certainty whatsoever.

By 9 A.M. we were rigged and ready. Bob directed our driver to park at the ferry terminal, where hydrofoils depart for Capri. A small cruise ship was just tying up. That was a good sign.

I banished Bob to the wrong side of the street. Since we had brazenly filmed here several months before, it was possible they'd recognize him. No visible video cameras, we specified, or they'd never offer the sale. We must all be extremely cautious because we don't know how an angry Napolitano crook might react. Neither do we know if any of the others loitering on the corner are their thugs. What we do know about is the proliferation of mafia gangs in Naples, their turf wars, and their violence.

From the maritime terminal parking lot, we observed the opposite side of the street with binoculars. A large news kiosk hulked on the corner, open for business as usual.

ABC *20/20*'s investigative reporter Arnold Diaz and I crossed to the corner where we hoped to find our prey, who'd hope to prey on us. The rest of the crew trailed us at a distance. First we paused at the news kiosk. With hundreds of magazines on display, it would be good for at least ten minutes, time in which we could scrutinize the characters who hung around. Most were selling knock-off watches and showed their wares eagerly.

I noticed two scooters parked on the sidewalk. Both had roomy, lockable storage bins perched on the back. Aha! These, I knew, were where the con men kept their props. Another good sign. Of course, scooters are everywhere in Naples; these could belong to anyone.

Arnold and I moved halfway down the block and examined a shop window full of watches. Our corner seemed quiet. Other than fake Rolexes and cheap leather jackets, there were no deals to be had. Perhaps it was too early. We ambled back toward the magazine stand, wishing for a proposition.

"Cell phone?" A middle-aged man held out a shiny new-model Nokia. "Try! Call your home. I sell cheap."

"Really? I can try it?" Arnold looked around to be sure the camera crew was in position. "How do I call America?"

"I don't know, better call Italy," the man said.

"I don't know anyone in Italy," Arnold said. "But it works? I believe you."

After a little negotiation, we settled on a price. Two cell phones for two hundred dollars. "We can call each other, honey!" I said to Arnold, as he counted out cash. He counted slowly, giving Glenn Ruppel, our segment producer, and Jill Goldstein, our hidden camera expert, time to move into position to catch the switch. The two looked so completely innocent, standing there against a shop window, not ten feet from us. Glenn's eyes

(continued)

roved everywhere as he pretended to be in an intense conversation on his cell phone. Jill seemed to be bored waiting for him. She looked down at her sneaker, turning her foot a bit as if examining the shoe. In fact, Jill was not looking at her shoe. She was looking into a hole cut in the top of her fanny pack, in which she had a video monitor. Jill had hidden button-sized cameras in the side of her clothing, in order to face away from the action. With the monitor, she could check that she was positioned correctly. Bob was across the street, watching the same scene he'd seen so many times before.

The salesman put the two phones in a box and looked around for his colleague, who came trotting over with transformers. They added these to the box, closed it, and put the box in a translucent plastic shopping bag. The salesman tied a tight knot in the bag.

Arnold handed over the money.

"Have you visited the castle?" the salesman asked, and pointed across the street to the thirteenth century Castel Nuovo. His English wasn't too good, but he got his point across. He pointed, and our eyes couldn't help but follow his broad gesture. In that instant, we knew, he and his accomplice swapped bags.

"Did they get it?" Arnold asked me. I glanced over at Glenn, still rapt in his phony phone conversation. He waggled one hand. What does that mean?! Sort of? A little? Don't know? What to do now? We couldn't very well back up and replay the scene. Arnold took the knotted bag and the deal was done. There was no handshake.

Grinning, Arnold immediately began to untie the bag. The salesman and his colleague, watching warily, hurried away. Arnold tore open the box and looked inside. A water bottle. No cell phones.

"Hey!" he shouted. "Come back! Stop!"

The two men jumped onto their scooters and roared off into the crazy Naples traffic. The five of us reconvened.

"Did you get it?" Arnold asked eagerly.

"I don't know, we're not sure," Jill and Glenn said.

"Why don't we try to interview a police officer," Bob suggested. "They're all around us. Let's see how they react when we show them the water bottle."

"Good idea," Arnold said.

We walked across the street to the passenger ship terminal, where we thought there might be a chance of finding an officer who spoke a little English. No luck, but with Bob's mixture of languages and the water bottle in the box as evidence, they understood perfectly.

"*Allora,*" the officer said, and threw up his hands. It was the all-purpose Italian expression that, in this instance, meant: *idiots! You get what you pay for!*

"But when I got to my cabin, I couldn't open the zippers. Four zippers on the bag and they were all stuck. That's when I knew something was wrong. I had to cut it open with a knife."

He showed us the zippers. They appeared to be glued or melted. He reached into the cut he'd made.

"All that was in the bag was this." He pulled out two boxes labeled *sale de cusine.* Salt.

"I thought I knew what I was doing, but he was just too slick for me."

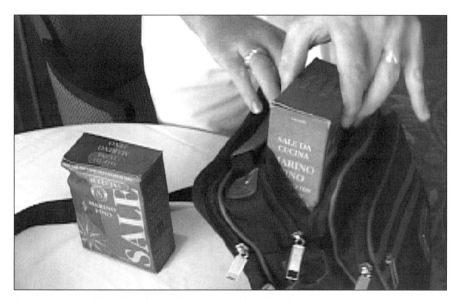

Ian, a cruise ship officer, shows his purchase. He saw the seller place the video camera into the bag—but he didn't see the switch. All the zippers on this bag were glued shut. Ian had to cut the bag open.

Unlike the opportunists and strategists I've described, these con artists do not steal wallets. Instead, they pretend to offer value for money. They get their victims to willingly participate, to pull out their own wallets and hand over their own cash. While getting rich, con artists can have a good laugh at their victims' stupidity. Hoodwink outwits greed.

And of course it is greed that drives the victim. Any citizen knows there's something illicit about buying electronics on a street corner. But he gambles: he's willing to risk the consequences, whatever they are, in order to get this killer deal, this too-good-to-be-true deal.

On the street, the bait-and-switch scam usually ends with rocks-in-a-box or buy-a-brick. But bricks-and-mortar shops perpetrate the bait-and-switch, too. The well-publicized case of West Coast Electronics, in New York, exposed a scam in which customers were lured to the shop with advertisements for a computer at a price too good to be true. The advertised item was never available and customers were routinely upsold on pricier, high-profit-margin machines of dubious pedigree. Upselling is not a crime, but false advertising is. Buyer beware.

In other versions of the scam, the unsavvy shopper just gets less than he bargained for. Underhanded merchants have learned new ways to extract dollars from buyers, especially overseas visitors. Goods may be sold with limited warranties or none at all, lack invisible features like the time and date stamp on a camera, lack a remote control, or lack other accessories that are routinely included with the item elsewhere.

Souvenir Sucker

Our friend Russell, a magician, works a considerable amount of time each year in Asia. A streetwise New Yorker, he knows pretty much all the tricks played from the East Coast to the Far East.

Russell was in Bali recently, between jobs. He was on a bus crowded with tourists when traffic ground to a halt. The morning was sweltering. Windows were open. Occasional clouds of dust wafted in, more welcome than rain, which would force the closing of windows and bring the interior humidity to Beverly Hills spa levels.

As traffic slowed, then stopped, a raging hoard of pleading faces surrounded the bus. Vendors reached up to the open windows offering their wares. Wood carvings, silver jewelry, and stamped batik sarongs danced in the windows like props in a puppet show. Vendors had only desperate moments to tempt these tourists before they and their dollars vanished down the road.

Always a sucker for souvenirs, Russell scrutinized the merchants, looking for something new. He was not disappointed. He noticed an intricately carved something glowing in the sunlight as its hawker flourished it. The expert salesman caught Russell's interest and pushed his way near. He proffered his wares for inspection. It was a hollow piece of bone—cow or sheep, Russell guessed—carved with delicate figures in classic Indonesian poses. So thin, it was, the light shone through the bone in warm amber tones.

"Twenty dollar," the vendor said, scratching a long dark scar on his neck.

"I'll give you five," said Russell.

"Ten."

"Okay, ten." Russell reached for his wallet and took out an American ten dollar bill while the vendor wrapped the bone and passed it through the window.

The bus began to move and the vendors scattered reluctantly, some trotting alongside the bus for another hopeful moment. Soon the bus picked up speed and the locals were left in the dust.

Pleased with his find, Russell unrolled his carving from its plastic bag. He stared at it.

It had looked so much finer a moment ago. Now, the blocky figures hacked into the bone felt sharp against his fingers. The delicate details were gone. He held it up to the light. No glow.

Cheated! Russell thought. *They got me, a world-wise New Yorker.* He rewrapped his booby prize and looked out at the passing lime-green terraced rice fields, the tall spirit houses, and offerings to the gods placed in the roadside gutters with care.

We ran into Russell in Bali as someone else might bump into a coworker at the grocery store. Together, we strolled along the waterfront of Cape Sari and through an open-air market. Fat pigs and goats lay suckling their broods beside stacks of bamboo furniture, while chickens stood waiting for sale, one to a bell-shaped woven basket. Souvenir T-shirts hung limply above varnished seashells and carved Buddha heads. Just a few years before, we remembered, only eggs and cloth were sold here. Now postcards outnumbered food items. As we browsed and wandered, Russell told us about his morning rip-off and, laughing, promised to show us his white elephant.

"Shit! There's the guy!" Russell pointed and, there, unbelievably, was the man with the scar on his neck, offering the same beautiful piece of carved bone. The three of us watched with fascination as the man made a sale, pulled a plastic bag out of his cloth satchel, and adroitly swapped artifacts.

(continued)

It was the classic bait-and-switch, expertly performed. Russell grinned, not at all displeased at having been duped this way.

"He's a magician!" he said. "Did you see how he used misdirection? Fucking great!"

For a highly skilled young street performer, Russell has been known to toss ten bucks into a hat, and that's all he'd paid this con man earlier. But he wasn't quite satisfied.

He strode up to the shyster who, of course, didn't recognize him at all.

"How much?" Russell asked, and the two repeated their earlier negotiations. Bob and I watched from a distance.

"You don't have to wrap it," Russell said, when they'd agreed on a price.

The vendor's face fell. "Yes, must wrap!"

"No. Besides, I want *this* one." Russell held onto the fine sample.

"And the guy started to panic," Russell told us later, with absolute glee. "And behind me, another vendor, a woman, began to laugh and point at us. You could tell she was happy to see this guy getting caught." Russell was laughing so hard he could hardly talk. Now he flourished the fine bone carving as the vendor had, triumphant. The sun was low and glowed through the delicate design of the salesman's floor sample.

"I'm gonna put them side by side on a shelf," he told us, "one beautiful, one crude, and a story to go with them."

Consumers aren't always aware of the difference between PAL and NTSC in video, and tuners built into computers or monitors may not function in the buyer's country. Slippery salesmen don't rush to make important details clear. Fly-by-night shops are regularly closed down by police, but they somehow manage to reopen under new names just blocks away. Hong Kong, long considered an electronics shoppers' paradise, is renown for this in its warren of tiny shops. Of course, there's good shopping in Hong Kong, too.

In the touts-on-the-take scam, lies and trickery trap tourists in dubious shops. The visitor to Bangkok stands on a street corner comparing his map to bewildering street signs. A well-dressed local approaches, apparently eager to help and make a good impression of his city. He's friendly and warm and in a matter of minutes has won the visitor's confidence. "By the way," he suddenly remembers, "did you know that today is the last day of Bangkok's annual jewelry promotion? A few government-selected shops are allowed to sell duty free! Come, let me take you. Hurry!" He flags the first passing duk-duk, the ubiquitous three-wheeled motorcycle-taxi, instructs the driver, and the tourist is, literally and unfortunately, taken for a ride. The tourist will certainly get a deal, but it will be wholly to the shop's advantage, with a healthy commission for its sophisticated tout. This scam, in endless variations, is nearly impossible for the police to stop, as the shops do nothing illegal. Most simply sell inferior merchandise at inflated prices. Others provide worthless guarantees.

Pavement Wagers

Copenhagen's pedestrian shopping street is an ideal venue for the three-shell game, also called the pea game. Several competing crews set up there. They choose locations in the middle of a block along the narrow lane, which is swarming with jolly people from all over the world, shopping, slurping ice cream, and munching ambrosial Belgian waffles as they meander.

A pair begins the game: a barker, and an operator. The operator drops to his knees, produces a small rubber mat not much bigger than a mousepad, and begins manipulating his pieces. Instead of the traditional walnut shell halves, he uses three matchbox trays reinforced with tape. His pea is an aluminum foil ball.

He slides the boxes madly around his mat, his hands a blur.

"Lef', ri', mi'l! One, two, three. Where'za ball?" He is sloppy—on purpose? One box goes sliding off the mat.

Immediately, a man places a bet and wins. A shill. Another man, another bet, a loss. Laughter rings out, but it sounds hollow and false. Hands fly over the mat, and in the process a box is briefly tipped, revealing the ball.

Quickly, an audience gathers. Everybody knows: a crowd draws a crowd. Excitement builds. Money changes hands. Bills are flashed and stashed.

"Totto-lotto, mini-casino! Wanna play? Twenny bucks!"

"Just looking."

"Lookie-cookie. Sir! Wanna play? Where'za ball?"

The barker's narration lures. The operator's manipulation tempts.

The three-shell game. A little betting fun draws a big crowd, but it starts with half a dozen shills.

Imagined winnings seduce. It looks so easy: you can see the ball! Bets are placed: an easy win, a stupid loss . . . and soon enough, a tourist tries.

Five team members immediately close around him. They joke in any language, whatever is called for. A moment of suspense and camaraderie is staged. The operator is on the ground with his game, kneeling before his rubber mat, hunched over his boxes and ball.

"One, two, three, four. Lef', ri', mi'l! Where'za ball?" He's tightly surrounded by the six standing men: the barker, the transitory player, and some shills. For a moment, no one else can see the game. The player chooses, a cry goes out in sympathy. The circle opens and the spectators are once again included as the loser slinks away.

But wait! Arms around the player's shoulders, a conspiratorial pat on the back. "You can do it! One more time, double or nothing!" So encouraging, so friendly, who'd guess these guys were in on it? Moments later, the player turns away, shakes his head, wonders how he could have lost so much so quickly.

Bob and I run after him.

"How much did you lose?"

"Fifteen hundred crowns!" (That is approximately two hundred dollars.)

"Where're you from?"

"Bhutan."

"Why did you play?"

"I've never seen this game. It looked fun."

"This is one game you can never win."

A small crew tries to get a three-shell game going on La Rambla.

"I know that now!" He hikes up his backpack and strides away.

Bob and I follow our noses to a waffle stand and wait for a fresh one hot off the iron. A rosy-cheeked girl hands it over, steaming and blackened, caramelized surface stuck to its parchment wrapper. Standing on a street corner, we savor the chewy sweetness of this European street snack. It has no relation to American waffles.

"See the guy in the pink jacket? Bob points with his chin, chewing.

"No."

"There near the trash can."

"That's an orange jacket." I reach for the waffle.

"Orange, then. He's a spotter."

"For the three-shell guys? How can you tell?"

"Just watch him. And his partner over there, in plaid. They're looking for police. They were there before, too."

We finish the waffle and watch a while longer.

"Now!" Bob says, and we're off. The orange and plaid guys walk full speed up the lane, weaving deftly through the oblivious crowd. We follow in their wake.

The spotters reach the tight knot of people gathered around their colleagues, but they don't stop. They don't even pause. They hurry to the

Shills and Shells

"It's the talk that's important," Serge insisted. Each forceful word sent a curl of smoke into his own eyes. "Not the hands. The skill is the talk." His fingers idly spun and twirled a matchbox as he spoke. "Why you want to know this? Why you ask me?"

Because we'd watched him work the crowds earlier in the day, watched him cheat a steady stream of happy-go-lucky vacationers. Because we'd watched his team of almost a dozen men take in bets of three dollars at a minimum and up to seventy-five dollars, and no one ever won. And because we hadn't expected this opportunity, this impromptu interview with an eminent operator.

It was past 10 P.M. when Bob and I began our stroll up Copenhagen's Vesterbrogade, away from Tivoli, away from the maddening throngs of holiday-makers, away from the Swedes who swarm across the border for a night of cheap beer. The wide avenue got darker and quieter as we walked west, the shops more utilitarian and drab.

As we approached and passed a small restaurant, a diner at an outside table leered at me, swinging his huge head like a dashboard dog's as I passed. His lewd look was piercing enough that I turned back, only to see the man's head swiveled backward on his shoulders, eyes still fixed on me.

"I've got to go talk to him," Bob said abruptly. Strange: I could have sworn he hadn't noticed the man's stare; neither is Bob the type to challenge a man for a glance. Feeling hostile and squeamish, I hung back, concealed and feeling protected by a sidewalk sign.

Bob was smiling! I crept a little closer. They were peaking in German. I made out a bit of it. Bob was asking the man about immigration policies in Denmark, but I hadn't the faintest idea why. They spoke for several minutes before Bob rejoined me.

"Who *is* he?" I asked, half mad, half curious.

"One of the three-shell guys we saw today."

"You're kidding! Did you ask him about it?"

"No, I just asked him about immigration. He's from Kosovo."

"But let's go back and ask him about the game!" I said, going from zero to zeal in an instant. "What luck!"

We returned to the con man and his partner as they sat before empty dinner plates, each enjoying beers and cigarettes. The big head swung around to look me up and down, unapologetically. Perhaps it was second nature for him to appraise his opponents.

Serge was reluctant to spill his guts to strangers. It took considerable chitchat before he warmed to us even a bit. Our conversation shifted back and forth between elementary English and rudimentary German.

Gently, we hinted that we'd seen him in Strøget, the pedestrian shopping street, that afternoon. He looked from me to Bob, questioningly. Yes, we'd seen him doing the three-shell game; he appeared to be quite proficient. We saw him take in large sums.

Serge smiled nervously, trapped in his seat as Bob and I stood at the edge of his table. His younger partner sat silently, lacking any understanding of English or German.

"I make the game also," Bob confided, "but only on stage. I'm a magician."

Serge visibly relaxed a notch. He balanced his cigarette pack on its corner and spun it under a fingertip, considering.

"There is not trick," he tried, "just talk and fun."

"I know the game. I'm interested in you. How many in your team?"

(continued)

"Eight. Sometimes ten. Many men to share money."

Serge had been operating the three-shell game for twenty years. First in his native Kosovo, then in Germany for six years, and finally in Copenhagen. Having fled the war in Yugoslavia, he had no papers in Denmark, he told us. What else could he do? How could he earn money?

"This job," he said, "it is just to make fun for the tourists." Palms up, fingers spread, shoulders hunched. "People see that it's easy to win; they *want* to play."

next corner, to alert their bookend pair of spotters. Yet, the gaming gang has seen them and that's all the signal they need. They scatter. In the blink of an eye the game is over, the gang is gone, and the crowd is left wondering what they were gathered for, if anything at all.

Videotape is a wonderful diagnostic tool when it comes to sleight of hand. In slow motion, we can see the phenomenal skill behind the Copenhagen teams' manipulation. In other words, they do more than simply mix up the boxes with great speed and confusing baffles. They provide onlookers with fleeting peaks of pea as it's shuttled around the mat, as it's switched from box to box, moved from corner to corner. The player knits his brow in concentration, trying to follow its progress. The operator's hands stop. The player is sure he knows where the ball is. Or is he? He hesitates.

If a player is about to make a winning bet, a shill quickly intercepts by turning over one of the boxes, throwing down his money, and ending the round. House odds rely on the operator's ability to hoodwink the spectators with bluffs and psychology.

In New York and Las Vegas, the games are played curbside, with bottle caps and a ball of sponge. The Spanish gangs we've studied in Barcelona's Plaça de Catalunya are a brutal incarnation. They use vegetable props: either the thick ends of carrots or small potato halves hollowed out to make shells. The game is played standing, on a rickety cardboard box-cum-table. Spotters are vigilant and malevolent. They want a crowd, but scrutinize the gathering individuals. Anyone who does not appear to be a happy-go-lucky tourist-type gets a threatening once-over, an in-your-face stare, or a menacing growl. Cameras are blocked and overly curious nonplayers are swiftly made to leave.

All three-shell gamers use the sophisticated techniques of professional magicians—or is it the other way around? In any case, it's a method that ensures the punter will never win. The pea is manipulated by any of several methods, some of which use principles of magic I will not divulge except to say they employ a simple gimmick that is neither smoke nor mirror. The most common trick utilizes a miniature version of palming; you can call it thumbing. It allows the operator to sneak the ball out of and

A Con's Con: "Your Chance Is Slim"

In his book *Billion Dollar Bunco,* Simon Lovell wrote:

> At the end of the 1800s one of the best-known shell men in the country was Jim Miner, also known as Umbrella Jim. He used to introduce his game with a wonderful little song, thankfully recorded in *Gambling and Gambling Devices* by John Phillip Quinn (a reformed gambler), which went as follows:
>
> A little fun, just now and then
> Is relished by the best of men.
> If you have nerve, you may have plenty;
> Five draws you ten, and ten draws twenty.
> Attention giv'n, I'll show to you,
> How umbrellas hide the peek-a-boo.
> Select your shell, the one you choose;
> If right, you win, if not, you lose;
> The game itself is lots of fun,
> Jim's chances though, are two to one;
> And I tell you that your chance is slim
> To win a prize from 'Umbrella Jim'!

into any of the three shells or boxes. He can place it in a seemingly impossible location and guarantee a player will never win.

At the shrill whistle of a Spanish spotter, spectators see more magic. From within their very midst, the operator vanishes and all traces of his game disappear. A flash and puff of smoke are all but real. Gaming pieces are gathered or flung away, and the cardboard box is flattened and tossed against a tree or trash can: nonincriminating evidence. The team disperses like panicked pigeons and, when the coast clears, reforms its gambling gaggle.

In the aftermath one day, Bob and I found a young German tourist weeping on a sidewalk bench. A girlfriend tried to comfort her, though she, too, was distraught. Through angry tears, the girl sputtered her tale: she'd lost too much money, goaded and cajoled to bet in a fast-paced game she only vaguely followed. She'd been separated from her friend, surrounded by strangers, and pressured to play.

Few tourists penetrate Desker Road in Singapore's Little India. Activities there are meant for the locals, specifically the tens of thousands of Indian guest workers in Singapore on two-year labor contracts. Bob and I go there for the food.

When we neared a half-hearted three-shell game, things suddenly livened—for our sake. More than a dozen men clustered around us to create

A Bad Bet in New Orleans

"Betcha twenny bucks I can tell you where you got those shoes."
"How would you know that?"
"Twenny bucks. Bet me."
"Okay, where?"
"You got 'em on your feet, on Bourbon Street. Pay up!"

action and excitement. Ten- and fifty-dollar notes were flung onto the table by shills betting on this cup or that one. The operator made certain Bob and I saw every move. The little red ball was clearly on the right—yet bets were being placed on the left and center cups as well as on the obvious right. Fools!—we were supposed to think. And sure enough, the cups were knocked over to reveal the ball on the right. This continued with patient repetition by the gang who knew that the foreigners needed convincing by demonstration. In time, they knew, we'd eventually see how simple it was to win, and place bets of our own with real money.

And so we did.

Our camera was hidden in an eyeglass case Bob held in his hand and pointed with nonchalance. As he pans over the shills, you can see their eyes flick toward us. The operator concentrates on his game. You can see his hands "downstairs" when Bob holds the camera low. He doesn't do

A nighttime three-shell game in Singapore's Little India.

Red Light Gamers

"I once won a hundred dollars," Joe told us in a Singapore bakery while wrapping bread loaves for us. "But that is because I am a regular customer only and I'm knowing their tricks."

Joe was not embarrassed to tell us that he hung out on Desker Road, known primarily for its row of brothels, in Singapore's Little India. A hundred Singapore dollars was worth about US$60.

"They are using black magic," Joe continued with confidence. "If you watch them, you'll see they are always putting their hands downstairs." He dropped both his hands heavily to his sides, below the level of an imaginary gaming surface.

In Desker Road, the three-shell games begin after dusk, when Singapore's huge population of Indian national laborers finishes work. The lane is narrow, too narrow for cars, and as night falls, the crowd builds. Open doors line both sides of the street. Within, bored women can be seen lounging in chairs, some with needlework or newspapers on their laps, though the rooms' red lighting seems insufficient for those activities. Orderly lines form outside the most popular establishments. "Better selection! More variety!" we're told.

The entire street has been makeshifted into an entertainment center. Ropes crisscross haphazardly above to support tarps in case of rain. Red paper lanterns glow. Table games intersperse the porn-CD displays, and the alley is packed with men.

The three-shell gamers stand surrounded by permanent participants. A cafeteria-type tray serves as surface atop a stack of plastic beer crates. A battery-powered fluorescent lamp hangs low over each game giving confidence to players: no tricks here, see?

"They are doing something under the table," Joe the breadman explained with naïve conviction. "They show you under one cup the ball. Because I am seeing it there, that one I never bet on. That's how I am winning."

The cups here are well-worn wood, bell-shaped, like simple chess bishops, with a small round ornament at their tops.

"The minimum bet is ten dollars only. If you play, don't win more than twenty! Then walk away. If you win a lot, they'll follow, then hammer you."

"You mean they mug you? You've seen that?" I asked our young breadman. Joe is small and sweet looking. He couldn't be more than twenty-five years old.

"I haven't seen. I've heard only."

"He knows because they've hammered him!" A girl came around from the ovens. She was smiling broadly. "I know because he's my brother. I've seen his black eye!"

"Yes, they've hammered me. But still I play. I am a regular customer," Joe said with pride. "They don't care who you are, Indian, regular customer, even tourist." That was Joe's subtle warning directed at us.

anything with his hands under the table: he just drops them to his side, away from the cups. Bob and I knew we wouldn't see any tricks until outside money was on the table.

I dropped a ten on the center cup, the obvious one. The cups were knocked over. The ball was on the left.

A skilled operator, such as this Indian in Singapore's Desker Road, never loses—except to encourage a player to keep gambling. His method is simple but highly practiced. When he finishes manipulating his cups or shells, when he drops his hands, if that is his style, the little ball is hidden between his fingertip and thumb. *All* the cups are empty. When he knocks over the cups, the ball is released—with precision timing—behind the cup of his choice.

We bet and lost once more, just to get it on film. Then, as I thought a tourist might, I smiled and handed my camera to Bob, so he could take a picture of me "gambling." The operator immediately switched off his fluorescent lamp and dismantled his table. We apologized and turned away. Although we hadn't won, I worried about getting "hammered" as we ambled further down Desker Road.

We came to a porn-CD seller who realized that ambiance is everything. His five-dollar discs were spread atop a cardboard box. Along the back and two sides of his display were a row of upside-down one-liter soft-drink bottles; there were about a dozen of them. The bottle tops had been pushed into small holes along the edge of the box top, and each held a tall, white, flickering candle. The bottle bottoms had burned away and the clear plastic cylinders, now gracefully curled and warped at their upper edges, reflected the flesh and flushed faces of the man's wares.

Further along we found a game we'd never seen before. At first glance, it looked like dreidel—out of place, but it *was* December, so the time was right. A vertical line divided the cardboard gaming surface into halves. On the left was drawn an 8, on the right a 9. The operator spun a small top, like a dreidel, which was marked with 8s and 9s. Just as the top came to rest, he clapped a wooden cup over it and slid it back toward him.

This simple betting game in Singapore's Little India is rigged with a magnet.

"If you see an eight, buy an eight. If you see a nine, buy a nine," he droned. Again, shills gathered and played with enthusiasm for our sake.

"Only eights and nines. Buy an eight or buy a nine. Wait till you see it." He allowed just enough time to give a glimpse of which way the top landed before slapping the cup over it and sliding it back.

Bills plunked down on both sides of the board: for eight and for nine, even though it was clear to anyone who watched which side was up.

So how does the operator ever win?

The house advantage is a magnet glued to the bottom of the cardboard. The operator knows how the top has landed, as do his players. When he wants to flip the top to switch its winning number, he simply slides his wooden cover over the hidden magnet and the top tips. Simple. Ingenious. Age-old.

And if the clientele believes the nine they saw has become an eight through black magic, the operator's advantage is more than magnetic.

Magic, sleight-of-hand, conjuring, conning . . . what's the difference? Vagrant wager games like these have been drawing crowds since time began. People now, like way back then, gather close, suspend belief, and open their purses. In a game of catch-the-magician, sleight-of-hand becomes gambling, and gambling becomes entertainment. Willing players pay the entertainer until their own fun, or money, runs out.

Three-card monte is a variation of shills-and-shells played with three cards: often a red queen and two black tens. The operator is called a broad tosser (because he tosses the queen) or a molly man (molly is a derivation of monte). He puts a lengthwise crease in each card, shows his players the three faces, then tosses them like mad, face down. The player's idea of fun is to bet money that he can follow the queen as it ricochets across the table like a pinball, under the super-skilled hands of the tosser. Since the tosser's expertise is tricky dealing, the odds are highly in his favor. Since deception, coercion, and feints are used, the odds are *all* in his favor. Not that a passerby understands that—induced to play by a shill's enthusiasm, seduced by the shill's effortless wins, encouraged by his idiotic losses.

Simon Lovell, a former card mechanic (cheat), explains how the tosser mixes "straight throws" with "hypes" or trick tosses, ensuring that players follow the wrong card. "But the tosser's moves are straightforward," he says. "The brilliance is in how the shills manipulate the mug." *Playlets,* Lovell calls them. Sneaky ploys to get a *deadhead* (a mug who won't get his money out) to play, to get a player to bet bigger, to give him confidence that this time he can't lose. Lovell describes these and many other con games in his book *Billion Dollar Bunco.*

"*Nobody,* repeat *nobody,* beats the game of monte," says Lovell. "It is a testament to greed and stupidity that the three-card trick has remained almost unchanged since its birth in the mid-1800s."

Like the three-shell game, three-card monte can be found in most big cities, particularly in areas with significant tourist traffic. Rod the Hop, my Las Vegas monte informer, is a former tosser whose demonstrations proved that drills teach skills for life. He used to set up in areas with less police presence. He favored the sidewalks outside large factories, especially on payday, "where there's eight hundred people going to lunch and they have to walk by you. A real good spot is outside military bases, where you've got a lot of young, naïve kids with nothing much to do and a little bit of money to spend.

"The moves are easy. You can learn it in a day and be good in a week. It's the presentation that's important. You have to have unflinching audacity and unmitigated gall. I don't get intimidated."

A traveler is more likely to encounter games in city streets or open spaces. In Manhattan, it's big on Canal Street. In London, it pops up regularly in Leicester Square and spontaneously all over. The version I've seen most often there is played with three five-inch disks of shoe rubber, one of which has a piece of white adhesive tape on its bottom. The tosser handles the disks as if they were cards, using the same double-dealing techniques. Using shoe rubber allows the game to be set up anywhere without fear of a breeze blowing over cards. As in the card variation, players are purposely given a glimpse of the target early in the scramble, a skillful slip is performed by the tosser, and players thereafter carefully track the wrong object with confidence.

I have called three-card monte a "game," but, like the three-shell game, they're games of no chance: tricks and traps. You'll see other players win and walk away, but they are, in fact, shills. *You* cannot win. If you win once, it's the tosser's intention in the hope that you, or someone in his audience, will bet big.

The Pigeon Drop

Birds and their excrement seem to figure frequently in the world of street thievery. While pigeon pooping, which I described in chapter 7, is unrelated to pigeon dropping, the explanation of which follows, both require a gull, someone easily tricked or cheated, a dupe, a person who is gullible. When we hear about people taken in pigeon drop scams, Bob and I wonder how anyone could be so naïve. Yet these swindles proliferate relentlessly, constantly reinvented to suck in the greedy.

Here's one from Singapore: The con man selects his mark and approaches. This time she is Ahmad Zuanah, a middle-class housewife.

"Excuse me, can you tell me how to get to the Wa Keo Me Temple?" The con man speaks with an unidentifiable accent, as phony as the name of the temple.

Confessions of a Tosser, as Told by Rod the Hop

The object of three-card monte is to make money. Each person in the crew gets an equal end. Some days it's good, and it's a street game so obviously you can only make as much money as what a person has in their pocket. But if you make two or three hundred dollars apiece a day, then you've done what you set out to do. Most of it has to do with grift sense, and your con and your presentation. That's more than the skill factor, I would say.

It's just a hustle. I mean, you just do the best you can and you prey on tourists or suckers who don't know they're breathing air.

What I look for in a sucker is, they've got money, number one. And that they're a sucker. I don't have a conscious thought pattern that goes through my mind when I see a sucker. I know a sucker when I see one. I just do. I've been doing it so long, I know a candy bar when I see one. That's all there is to it.

But by the same token, I know someone that's not a sucker, or might be a cop, or somebody that knows the game. I can just feel it. I just know a sucker when I see one and my crew does too. You know that when you pick a crew. I don't go out and say, yeah, he looks like a pretty good thief and has a lot of grift sense, I'll get him. The deciding factor whether you have a good crew or a bad crew is how much grift sense all your partners have. But most of the time you're not going to hook up with someone that doesn't have grift sense.

You'll find the game in the back of buses, train stations, things like that. Very seldom do you see it in the streets, 'cause if it's windy it'll blow the cards open.

I used to go outside a factory. Believe it or not, all you have to do is set up a box and start throwing cards and people will just stop by to see what you're doing. You don't have to say anything. Then you start betting with the shills. And pretty soon people get to realize that it's a betting game. I'll keep throwing it, and my shills will be betting, and they'll be winning, and the sucker sees them winning, and so they want to bet. And I might even let the sucker win some if I see other suckers that might have more money.

So, the red card's on the bottom of the two cards and the black card's on top. When I throw the cards down, I'll throw the top card instead of the bottom card, which is the red card. But first, just to get into the rhythm of it, I'll do it for real. I'll throw the red card on the bottom, and let them watch where it is, very slowly, and they're watching and wondering where the red card is. And there's no question where the red card is.

And they'll want to bet, so I'll say, well here, let me do it again. And then I'll pick them up and they'll say, oh gosh, I was right. I knew where the red card was. And then I'll do it again, and now they'll want to bet. When I don't want them to win is when I'll throw the top cards. And then obviously they'll lose.

You would think that a normal person would think, *wait a minute, I knew where the red card was. I bet on it and I lost. Why?* Well you'd think a guy would just quit. But no, not suckers. Suckers go, *wait, this time I'm really going to watch him.* And then they'll bet more money, and it just goes on and on until they don't have any more money. So I try to entice as many suckers as I can to bet on it. Then, when everybody's out of money, I take the cards, stick them in my pocket, and walk away. And then we'll go somewhere else.

I'm where there's people. Where there's people there's money, and where there's money there's me. And that's where you do con games. You can't do it if there's no

(continued)

customers. Where there's people, there's suckers, and where there's suckers, there's people like me.

The reason people try to beat this game is because of the skill of the operator. It's my presentation. I say, "Look, I want to show you something." First off, I say, "This isn't three-card monte." Because then you're thinking, *this is not three-card monte.* I tell them that you win on the red and you lose on the black. Now watch. Here's a red card. I'm just going to set it right there. Then here's a black card and I want to set it right there, and just switch them. Now where's the red card? Will you bet on something like that? Well sure you would, if you were a betting man. But if you're not a betting man, you're not going to do it.

And this is a cliché that everyone uses, that you can't beat an honest man. Well, you can't beat someone that's not trying to win your money. You can remember that. As a hustler, and doing the three-card monte, I cannot get my money from someone that's not trying to get my money first.

This is a real old game, this three-card monte. I know it's at least a hundred years old. It's in a book a hundred years old, published in 1902. But each generation that's never seen it before thinks they can beat it. There will always be suckers.

Look, three-card monte is a great little hustle in the street. And, frankly, I don't do it any more because there's not enough money in it for me. It's only as good as how much money a person has in their pocket at that time—right now. How many people walk around nowadays with eight hundred dollars in their pocket, or a thousand? Or even three hundred? You know what they got? They got about six dollars and fourteen credit cards. That's what people have nowadays. They don't carry around cash. The only people that carry cash nowadays are criminals.

The one good thing about three-card monte and the three-shell game and the short cons like that is it's a good training ground for con men, for grifters. It's a prep school, if you will. Most people grow out of it.

If you're a tourist and you see a three-card monte, don't stop and look at it and think, *well I know that he throws the top one sometimes and maybe sometimes he throws the bottom one,* or whatever. I'm telling you right now. Do not play it. Cause it's a guarantee, you cannot win. It's simple as that. And that's my advice. I can promise you, you cannot beat it. Just go on down the road when you see it.

"What is it called?" Madam Zuanah asks, scrunching her face in puzzlement.

"Wa Keo Me Temple, I think, or is it Wa Teo Ma?"

"Sorry, I don't know what you mean."

A passerby overhears and stops to assist. He looks like a local businessman.

"You must be looking for the Wa Teo Me Temple! I can tell you where it is." The passerby offers some convoluted directions.

"I'm so grateful. Let me thank you—both of you—by giving you each one of these." The con man takes a little pouch from his pocket and gives them each a small stone. "These will solve your problems, but—do you know how they work?"

"Tell us," the passerby says eagerly, with a conspiratorial glance at Madam Zuanah.

"For this lucky charm to work, you must each go and buy some needles. But, wait! This is important. You must go like a pauper to buy the needles. The stones will lose their power if you carry valuables with you."

The passerby looks at his watch. "May I go first? I haven't much time." And he quickly removes the watch, a ring, and the money from his wallet. With both hands and the slightest inclination of his head, he holds them out toward Madam Zuanah.

"Would you hold these for me? The shop's just there."

Madam Zuanah takes the man's valuables and waits while he goes to purchase needles. He returns smiling, and she gives him his money and jewelry.

Now the woman removes her bracelets, wedding ring, and necklace. She puts them in her handbag, offers the purse to the businessman, and goes to buy needles.

When she returns . . . well, need I say more?

Later, Madam Zuanah cursed herself for trusting the men.

"I've read about the stupids who've been cheated," she said. "I told my husband that if someone ever gave me a stone, I would throw it away."

Yet, Madam Zuanah fell for the scam. The participation of the accomplice as passerby was vital, as it was he who garnered the woman's confidence.

As Westerners, we probably find this story outrageous, silly, superstitious nonsense. Beware: someone, somewhere, has devised a pigeon drop just for you.

How about the one in which someone needs to change a large amount of foreign currency, and will give you half the money to do it. You see, he doesn't have a proper ID just now and . . . you know. You're given *all* the foreign cash to go exchange, but must offer collateral while you're away. You give your gold chain, perhaps, as security, to prove you'll be back in a moment.

Or, someone has a winning lottery ticket, but she's afraid to go in and claim it because she's in the country illegally. She'll split the winnings if you'll do it, but first put up something of value in good faith.

How about the guy who finds a sack of money on the street, doesn't know what to do with it and needs your help.

There are endless variations of the pigeon drop. They all have the same basic formula: someone wants to give you something—money, gold, a lucky charm—usually in thanks or in conspiracy. In good faith, you must give a valuable in exchange, even if just temporarily.

A modern-day version of the pigeon drop has moved off the streets and, while it used to operate through postal mail, now takes advantage of the Internet. Commonly called the Nigerian scam, the solicitation arrives

Subject: URGENT AND CONFIDENTIAL BUSINESS PROPOSAL

From: Dr. Mohammed Abacha <mohammed_abacha1@mail.com>
To: <bambi@bobarno.com>
Date: Tuesday, October 22, 2002 5:53 AM

I am Dr Mohammed Abacha, the son of the late Nigerian head of state General Sani Abacha.

But hope this confidential business proposal will not meet you in a surprise, as I hope the news has been passed round the whole world about how I've been in detention for past years and just been released in weeks back.

Upon my released from the detention in few weeks back, I came out to discover a reasonable amount of UNITED STATED DOLLARS in my late father's strong room.

The sum which I discovered in a two big box, after counted, resulted to (US$50,000,000.00) FIFTY MILLION UNITED STATED DOLLARS.

For the safety of the fund and to avoid another allegation being layed against our family, I quickly compiled the fund in a two trunk box and ordered a diplomatic channels organisation here in Nigeria, to assist me moved it to a private security company in abroad under "NON-INSPECTION" charges.

Now, the fund is lying in the vault of a security company in abroad, waiting for clearing and collection.

Upon your interest to assist me travel and clear this consignment, I will forward you further details about the transaction but with the following conditions:

1) YOU MUST CONFIRM TO ME YOUR FINANCIAL ABILITY TO HANDLE THIS TRANSACTION, AS YOU KNOW THAT IT INVOLVE HUGE AMOUNT OF MONEY.

2) YOU CONFIRM TO ME YOUR ABILITY TO TRAVEL ABROAD AND CLEAR THE CONSIGNMENT FOR ME.

3) YOU MUST CONFIRM TO ME THAT YOU WILL KEEP THIS TRANSACTION STRICTLY CONFIDENTIAL AND FASTER AS TIME IS NOT ON MY SIDE AT ALL.

Kindly indicate your interest in this transaction by calling me immediately on my private line: 234-1-7752206.

Waiting to hear from you.

Yours Faithfully,

Dr Mohammed Abacha

by e-mail in the shape of a detailed formal letter pleading for a sympathetic (greedy) assistant who will help the abused, imprisoned, nearly killed writer smuggle millions of dollars out of Nigeria in exchange for a generous fee or commission.

In one set-up, an American oil consultant with the "Nigerian National Petroleum Corporation" dies intestate with twenty-five million dollars in a numbered bank account. The writer, a bank manager, has earnestly searched for next of kin to no avail. Without a claimant, the funds will shortly revert to the Nigerian government.

"Consequently," he wrote to me, "my proposal is that I will like you as a foreigner to stand in as the next of kin so that the fruits of this old man's labor will not get into the hands of some corrupt government officials."

Aha. I'm to be in cahoots with "Mr. Gerald Omah, manager of Orient Bank of Nigeria, Lagos branch." For my invaluable and trustworthy participation, he tells me, "The money will be paid to you for us to share in the ratio of 60 percent for me and 40 percent for you." And to assuage my worries in advance, the generous Mr. Omah adds, "There is no risk at all as all the paperwork for this transaction will be done by the Attorney and my position as the Branch Manager guarantees the successful execution of this transaction."

The next step in this, or any, version of the Nigerian scam requires me to provide my banking details "so money can be deposited". But first—a few minor details must be finalized: affidavits, fees, taxes, bribes, and would I wire funds immediately please? All expenses will be reimbursed. If I do send money, I'll be requested to send more and more. And, by the way, those bank details, please? The con artists will get as much out of me as they can: passport and driver's license information, my signature, my social security number.

Coincidentally, ten months after Mr. Omah wrote me, I received an identical proposal from a Mr. Tunde Badiru, "branch manager of Stallion Bank Nig Ltd. Idumota Branch," written in the identical words. I can only assume that this letter template, and others, are sold in Nigeria as get-rich-quick schemes. I have received numerous variations of the Nigerian scam proposal, and they all follow the pattern: a detailed explanation that includes obscure facts, a huge amount of money that I will acquire, and a sentiment such as, "Time is of the importance and I am desperately looking for a person to assist me in this confidential business." I have received similar letters from other African countries and, most recently, one from the Netherlands that informs me that I have won a lump sum lotto payment of $22,500,000 in an "International Promotions Program," and all I need to do is claim the prize immediately.

I picture the greedy gull sitting at home, perhaps losing a few thousand dollars in bogus expenses in the vain hope of snagging an instant windfall of millions. But in a recently publicized case, the office manager of a mid-sized law firm wiped out her employer's entire savings and operating funds. In another, a church paid out eighty thousand dollars in anticipation of a huge foreign bequest. Other ready lambs await.

Often, a Nigerian scammer requires his dupe to travel abroad to collect crates of cash. According to the Federal Trade Commission, most of these cases result in the fleecing of the victim. But victims enticed to visit Nigeria in order to conclude transactions are sometimes kidnapped for ransom. The pigeon drop gone abhorrent.

Con artists who practice the pigeon drop and the bait-and-switch and all the variants of those are the epitome of their label. They are the ultimate confidence men, both seeking and pretending to offer the trust of a stranger. *We're in this together,* they intimate. *It may be wrong, but it's you and me against the bad guys.* The pavement wager gamers rely on their shills to inspire confidence while they promise the chance of easy money. As the victims of all these con artists count cash into the hands of their covert tricksters, they expect to receive value for money. They expect to get rich, get a killer deal, win big.

The moral of this chapter might be *if it seems too good to be true, run!* But greed drives the victims of these con artists, and greed trumps reason. For the con men, that spells advantage: for a gull blinded by greed is a victim indeed.

Theft Thwarters #7: Con Games—Play and Pay

- Let logic inform greed.

- If it seems too good to be true, run.

The Bait-and-Switch Scam

- Electronic equipment surreptitiously offered on street corners is tempting, but you'll walk away with a sack of salt and wonder how it happened.

- Everybody and his brother seems to know a special-price store with a special sale and, strangely, "You must go right now!" Don't bother; it's just a scam.

- If you buy art or furniture to have shipped home by the store, take a picture of it just to be sure you get the right items. The very act of photographing seems to increase your odds.

Pavement Wagers

- You cannot win. The three-shell game, three-card monte, and others are designed to extract your money. The operator is in complete control and fellow players are shills.

The Pigeon Drop

- Do not agree to split a stranger's windfall. Do not participate in a street-side get-rich-immediately scheme. Do not give anything of value to a stranger to hold "in good faith". This applies to U.S. Mail and e-mail solicitations, as well.

Identity Theft: You've Got a Criminal Clone 9

Imagine driving along, perhaps in your own neighborhood, in a bit of a hurry so you creep a fraction over the speed limit. Unlucky you. A cop pulls you over, just when you don't have the minutes to spare. You hand over your driver's license and registration, along with an exasperated puff of air. Next thing you know, you're being handcuffed and folded into the back of a squad car.

Why?!

"We have a warrant out for your arrest," the cop says, and hauls you in. You have no idea what's going on.

This is identity theft of the newest variety: *criminal* identity theft.

Criminals use a stolen identity when they're arrested, then are released under the same stolen name. When they don't show up for court, a warrant is issued for their arrest. But *they* are *you*. "Someone could steal your identity without you knowing it, go to jail, get released, and you end up getting arrested on a warrant when you're stopped for nothing more than a broken taillight," explained Lieutenant Bob Sebby of the Las Vegas Metropolitan Police Department, which has processed several high-profile cases.

"There's a market now for stolen identities where the thieves do *not* commit financial fraud, which would alert the victims. They just want a clean, anonymous identity to use when they commit their other crimes," he said. Unless you have reason to check your police record, you'd never know about your false criminal history.

That's what happened to Californian Bronti K. in a well-documented case. First he was fired from his job for shoplifting, a charge he knew to be false and proved with military documentation. Then, trying to find new work, he was turned down for one after another opportunity, and not one employer would tell him why. He began to lose confidence in himself, and, eventually, as bills mounted with no employment in sight, he lost his home.

According to the Federal Trade Commission, identity theft is America's fastest-growing crime. Until recently, it meant credit card fraud, bank fraud, phone and utility fraud, and other financial crimes perpetrated in the name of another party. *Criminal* identity theft, as it's being called,

Look-Alikes

American whiz player Johnnie Downs considers the cash in a stolen wallet pocket money. He's more interested in getting a "spread," a collection of identity documents. "I can take one sting and it might only have one dollar in it, but if I got a nice spread I can get fifty thousand dollars off it. In a day! Credit card, driver's license, checkbook, and social security card: that's the spread."

As a teenager, he began with simple credit card fraud. He found a complicit shop owner who let him buy jewelry with stolen cards. Later, he learned how to get cash advances. "The game had stepped up another level," he said.

"I do 'look-alikes'. I get five women working for me, because it's always easier to get a woman's purse. I get a blond, a brunette, a black-haired, a heavy-set blond, and an older woman with gray hair, just on stand-by, waiting. Once I get the good spread, I dump it off to the right woman, let her do what she needs to do. That's where the big money come in."

The look-alikes are called "writers" because they sign for the cash. They're also called "steppers" because they "step up" to a teller or cashier. Johnnie maintains a network of these writers all over the country. If he has male writers on standby, he'll concentrate on stealing from male victims.

"Whatever kind of hide or poke or sting you get, it would match one of those ladies. You would call them and tell them, 'here we come. We just ran five thousand dollars in one casino and five thousand dollars in another. You have to go and pick up the cash.'"

Back up, Johnnie. How does this work?

"We get in the car, we go to work, we see a good victim on the street, maybe walking to the bus stop. We get out of the car and go behind the victim and see if the victim is going to go through any doors, jam herself up getting on the bus, or anything of that nature. Since we have the writers that are female on hold, we are strictly looking for females now, right? Because that's what we're doing, what we call look-alikes. So whatever type of a wallet we lift, we'll have almost an identical look-alike and we won't have to change the driver's license. We just have the look-alikes on standby with the phone. So all we have to do is get the spread, run the check, get the approval, go and pick them up and let them pick up the money.

"[In a casino,] you go up to a little computerized box that's connected to the head casino cage. It's a thing that's being done regularly in Las Vegas. So it's not unaccustomed for people to try to get five thousand dollars, three thousand dollars off their credit card. I find this little box somewhere on the wall inside the casino, then I run the credit card through it and try to get it approved for either five thousand dollars or twenty-five hundred dollars.

"All you need is a driver's license and a major credit card. That's it. The machine tells you that your check has been approved and you can go to the head casino cage to pick up your money. [The writer says] 'I have a cash advance to pick up,' and they say, 'What's your name, Ma'am? Give me your Visa, and give me your driver's license.' The cashier's going to probably ask her for a home phone number and a work phone number. I always have my slip where I have all fifty states with all the zip codes in them, and area codes.

"I'm not going to send nobody in there for fifteen hundred dollars when you got to split it four ways. That's not worth it. I'm not splitting fifteen hundred dollars four ways, unless I'm really desperate for some money. After I stole a wallet? It's too big a risk. We got to get at least thirty-five hundred dollars."

(continued)

> Johnnie can also get cash from a spread at a bank.
>
> "If there's not a social, you can gather the information to get it. You may have a connection or have an associate that works in another city that has connections in the DMV and they can draw the social up for you. But if you don't have a social, it's not a good spread, because when you go to the bank, you must have the social. The social must complete the spread.
>
> "I'll go to the bank and say, 'Excuse me, I'd like to check the balance on my account please.' And the lady will say, 'Let me see your driver's license, and what's your social security number?' So you slide them the driver's license, you give them the social, you know they don't have to leave from in front of their computer. They write the balance on the piece of paper and they slide you the information. That's when you know that they believe you say who you are. Cause now they gave you this person's information, how much money they have in their checking, savings account. You say, 'Well I'd like to make a withdrawal for fifty-five hundred dollars.' No problem.
>
> "I got a 1-800 number. I could check your credit card right now, and get an approval code, or find out if it's stolen or not. Just dial a 1-800 number and deal with computers. They say 'put in your merchant number, put in your credit card number and your expiration date, put in your amount.' I have the credit card numbers, so I could call and get approval codes from laying in my bed."

adds a chilling new twist. Not only is an innocent person burdened with a criminal history he doesn't deserve and can't expunge, but an unnamed scofflaw goes scot-free and disappears into society.

Statistics for identity theft are hard to come by, particularly since the individual offenses are categorized differently by the interested government agencies. There is no universal standard for reporting the crime, and even credit card companies know only what their issuing banks tell them. True figures are minimized by businesses that don't want to scare off consumers and don't want to reveal their weaknesses to hackers. And they're suppressed by credit bureaus and credit card companies with a vested interest in the status quo.

In March 2002, the United States General Accounting Office (GAO) presented a Report to Congressional Requesters cautiously called *Identity Theft: Prevalence and Cost Appear to Be Growing.* "No single hotline or database captures the universe of identity theft victims," the report said. "Some individuals do not even know that they have been victimized until months after the fact, and some known victims may choose not to report to the police, credit bureaus, or established hotlines. Thus, it is difficult to fully or accurately quantify the prevalence of identity theft. Some of the often-quoted estimates of prevalence range from one-quarter to three-quarters of a million victims annually."

The Identity Theft Resource Center, a nationwide nonprofit organization, puts the number of victims at seven hundred thousand in 2001. By

ID Theft Statistics

- In 1992, the credit reporting agency TransUnion received only about thirty-five thousand calls about identity theft from victims and those concerned about potential crime. In 2001, they received more than a million calls.

- It is estimated that 700,000 to 1.1 million people became victims of this crime in 2001. That number is based on various reports, including those from members of law enforcement.

- The Secret Service estimates that in 1997 consumers lost more than $745 million due to identity theft.

- A Florida grand jury estimated that the average identity theft crime costs the business community about $17,000 per victim. If we use the lowest estimated number of victims (700,000) that means a loss of $11.9 billion in 2001.

- This number does not include victim costs, including legal assistance and judicial and law enforcement time in investigating and trying cases.

- A GAO study on identity theft (GAO-02-363, issued March 2002) discussed costs to federal agencies. The executive office for U.S. Attorneys estimated the cost of prosecuting a white-collar crime case was $11,443. The Secret Service estimates the average cost per financial crime investigation is $15,000. The FBI estimates the average cost per financial crime investigation is $20,000

- On average, victims spend 175–200 hours and $1,000 in out-of-pocket expenses to clear their names. (Privacy Rights Clearinghouse and FTC)

Compiled by the Identity Theft Resource Center, San Diego, California. Used with permission.

all accounts, the crime has reached epidemic proportions and continues to increase.

Identity theft is the appropriation of a person's name and other personal data for unauthorized use, usually for financial gain. Pretending to be that person, the impostor may charge purchases on the victim's credit card, open new credit accounts, rent an apartment, obtain loans for major items like cars and houses, and, as mentioned earlier, commit crimes. The criminal clone leaves financial and emotional rubble in his wake: for the victim, a tangled mess of false accusations, a ruined credit history, a full-time job of restoring his good name, years of lingering repercussions, and, for some, a false criminal record that cannot be repaired.

The emotional toll is impossible to measure. The GAO, in its report, wrote of finding feelings of invaded privacy and continuing trauma. Those who've experienced it firsthand choose stronger words. "It destroys your whole life, it's so violating," said Michaela L., an unusually persistent victim who hired her own investigators and pushed her complicated case through to trial. "People say 'get over it,' but they don't understand. I'm screaming in my sleep. It's me, it's my being that was invaded."

I've written about victims of pickpockets who were "devastated" by the theft of their cash, credit cards, identification, passport, and airline tickets. Those losses are *nothing* compared to the wreckage the identity thief inflicts.

"I'm a victim and it's been a nightmare," Cheryl R. wrote me. "I am still not able to get my credit cleared up. The person who did this to me was arrested after many months of my persistence with the Los Angeles Sheriff's Department but she got out of jail immediately. How can I be sure that she won't do this to me again in a few years?"

Sorry, Cheryl. You can't be sure.

In some of the nastier cases, thieves will impersonate a victim until her credit dries up or the trail gets hot, then move into another person's identity until the first victim clears up the mess and re-establishes credit. Some victims are re-attacked months or years later. It's not only a nightmare, it can be a neverending one.

Like most victims, Cheryl had no idea that she had an alter ego until she applied for a loan. In the process of refinancing her house, the mortgage banker called and said, "Your husband's credit report is stellar, but yours is awful!" Cheryl, a retired loan underwriter herself, was astounded. She'd always maintained an unblemished payment history. She was unable to get the loan.

"There is a value, an intrinsic value, in who you are," said Edward Wade, a privacy and identity expert who wrote *Identity Theft: The Cybercrime of the Millennium* under the pseudonym John Q. Newman. "I'm talking about how we define a person in the world, which is by name and number, your name, your birth date, your Social Security number, things like that. That is actually the most valuable possession that you have. Thieves will want to steal this because they can then take this and use it to get credit, to rent an apartment, to live a life that they themselves are unable to get, because they don't have the necessary background. But through your hard work, they can live it vicariously through you. The problem is, when they're done, they leave your life in tatters. And then you have to go and fix it."

I Wanna Be You

How does an identity thief become you? It's frighteningly easy in this age of instant credit, free-floating data, Internet access, and lingering trust from the easy-going era in which we were raised. All a thief needs is your basic, nonprivate information, meaning your name and address, and the bit that should be confidential but is not, meaning your Social Security number. In too many cases your Social Security number is right there for the taking. It's on your health records, in your wallet, possibly on your driver's license, possibly on your school ID card. And if it's not easily available by rifling papers, it can be purchased, legally, for a small fee.

Let's look at the low-tech ways a you-wannabe can acquire the few necessary starter facts once he becomes or recruits a data miner and starts digging.

Document Theft

A pickpocket steals your wallet, as in Nancy S.'s and Bronti K.'s cases. A hotel maid takes a document, as in Michaela L.'s case. A burglar breaks into your home. A worker you've allowed into your house takes a bank statement, health insurance bill, or pay stub. A personal document is stolen from your desk at work, possibly by a coworker, a temporary employee, a maintenance worker, or even a customer. Envelopes are stolen from your mailbox, incoming or outgoing.

"When cars are broken into, they're not looking for the stereo," said Lieutenant Sebby. "They're looking for paper: bills, bank statements, information. It's far more lucrative."

Some years ago, a thief would steal a wallet, remove the cash, and toss the rest. Now, the cash is just a bonus—it's the documents they want. "We just collared a guy who gets five hundred dollars for each good credit card," a New York pickpocket cop told me.

"On the street they call it 'a set of works' when they get a wallet with a credit card, driver's license, and Social Security card," said Sergeant Randy Stoever of the New York Transit Police, Manhattan pickpocket unit. "Even 'dead work,' a set with a canceled credit card, is worth about seventy-five dollars to a pickpocket."

Mail Diversion

A change of address form can be filed with the post office or called into some credit issuers.

Shoulder Surfing

The same techniques used at ATM cashpoints are practiced to acquire other data, as in Cheryl's example, where her impostor turned out to be a previous classmate. Sitting side-by-side, the charming student (read: con artist) had ample time to peek and copy Cheryl's vitals as they both filled out state-required forms.

Dumpster Diving

What's in your trash? If you're not making confetti out of every sensitive document you discard, your data is available to any garbage grubber with rubber gloves. You've never seen a trash picker? That's because they favor

You've Been Pickpocketed—But That's Not the Worst of It

When Nancy S. was bumped at the free pirate show outside the Treasure Island hotel and casino in Las Vegas, she didn't think anything of it. "You know it's wall-to-wall people there," she told me. "An hour later I went to lunch and found my wallet missing from my purse."

Thus began Nancy's nightmare and a thief's windfall. Besides $100 cash, the criminal acquired a few credit cards and Nancy's driver's license, on which was printed her Social Security number. With that, the fraudster set to work, opening a cell phone account and a credit card account and racking up charges. The thief applied for additional credit on the Internet. Nancy's credit report, when she finally saw it, listed numerous credit inquiries initiated by the thief's purchases and applications.

Nancy got off relatively easy, as far as ID theft goes. Yet, when she obtained a new Nevada driver's license, she chose to include her Social Security number on it, again, against all advice. "For convenience," she explained to me.

It's tempting to imagine the pickpocket wreaking this havoc himself, but it's unlikely. The pickpocket, a non-tech thief, most likely kept Nancy's cash and sold her vital information to an organized crime ring.

business refuse: fewer fish bones—richer in data! How do the companies you patronize safeguard their documents? What about your dentist's trash? Your pharmacy's?

Who'd think of these myriad opportunities?

The identity thief.

Scamming

If the identity thief (or part of his ring) is con-inclined, all he needs to do is ask and he can collect all the data his malevolent heart desires. Like the express kidnappers in Argentina whom I described in chapter 7, a clipboard seems to spell trust and encourages citizens to spill their guts. Scammers pretend to do a survey, pretend to offer credit cards (just fill out this form!), pretend to be your bank calling about record updating, pretend to offer an apartment for rent, pretend you've won a prize. They'll say anything to gain your confidence and your confidential data.

Skimming

For the data collector, skimmers are especially useful in business contexts where addresses are recorded, which is to say almost any neighborhood business in this age of information brokering. More on that later. A skimmer is a battery-operated device smaller than a deck of cards with a slot for swiping credit cards. It reads and stores data embedded in the magnetic strip on the back of the card. Restaurant waiters are the typical recruit, given the contraption and requested to swipe each credit card as they take customers' payments. At the end of the shift, the data collector shows up with a computer and downloads the skimmer's memory, which might hold the information from a hundred or more cards.

This is effective data collection; and the waiters, for the data collector solicits many of them, may not even understand the purpose of the exercise for which they receive a nice little tax-free chunk of change. Restaurant and service station employees are reportedly earning over $100 for each credit card they skim.

Meanwhile, the customer has no way of knowing that his credit card has been skimmed. Some privacy advocates and security experts recommend that you never let your credit card out of your sight. I find this advice impractical to the point of impossible, but it's a question of compromise: convenience in exchange for risk. Each of us must decide where to live along that scale. While I might hand my credit card over to a waiter for processing, you might decide to follow him to the charge machine and supervise the transaction.

Exchanging

"Whose credit card is in your wallet?" asked Lieutenant Sebby as we finished lunch in a Strip hotel restaurant. He'd been pointing out the card verification value on our American Express card and his MasterCard. These are the extra digits printed at the end of your account number on the back (on the front for American Express cards) that have specific security functions. "I just handed you back your card," Sebby said, "and you stuck it in your wallet without looking at it. That's what 95 percent of people do." Sebby explained a scam in which a waiter carries a small collection of cards and rotates them, returning, instead of your gold AmEx, someone else's, which has already been fraudulently maxed out. If you fail to catch the "mistake," he passes your card to a colleague who gets to work on it. If you do check your card, the waiter's apology and correction is enough to subvert any suspicion. The waiter's risk is getting caught with a pocketful of credit cards.

Check Writing

Check writing? Absolutely. Look at all you're providing on one neat slip of paper: your name, address, telephone number, bank name, and bank

A Credit Card Fraud Primer:
Excerpts from Instructions on the Internet

[These frightening instructions, along with others for lock picking, car breaking, and bomb making, are posted on the Internet. My comments are in brackets.]

Obtaining a credit card number: There are many ways to obtain the information needed to card something *[fraudulently use a credit card]*. The most important things needed are the card number and the expiration date. Having the cardholder's name doesn't hurt, but it is not essential.

The absolute best way to obtain all the information needed is by trashing *[searching though trash]*. The way this is done is simple. You walk around your area or any other area and find a store, mall, supermarket, etc., that throws their garbage outside on the sidewalk or Dumpster. Rip the bag open and see if you can find any carbons at all. . . .

Another way is to bullshit the number out of someone. That is, call them up and say "Hello, this is Visa security and we have a report that your card was stolen." Or think of something to that degree. . . .

Ordering: The type of places that are easiest to victimize are small businesses that do mail order or even local stores that deliver. A personal tip: When I call to make an order, it usually goes much smoother if the person you are talking to is a woman. In many cases they are more gullible than men.

The name *[of the cardholder]* is really not that important because when the company verifies the card, the person's name is never mentioned, EXCEPT when you have a Preferred Visa card. Then the name is mentioned. You can tell if you have a Preferred Visa card by the PV to the right of the expiration date on the carbon. The phone number to give them as your home phone could be one of the following: a number that is ALWAYS busy, a number that ALWAYS rings, or a pay phone number.

[The writer goes on to extol the virtues of Visa vs. Mastercard vs. American Express, and how to estimate an expiration date.]

The address: More commonly referred to as the 'drop'. Here is a list of various drops: the house next door whose family is on vacation, the apartment that was just moved out of, the old church that will be knocked down in six months, your friend's house who has absolutely nothing to do with the type of merchandise you will buy and who will also not crack under heat from feds, etc.

[He warns against using a P.O. box, and then instructs, in detail, how to verify a card, i.e., find out if it has been reported stolen, and how to estimate the credit limits on the account.]

Stolen cards: Mastercard and Visa come out with a small catalog every week where they publish EVERY stolen or fraudulently used card. I get this every week by trashing the same place on the same day. If you ever find it [*while*] trashing then try to get it every week.

Excerpted from the *Anarchist Cookbook* IV, ver. 4.14, released in June, 1994 account number. Is your driver's license printed on the check, or did a clerk ask for one? If so, she may have noted your birth date, as well, and possibly even your Social Security number if it's on your driver's license. All that and a signature specimen, too.

Fraudulently Obtaining Credit Reports

Car lots, apartment houses, and employers all have legitimate cause to access credit reports of potential loan applicants, renters, or employees. Who else has access to that credit report once it's printed and lying around? Is it safeguarded? Worse yet is the unauthorized order of someone else's credit report, who has no relationship with the business at all. This can happen one by one by underhanded employees of small businesses, or *en masse,* as in the late November 2002 bust of Philip Cummings, who stole thousands of individuals' credit reports in unauthorized downloads

For the tech savvy, obtaining a person's private data is a cinch. Everything's available on the Internet, much of it free, some for a small fee.

E-mail

As in low-tech scamming, a con artist can always try asking for your information. E-mail is highly effective. It costs nothing to send out hundreds of thousands of solicitations. All the scammer has to do is promise some sort of value for your information. The Nigerian scammers are famous for this. Generic letters claiming you've won a prize, a vacation, or a lottery are in the same category.

One recent scam specifically designed to collect credit card data, Social Security numbers, and more, started with an e-mail confirming an expensive eBay purchase. Recipients were invited to confirm or cancel the purchase by going to a Web site, where they were instructed to fill out a form. Once they submitted the form, they were satisfied by the next screen: "Your order has been canceled." While responders were never billed for the item they supposedly canceled, all fell for the con, and all put themselves at risk of identity theft.

False Merchant Sites

These ask for personal data for membership identification purposes and, on adult sites, may request a credit card number in order to access site content. These insidious data-collecting sites may not actually charge a customer, but exploit the wealth of data they collect in other ways.

Internet Searches

Anyone can purchase almost any piece of data about anyone, for a fee. You and I may not know where to look for a Social Security number, but give a name and address to the IT person in an ID theft ring and he'll get it. A Social Security number, of course, is the ticket to getting everything else. Much of what you may assume is private information is actually public record, and the Internet makes it simple to access, as opposed to trips to government records departments.

Birth and death records, divorce decrees, bankruptcies, driving records . . . did you know that your credit report is open to the public? Yes, it is. Not the section documenting your payment history, but the part called the header: that includes your name and address, previous addresses, unlisted phone numbers, Social Security number . . . with all that, what else matters? More on this later. Anyway, a single piece of information about a person can become an entire dossier for just a few hundred dollars.

Continuing online, a small-time crook can go to counterfeiting Web sites to obtain real-looking driver's licenses. Yes, these sites are there for anyone and operate on the fringes of legality by selling their products as "novelties". Driver's licenses can be customized for any state or, why not an international driver's license? If the fraudster is manufacturing new credit cards in your name, he can download an algorithm generator—software available on the Internet, which will generate real credit card numbers. With a minimum of effort and a minimum of funds, an amateur Web sleuth can get everything he needs about *you*.

Docs 'R' Us

With your personal data now in the criminal's possession, it's time for document production. There are two types. Counterfeit documents can be homemade, ordered from an ID shop, or ordered on the Internet. This is a common way the thief gets his "breeder document," the fake he passes in order to start collecting legitimate IDs from other agencies. He might start with a fraudulent birth certificate, for example. These are easily forged with a computer, graphics program, and a printer. As there are fifteen thousand or so different types of birth certificates in the United States, a forgery has a good chance of passing. With a birth certificate, our thief can now walk into the Department of Motor Vehicles of his choice and obtain a real driver's license or state identity card. This is the second type of documentation: it's real, but authenticates the wrong person. The driver's license will bear the thief's picture, your identity, and a drop box address.

And that's all he needs to start opening instant credit accounts. He can get a cell phone, buy the computer of his dirty dreams, and all the software and other counterfeiting equipment he needs in order to run his own little ID theft business. Or whatever.

He may as well rent a decent apartment in your name—you can afford it—and turn on utilities in your name, too. And, perhaps, in order to protect his new identity, he'll also rent a cheap apartment as an address to which he'll ship all the goodies he orders on the Internet.

If he manages to get your credit report (or if he already has your existing credit card information), he may practice a bit of account takeover activity. That means he'll charge purchases to your existing credit accounts, drain your bank account, and possibly even suck the equity out of your house. But these activities are risky and short-lived: you're bound to notice the illicit transactions on your statements—*if* you get them, and *if* you look at them.

Organized ID theft rings work on a large scale, churning out credit cards from blanks. In southern California recently, federal and local law enforcement raided the luxury apartment of Jeremy Cushing, a ringleader who'd rented the place under a stolen name. Within, they found a high-tech production line for manufacturing false documents. Equipment included a computer, scanners, printers specific for making fake checks, and printers for making credit cards.

According to FTC reports, credit card fraud is by far the most prevalent manner in which a victim's information is abused. Much of the high-volume credit card production industry is centered in Asia and Russia. Excellent counterfeits are manufactured with most, but not all, of the safety features. So many are made in Vietnam that they're being shipped to the United States in bulk containers. The *New York Times* reported that the price of bulk, ready-made credit cards fluctuates between forty cents and five dollars apiece, depending on the level of information authentication. Prices drop with volume, and purchases come with guarantees that the numbers are valid.

But, as in Cheryl's case, new documents are not always necessary for the crime. With a minimal amount of information an impostor can open credit card and other accounts and use a new address. According to Cheryl's credit report, the faux-Cheryl attempted to open twenty-two credit accounts, including for cell phones and car loans. She succeeded in opening two fraudulent credit card accounts and one merchandise account, on which she charged a total of eight thousand dollars.

"The Los Angeles sheriff's deputy assigned to my case said mine was minute compared to most others," Cheryl told me. But it's been complicated nevertheless. Using the checks attached to one of the credit card accounts, the impostor had made minimal payments on another. Now one creditor, Capital One, still refuses to remove its bad debt from Cheryl's credit report. It claims that since minimal payments were made, the debt cannot be considered fraud.

"I still can't get credit in my name," Cheryl said, "and because of the frustration and embarrassment involved, I don't even try any more." She refinanced her house in her husband's name only, and now worries about how she'd ever get along without him.

And the Victim?

"You're not the victim in this case," Michaela was told at her impostor's hearing, "you're a witness." Cheryl heard similar sentiments. "How much did you lose?" she was repeatedly asked and, "Well, you're not out any cash, are you?" No one wants to hear about time spent and emotional trauma.

In the courtroom, the judge in Michaela's case asked, "Can someone tell me what makes this crime so heinous?" He got an earful from Michaela.

"Identity theft victims suffer the reprobation rape victims did years ago," said Linda Foley, executive director of the Identity Theft Resource Center. "The burden of proof is on the victim. 'You must have done something to cause this,' others imply. It leaves the victim with a profound sense of powerlessness and betrayal."

"I was on the phone every day, almost all day, for six solid weeks," Michaela told me. "I was trying to stop her, trying to clean up after her, and trying to find her." Michaela did find her impostor, dug up her prior record, and tracked down a Blockbuster store video that showed her making a purchase in Michaela's name.

As a small business owner, this non-victim lost "an astronomical number of business hours, huge amount of income, untold opportunities, several clients, and quite a bit in out-of-pocket expenses."

"People don't understand the extent of this crime," Michaela said. "They're brainwashed into thinking all they'll lose is fifty dollars and then be done. Wrong! A fraudulent credit card charge is your first clue that it's just beginning."

Victims of identity theft are usually not liable for fraudulent charges. Banks and credit card companies advertise a fifty-dollar cap for liability, and in most cases waive even that. In fact, zero-liability accounts are the latest seduction in ad campaigns.

Okay, the "non-victim" isn't liable for the fraudulent charges. Still, the list of short- and long-term damages is appalling. The Privacy Rights Clearinghouse and the FTC have found that victims typically spend 175 to 200 hours and one thousand dollars in out-of-pocket expenses in efforts to clear their names. Costs are for photocopying, notary fees, certified mail, and telephone charges. Some victims also hire lawyers and private detectives.

Lieutenant Sebby says it takes an average of four years to clean up the mess. As new charges are discovered, victims must repeat trips to Kinko's for copies, to banks for notarizing, and to the post office for sending certified mail. As well as all the hours lost to the frustrating job of repairing the damage, add reduced productivity at work.

Other early consequences to the victim include denial of credit, financial services, and employment, so he may not get the house he was trying to buy or the job for which he'd applied. Victims suffer harassment by debt collectors and creditors, are often treated with disdain and condescension, and sense others' doubt of their credibility. The unluckiest victims (15 percent and rising) are subjected to criminal investigation, arrest, or conviction.

By any definition, a person whose identity has been unlawfully used by another *is* a victim.

For the long term, he's stuck with a bad credit report that will likely dog him for the rest of his life. He may place a fraud alert or a freeze on his credit file, but that has limited value and a limited life span. Even a new Social Security number will not erase history, and even with a new name, a drastic measure, his address will link him to the negative file. Once a victim, forever a bad risk. If he can get future financing, it will often be at usurious rates. And if he's been saddled with a record of the impostor's crimes, it could be for life.

And the emotional damage? Who can quantify it? "I don't know who to trust and who not to anymore," wrote Linda Z. in her victim's impact statement, submitted to the judge who presided over her case. "Since this crime against me has taken place, I have distrusted every attempt to gain my personal information, even when necessary—from doctor's offices, merchants, and even potential employers. . . .

"From this date forward, in order to get a credit card, a loan, to purchase a major ticket item, to rent an apartment or buy a house, I will be faced with miles of red tape, suspicions and weeks of notarized documentation."

In some ways Linda Z. was fortunate. Most victims never receive closure, never hear of their impostor's arrest, conviction, or sentence.

Linda Foley has watched this epidemic grow since she founded the Identity Theft Resource Center in 1999. "Identity theft is a high-profit, low-risk, low-penalty crime. Thieves see this crime as the smart way to make money," she said. "The crimes are becoming more complex, reaching more victims, and causing higher value damage of greater complexity, which is taking victims ever longer to untangle."

The Info-Market and How Your Data Dribbles Out

To marketing people, your personal data is a goldmine. To merchants, who collect and sell the information, details about your life have intrinsic value. To information brokers, lately dubbed info-traffickers, your most intimate detail is their bread and butter.

What seems innocent becomes insidious. You fill out a questionnaire and they'll send you a free whatever. Answer details on a warranty card and you'll be rewarded. You sign up for a store discount card and the application asks how many in your household and what ages. You become a "member" of a travel information service and are asked where you go and why, who travels with you and how often. You sign up for a free trade magazine subscription and the form asks your profession and income level.

Alone, none of these innocuous queries is detrimental. However, info-traffickers combine them and attach more damaging details.

Consider the supermarket. Now that we have bar codes, itemized receipts, and store membership cards, your purchase of extra-dry deodorant, pharmaceuticals for herpes and depression, and large supply of zipper baggies is gathered, attached to your name, and put on the market. (What suspicions might be raised—are you a nervous, psychotic drug dealer?)

Who wants to know all this drivel? Who cares what you buy, how you answered the silly questions? Wait—there's more.

Your bank knows how much you deposit each month and from whom, who you pay, and how much. Wouldn't you expect that information to be kept private? It's not. It's sold, and the bank makes money on it. Did you give them permission to sell the details of your personal finances? What about your health issues, entrusted to your insurer? Your investments, which only your broker knows?

When you complete applications or answer questionnaires, you do so for an express purpose. Perhaps to get a bank account, become a member of an association, or in order to receive a service. If you knew that your data would be packaged and sold for profit, then end up in the hands of telemarketers (for example) who pester you with dinnertime disturbances, would you answer all the questions? Was the benefit you received worth it? What will happen to your information next? What other databases will it be packaged with before it's sold on to junk mailers who want to fill your mailbox with offers for credit cards, refinancing, debt-relief, and vacations to Bermuda? How can we hope to keep our Social Security numbers and mother's maiden name secure when they're bought and sold on the open market?

Once our private particulars leak out, they're free as flies and reproduce just as quickly. There's no retrieving them, no protecting them, no regulating their use or abuse. Like anyone else, organized identity theft rings can obtain the juicy data for efficient, high-volume rip-offs.

With easy access comes tamperability. As errors are introduced into our histories, bad debts, for example, or fraudulent accounts, or wrongful address changes, they proliferate as that information, along with the legitimate, is bought, sold, traded, and shared.

Your little bits and pieces are for sale to anyone who wants them.

Why? Why is all this private stuff available? Some is public record, because our government is transparent and accountable, and the price we pay for that is visible information. Other data is gathered and brokered

Personal, but Not Private

In addition to records of birth, death, marriage, divorce, Social Security number, mother's maiden name, judgments and liens, medical history, professional licenses, and vehicle information, here are a few examples of information traded on the Internet for approximately ten to sixty dollars per menu item (discounts for multiples!):

If you submit:	You can get:
an unlisted phone number	name and address of its owner
a name and address	the person's unlisted phone number
a pay phone number	the location of the pay phone
a post office box address	name and residential address of owner
a pager number	the billing name and address
a name and state	the person's driver's license records
a name and address	the person's prison records
a corporation's name	corporate status, name of owners, etc.
a residential address	the price paid for the house
a name and address	the person's bank balance
a name and address	the stocks, bonds, and securities he owns

by big business. The knowledge of *you* becomes income for them. They solicit it under the guise of a specific use. They collect it. They sell it for monetary gain. And other businesses buy it for target marketing, for deciding to whom they'll send preapproved credit applications—the theft of which is valuable bounty indeed (as in Michaela's case)—and for deciding to whom they'll pitch financial services or a cruise to Alaska.

If our intimate details are so available, how can we protect ourselves from identity thieves? We can't. We can take some measures, but, for the most part, it's out of our hands.

"ID theft begins and ends with the business community," says Linda Foley. "Consumers do not send themselves the preapproved credit applications which are stolen from their mailboxes. Consumers do not ask to submit unnecessary information on application forms. It is not my obligation as a consumer to stand guard over the file cabinets or computer systems where sensitive data resides. It's up to businesses to safeguard consumers' information as they would the company's own proprietary information."

But, it's financially beneficial for businesses to freely trade our information, and they have no intention of regulating themselves. That's why Foley's Identity Theft Resource Center and other organizations are working toward legislation as a means to protect the privacy of individuals. Simple, reasonable measures would help, such as requiring responsible information handling by businesses, including document disposal.

Truncating credit card numbers on receipts. Stopping the use of Social Security numbers as identifiers, and prohibiting their commercial sale. These are just a few of many potential improvements to the security of our identity.

Privacy advocates are furious about duplicitous acquisition of personal data. The trafficking of it without our knowledge or consent is, in a sense, a form of theft. After all, *I* would never reveal to casual friends, let alone strangers, my salary, bank and mortgage balances, medical details, or anything else I consider private. Neither have I authorized the broadcast of that private data.

"The reality is, that information is mine," Foley continues. "I *lent* it to a company for one specific purpose. Unfortunately, some businesses have the arrogance to believe that it has become *their* information to do with as they choose. And that's one of the reasons we see consumers so outraged over this invasion of their financial and personal privacy. It is businesses' inherent disregard for protecting that information that upsets so many of us."

That's because we assume our confidential information will be treated appropriately. One, that it won't be blabbed, and two, that it will be safeguarded. Protecting information means limiting its accessibility: in the way it's used, the way it's disseminated, and the way it's stored. Case in point: when I asked a question too tricky for the teller at a bank I use, Wells Fargo, she sent me to the cubicle of a higher-level employee. He invited me to sit in his client chair while he went to investigate my issue. He was away for ten or so minutes, and I was left alone in his cubicle, where several loan applications were spread over his desk. *Everything* is on loan applications . . . the confidential financial histories of people in my community, perhaps even people I know. If data were dollars, that bank manager would never have left his desk with such value unprotected.

Well, he shouldn't have done that, Wells Fargo higher-ups would say. But company policy is not the same as company practice.

Business Fixes

The way it is now, an identity thief can find or buy whatever information he needs in order to commit his crimes. Must our private data continue to dribble out unregulated? Businesses can do several things to help us protect our core bits.

They can safeguard the information we entrust to them: that which we tell them, and that which they learn through our dealings with them. They can treat customer data like the valuable and confidential asset it is. They can collect only what is necessary, handle it responsibly, and protect it.

They can allow us—no, make it easy for us—to opt out of their information sharing. Most of us aren't even aware it's going on, or we don't realize the shocking extent of it. How about full disclosure? *"Be aware before you purchase your drugs for psychosis at this pharmacy: we sell your records to insurance companies, employers' background search services, and direct marketers."*

Fat chance. Businesses, government agencies, the insurance industry, auto industry, credit card companies, credit reporting agencies, and others make big bucks on information. They want to own it, use it, buy it, sell it, and manipulate it to their financial advantage.

They can restrict the use of the Social Security number as an identifier. It should not be on our driver's licenses, it should not be our school ID number, it should not be printed on reports or other documents unless absolutely necessary.

The way it is now, an identity thief can get instant credit at a store, walk out with a few thousand dollars worth of merchandise charged in my name, and I'd never know it until the first bill was months overdue. Since the thief would use a different address, I might not learn about the impostor's activities until contacted by a debt collector. Store credit issuers could do much more to verify the identity of an applicant, not just his documents, before granting easy credit. For a start, compare the address on the credit application with the one on the credit report. Try calling the phone number on the credit report.

Perhaps credit shouldn't be instant. That would be an inconvenience to the customer, who couldn't walk in and walk out with a big-screen TV. It would be a risk for the store, which could possibly lose the sale. And it would be a hurdle for the fraudster, who likely wouldn't hold up to a higher level of scrutiny.

An identity thief can easily obtain instant credit at a store and the victim wouldn't be notified by the credit reporting agency that the store requested her credit rating. If she had been advised that XYZ Outlet had inquired about her credit rating, she'd have cause to be suspicious and could immediately investigate. Credit reporting agencies should inform the subject of inquiries when they're made.

Currently, a fraud alert, or freeze, on an individual's credit report is considered an advisory. Credit issuers may or may not see the alert, and are not bound by it. Credit reporting agencies should prominently red flag a file containing a fraud alert. Credit issuers should not grant credit when a report is red-flagged—not without a much higher level of verification.

But credit card companies don't want to frighten consumers. They want card use to be as smooth and simple as possible. They tend to minimize the significance of fraud and the importance of security measures. Bob and I use a credit card for most purchases, and we are rarely asked for identification; my estimate is that it occurs for about 10 percent of our charges. Clerks rarely compare signatures, and when they do, it's cursory.

"When it comes to fraud, credit card companies mask the real number because they make money each time a card is swiped. Requiring stricter identification would slow down the process and result in fewer swipes," said Werner Raes, a detective on the economic crimes detail of the Anaheim Police Department in southern California. Credit card companies could embed a photo on the card. Card use could require the entry of a PIN, as is done elsewhere in the world. Credit card companies could require that identification be examined. They should truncate account numbers printed on receipts (this is beginning to happen).

Biometric Technologies

When I cashed my literary agent's check at a bank I don't usually use, I was asked for a fingerprint, a quick and simple biometric safeguard. Lieutenant Sebby thinks this should be standard practice, and that further use of inkless fingerprinting would drastically reduce financial crime.

Detective Raes also believes in biometrics as a solution to identity fraud. He favors the retinal scan, which is not yet in widespread use. Although it's considered an accurate measurement, it's invasive (a light must be shined into the eye), and requires the cooperation of the subject.

Biometrics is the capture of an array of biological measurements unique to an individual. The result can then be used as an identifier. Fingerprints are the most commonly used biometric, and DNA analysis is another. Facial recognition software is in use, but is said to be the least reliable, since images are captured under differing conditions, at different angles, in varying light and shadow. Voice recognition cannot be fooled by impersonation, but it can be by a recording. Iris scans are thought to be highly accurate but, like retinal scans, require the cooperation of the subject.

Gait recognition and vein patterns also have potential use as biometrics. Hand scans are in use but are not very accurate or effective. The U.S. Immigration and Naturalization Service uses the hand as identification for frequent international travelers. Bob and I have the infamous INSPASS, for which we submitted to hand scans. In two years of hoping to bypass long immigration lines at U.S. international airports, the machines have never worked.

The explosion of remote shopping, working, and communications via phone and Internet is displacing the oldest and most complex form of biometrics. "Hey Bambi, long time no see!" But even this analog version is fallible: "I didn't recognize you for a minute—did you cut your hair?" If I'd changed my voice, iris, or gait, I might have succeeded in evading my techless authenticator.

Financial Fraud

"Identity theft is perpetrated by opportunists, organized crime, and local gangs," said Lieutenant Bob Sebby of the Las Vegas Metropolitan Police Department. He described the following financial crimes.

Scam: An organized crime ring targeted upscale fitness clubs in southern California. At each club they bought three-day membership passes. The thieves went into the locker rooms with lock picks taped to their fingers, popped the hasp of the locks, and opened the lockers. They stole one credit card from each locker, so victims wouldn't notice right away. One doctor's wallet contained twenty-one thousand in cash and sixteen credit cards. Only one credit card was taken, no cash.

The same or other thieves hit cars in the health clubs' parking lots, where people thought their belongings were more secure.

After obtaining a stash of credit cards, the thieves flew to Las Vegas, where they maxed out each card by getting cash advances at several casinos.

How do cash advance machines work in Las Vegas casinos? There's a special machine at which you swipe your credit card. After the machine processes the request, the screen says, "Your check is ready, go to the cashier and show ID." The thieves showed counterfeit identification to the cashier and were given cash. Each fraudulent cash transaction is twenty-five hundred dollars to five thousand dollars on average. They're made by a runner whose "manager" stands waiting just outside, just out of camera sight.

Scam: A fraudster gives you nine thousand to go to your bank and get a cashier's check. Using a computer, he scans the check and makes ten copies. He cashes each fake at a different casino. Even poor copies are typically accepted. Later, he gives you back the original check to redeposit.

One million dollars per month is reported in fraudulent cash advances at Las Vegas casino cages. It is estimated that losses are actually double that.

Scam: A con artist answers a classified ad for a car. He makes a lower offer, which is refused by the seller. The con artist calls every day and eventually offers a cashier's check for just under the asking price. The seller, like most people, assumes that a cashier's check is the same as cash. He sells the car for the cashier's check.

The con artist's cashier's check is forged. By the time the seller learns he took a bad check, the con artist has taken the car to a dealer and sold it for cash. The seller reports the car stolen. The car dealer, meanwhile, has resold the car, and the new owner has no idea he's driving a stolen car until he gets stopped or in a wreck.

A recent variation on this theme: the scammer answering the ad said he was calling from Africa. He said his cousin, in the United States, owed him eight thousand dollars. The cousin would send the sellers a cashier's check for eight thousand dollars. Sellers should deduct the price of the car (sixteen hundred dollars in one case), and wire the balance to buyer's bank in Africa. The sellers didn't find out until later that the eight thousand dollar cashier's check was a forgery. They lost the sixty-four hundred dollars they wired to Africa.

As an identifier, biometric technologies have the same challenges as tangible ID cards, and more. The first is ascertaining that the person initially enrolling is who he says he is. If he enrolls with a forged or stolen birth certificate, the entire system is compromised. It's not difficult to confirm (match) the identity of enrollees with an established database. That is, for the database to answer the question *is he who he says he is?* Much trickier is asking software to identify—that is, to answer the question *who is he?* With a gigantic database to sort through, the process might take more time than is possible in some applications.

Sad to say, bodies deteriorate. With age, with weight gain or loss, body metrics change. Also, biometrics can be evaded. False registration is one method; intentionally altering a body metric is another; hacking into a database is another. For facial recognition, wearing a brimmed hat or a false beard might be enough to throw the system. Fingerprints can be eroded with chemicals.

Like the metal detectors at airports, biometric matching can be tuned for sensitivity, producing either a high rate of false-acceptance or a high rate of false-rejection. It may become slow, and requires the brains of technicians.

Nevertheless, biometric systems are coming into use for purposes such as check cashing. One system takes a fingerprint and photo of each customer, and compares records with a huge national database.

Most privacy advocates oppose biometric solutions, concerned, among other things, that absolute identifiers have the potential for creating broad records of every aspect of our comings and goings and doings, and that this wealth of information has too great a potential for misuse. They also argue that biometrics would not solve the problem of identity theft, would be too costly to implement, and would fail to work for the elderly, a large at-risk subset.

In our huge world of electronic record keeping, our identities are faceless words and numbers that can be boiled down to ones and zeros. Those, it turns out, are easy to rip off. It seems that we cannot have anonymity, plus identity, without the threat of identity fraud. In other words, we need a body. If not face-to-face identification, we may very well have to rely on biometrics, somehow.

Help Yourself

Linda Foley, who speaks with a steady flow of identity theft victims, says they usually don't know how their data was obtained. Detective Raes believes the most common way thieves get personal information now is by database intrusion. Yet, four of the victims whose experiences I've described in this chapter could have played more of a role in preventing their own impersonations. Bronti and Nancy were pickpocketed, Michaela left a completed loan application in her hotel room, and Cheryl inadvertently let a classmate shoulder surf.

We all have sensitive documents to look after, but copies of those, in various forms, on paper and on computer media, are in others' charge, multiplied by a hundred, or a thousand, or more.

Even with the risk of identity theft so broadly out there and out of our hands, it's still worth taking every reasonable precaution to safeguard our good names. We cannot build walls around us, and most of us want to live in this world comfortably, taking advantage of its relatively new conveniences. If we live our lives holding onto the notion that our personal data is precious and valuable and highly desirable to a rotten subclass, we can lessen the risk of becoming a victim.

Guard Your Documents

Start with your purse or wallet. Slim it down. Under no circumstance should you carry around your Social Security number. Neither should you allow it to be part of your driver's license, school ID, or any other document you keep with you. If you're afraid you'll need to know the number and might forget it, see the Special Tips for Seniors at the end of this chapter.

Lieutenant Sebby recommends that you carry only one credit card. Bob and I carry two. When you use your credit card, check that you're given back your rightful card.

Consider where you leave your belongings. Obviously, after reading about the opportunists in chapter 5, you won't leave your things hanging on the back of your chair or under it. But how careful must we be in the course of an ordinary day? Think of the common risks to which a woman subjects herself: At work, where is her purse stored? At the supermarket, is it ever unattended in the shopping cart? Left momentarily in a shop's dressing room? What does a woman do with her purse at a friend's party? In each instance, assumptions are made: *the people around me are as trustworthy as I am.* How many ID theft victims were acquainted with their impostors? Cheryl's impostor was a classmate in a computer course. Linda Z.'s was her employer.

Fiercely protect your Social Security number. Don't use it, or any part of it, to log into bank or other Web sites. Do not have it printed on your checks.

Examine your bank and credit card statements promptly, to be certain there has been no unauthorized activity. Order copies of your credit report once a year from all three of the main credit reporting agencies. (Contact information is provided at the end of this chapter.)

Destroy Before Discarding

Shred. And shred crosswise.

Expired credit cards should be cut into pieces.

Dispense Information Stingily

Be aware of the tremendous data trail we leave as we go about our lives. *Data shadow* is the lovely term coined by Columbia University Professor

Alan Westin in his 1967 book, *Privacy and Freedom,* and refers to the records made by most of our daily activities. Much of these are a trade-off for convenience.

Choose what you want to reveal and ask yourself, what are the risks of sharing this piece of information? What are the benefits? Is it necessary? Is the trade-off worth it?

"Give the spurious to the curious," says privacy and identity expert Edward Wade. Who says you have to answer every nosy inquisitor with honest answers? Then again, it's a voluntary exchange . . . perhaps you'll choose to answer "required" questions only.

As proof of identity, your mother's maiden name is a weak key. What's so secret about it? In small towns everyone knows it, and it's easy to find on genealogy sites. The mother's maiden name question is not a portal to your history, it's meant to be a password. Therefore, make up a new one.

Don't give your PIN to anyone. A bank employee will never need it and never ask for it.

Opt Out

Banks, financial service companies, and insurers prefer that you don't. They have a financial interest in sharing your data. Their so-called privacy policies are buried in fine print and worded to baffle. Opting out of information sharing means the burden is on the individual, but these institutions and companies don't make it easy. While they could provide a postcard, a phone number, or a Web site, most require an old-fashioned letter sent with a stamp. Because they make money sharing our information, they don't want to make it convenient for us. On top of that, many institutions require an annual opt-out renewal. We'd need to keep a calendar just to track opt-out update times.

You can opt out of those maddening preapproved credit card offers as well. Not just annoying, the applications are downright dangerous. They're a favored booty of ID thieves who grab them out of mailboxes. Call 888-5-OPTOUT (888-567-8688) and be prepared to give your Social Security number. You will receive a confirmation form in the mail, which will alert all three of the main credit reporting agencies that you'd like to be excused from their offers.

It's possible to put a freeze or a fraud alert on your credit file, even if you haven't been a victim of identity theft. This action has advantages and drawbacks. On the plus side, no one will be able to change your address on your credit report, or open a credit account without your specific approval. A potential negative is that you, too, will be denied instant credit. And, although it shouldn't happen, you may also be denied credit by others. Credit issuers assessing you as a risk may read your entire credit history, or they may request only your credit rating. If they see that a fraud alert or credit freeze has been placed on your file, some may not want to bother with the double checks and verifications that should go with those. Neither do the alerts require mandatory action on the part of the credit issuer. Alerts are not guaranteed to prevent new fraudulent accounts, it is not certain that a credit issuer will see the alert, and the issuer may choose to ignore it.

While you're at it, why not get off junk mail and telemarketers' lists, too? Addresses for these are at the end of this chapter.

Internet Safety

If you don't go blabbing your secrets everywhere, the Internet is almost as safe a community as any other. Would you know a con artist if you met him face to face? Would you recognize an illicitly cloned Web page built to suck up information while pretending to be legitimate? Sure, there are tricks out there in cyberspace, just as there are in the tangible world. Shady dealers can appear respectable in the great equalizer of the World Wide Web, and anonymity is a con artist's best friend.

You don't have to shop on the Internet to be at risk. The databases of companies with whom you do business, online or offline, are hackable. Your information can be compromised whether *you* choose to access it or not. System penetration is a risk, by outsiders and by insiders, allowing proprietary information to be stolen or tampered with.

Regardless, no one should pass on the opportunity to use this incredible power and resource. Risks, warts, and all, we have phenomenal worldwide knowledge on the most esoteric combinations of subjects you can dream up, right at our fingertips, for pittance. You can use the Internet as a shopping research tool, then, if you're nervous about paying online, pick up the phone to make your purchase.

Or, you can simply take a few precautions. Remember that most credit cards advertise a $50 cap on your liability for fraudulent charges, and many waive that. Also, many card companies promise zero liability for Internet fraud. That doesn't mean we don't pay for it—we do, indirectly, in higher fees and higher merchandise prices.

When you shop on the Internet, consider the merchant. If you're not already familiar with the company, check to see that a physical address is revealed somewhere, or call to see that you can reach a person. If you choose to make a purchase on the site, check that the page is secure by looking for a closed lock icon at the bottom of your browser. You can click on the lock icon to read the site's security certificates. Also, the beginning of the URL (address of the page) will change from http to https.

Some credit card companies offer special-use numbers that take the place of your credit card number. You can get a single-use number that is good for one purchase only and will charge to your regular account.

Or you can get a limited value number, which will work until the dollar value is reached and will also charge to your account. This latter can also be assigned to another person, as a gift, for example, or for a student's shopping spree.

When you register or log into a Web site of interest to you, you can use an alternative e-mail address. Using one of the free e-mail services like Hotmail or Yahoo will protect your main e-mail address from being bombarded with junk. (Well, you can hardly protect yourself from junk e-mail; it will find you.) Watch for the tiny, pre-checked box that says something like *Yes, send me junkmail!* and uncheck it, or let the mail go to your alternative address.

Remember, too, that not every Internet questionnaire needs to be answered in full.

What about all those passwords that allow you entry to various sites? As you acquire ever more, you probably make note of them somewhere. Devise a code for yourself so they're recorded in a way only you can decipher. We're not trying to stop a world-class hacker, just to make it a little tricky for the guy who finds himself alone with your laptop for an hour. How do you code your passwords? Perhaps you never use the letter E, so if you write peOpLE, what you actually use is pOpL. Or perhaps you never use the first letter in the password you write, or any instance of it, so peOpLE would become eOLE. Or perhaps you never use vowels, but sprinkle your notes with plenty of them. And perhaps you throw in some numbers, but trick numbers: you add 3 to whatever number you write. Whatever you decide probably won't stop a pro, but it might be all you need.

Then there's computer security. If your computer is connected to the Internet via DSL, cable modem, or T-1, you should use firewall software to keep hackers and intruders from accessing your data. Keep your virus protection software up-to-date so your computer doesn't send out potentially damaging material on its own. Depending on where you leave your computer and who has access to it, you may wish to disable password saving, creating an extra step for yourself and an extra layer of protection, too.

When you sell, give away, or otherwise retire a computer, you need to delete your data from its hard drive. Simply deleting the files is not enough, however. They'd be easy to recover. The drive would need to be overwritten or wiped clean with special software in order to permanently erase your data files.

Credit Card Risk

As long as you don't mind leaving a trail of records, credit cards are an extremely safe form of payment. When used in person, additional information is usually not required, unless you're opening an account or unless you need to give your address for delivery. For a phone order, the merchant will need to verify your billing address, and obtain your shipping address if it's different from the billing address. He may also ask for the extra digits at the end of your account number. These digits wouldn't be visible to anyone without the actual card. They're a form of security.

Do you ever get those "convenience" checks from your credit card company? Thieves also love to snag these from mailboxes. Call your credit card company and have them quit sending them. And, when was the last time you got a cash advance (at exorbitant interest rates) on your credit card? "It's usually good for 75 percent of your available credit," Lieutenant Sebby said. Call your credit card company and disallow cash advances.

Check-Writing Risks

As I mentioned earlier, checks give far more information than you might like to give to a stranger. With a check (or money order), a dubious merchant can collect funds, shut down, and disappear before his customers even wonder where their merchandise is. For remote purchases, use your credit card. In person, if your debit card is accepted, it's a better option than a check, according to privacy experts. Banks suggest that you press "credit" instead of "debit" when paying with a check card. The benefits of this procedure are that you will not have to enter your PIN in public, and you will have dispute rights you would not have by pressing "debit". Debit cards usually carry a stricter responsibility for the account holder. Banks want to be notified promptly of the loss or theft of a debit card. If you don't notice or report its loss within a day or two, your liability could be greater than if it had been a credit card.

If You Become a Victim

If your wallet is lost or stolen, take immediate steps to prevent account takeover. Call your credit card companies and your bank if you carried an ATM or debit card or if you also lost your checkbook. Call all three of the main credit reporting agencies and put a fraud alert on your file. (As of May, 2003, one call to Equifax, Experian, or TransUnion is supposed to be enough. The credit bureaus say that they will notify one another.)

In its March, 2002, report called *Identity Theft: Prevalence and Cost Appear to Be Growing,* the United States General Accounting Office (GAO) stated that "a senior official" of one unnamed credit reporting agency claimed that "virtually all individuals whose wallet or purse is lost or stolen will call a credit reporting agency as a precautionary measure." Bob and I know that isn't true. We speak with a steady flow of people whose wallets have been stolen, and the majority of them do not know to call the three main credit reporting agencies.

If you're abroad, you'll need to contact the nearest American embassy or consulate in order to replace your passport. It's important to report a theft to the nearest police department and to the embassy or consulate if you're abroad. Victim reports enable agencies to tabulate incidents, which will help cities understand the extent of their street crime problems and allow the U.S. State Department to accurately warn U.S. citizens of risks. A police report is also required for any insurance claims you might make.

After reporting your loss and replacing your lost documents, watch your bank and credit card accounts for unauthorized activity. Order your credit report from each of the three main credit reporting agencies. It's commonly recommended that you examine your credit report once a year, regardless.

If you do find that your identity has been appropriated, call the fraud hotline at the Federal Trade Commission. Several other excellent organizations that will guide you and direct you to further resources are listed at the end of this chapter.

Theft Thwarters #8:
Identity Theft

- Ferociously guard your Social Security number.

- If your driver's license number, school ID, or other identification is your Social Security number, get it changed.

- If your Social Security number or driver's license number is printed on your checks, get new checks without those numbers.

- Remove unnecessary documents from your wallet, particularly your Social Security card.

- Don't give your ATM PIN to anyone. A bank employee will never need it and never ask for it. Shield the keypad as you enter your PIN at an ATM.

- Safeguard your documents. Don't leave your wallet (or purse) unsecured. Don't leave sensitive documents unsecured at home, at work, or in your car.

- Use a locking mailbox. Deposit outgoing mail in a U.S. Postal Service box.

- Investigate if your monthly statements fail to show up when you expect them.

- Scrutinize monthly statements promptly as they arrive to be certain no unauthorized activity has occurred.

- Be stingy with your personal information, especially on unsolicited forms or surveys.

- Never give personal information over the phone, unless you initiated the call and know exactly with whom you're speaking.

- Opt out of information sharing whenever possible. Read your banks', insurers' and others' privacy statements and follow their directions to limit information sharing.

- Opt out of preapproved credit solicitations by calling 888-5-OPTOUT (888-567-8688) and be prepared to give your Social Security number.

- Consider putting a freeze on your credit file.

- Treat any cashier's check you receive like a bank check, not like cash. Be certain it fully clears before assuming all is well.

- Shred sensitive documents before discarding them. Cut up expired credit cards.

- As proof of identity, make up a new "mother's maiden name" as a password.

Internet

- Don't use your Social Security number or any part of it to sign onto Web sites, including your bank access.

- Treat any e-mail offer of riches from a stranger as suspect. Never reply with any personal details. Better yet, never reply. Ignore e-mail from anyone you don't know.

- Be skittish about Web sites that want personal data. Be sketchy filling in electronic forms unless you know the company you're dealing with. Don't give your credit card number in order to enter the content area of adult sites.

- Look for an online merchant's physical address before doing business with the company.

- See that your financial transactions take place on secure pages. Look for a closed lock icon, and a URL that begins with the letters "https."

- Consider using a single transaction account number from your credit card company.

- Consider using an alternative e-mail address through one of the free and anonymous e-mail services like Yahoo or Hotmail.

- Consider unchecking the default request to be on mailing lists when signing onto Web sites.

- Store your list of passwords in some sort of code.

- Make sure your computer is secure with firewall and virus protection.

Credit Cards

- Carry the minimum number of credit cards, preferably only one or two.

- Although you may not want to go as far as following your credit card around (at a restaurant, for example), be aware that skimming does occur. At least check to see that you received your own credit card back after a charge, instead of someone else's by mistake.

- Have your credit card company quit sending "convenience" checks.

- Disallow cash advances on your credit card account.

- Thank store clerks who require identification and check signatures on credit card transactions.

Check Writing

- Try to reduce the number of checks you write. Instead use your credit or debit card when possible.
- Never put your Social Security number on your checks.
- To limit liability, be sure to report a lost or stolen debit card promptly.

If Your Wallet Is Lost or Stolen:

- Call your credit card companies and banks.
- Call the three main credit reporting agencies and put a fraud alert on your file.
- File a police report.
- If you're abroad, contact the U.S. embassy or consulate to replace a lost passport and to report the theft.
- Watch your bank and credit card statements for suspicious activity.
- Order your credit report from the three credit reporting agencies. Examine all three reports annually (recommended for everyone).
- If your identity is appropriated, call the FTC's Fraud Hotline.

Special Tips for Seniors

The Identity Theft Resource Center recommends the following safe-wallet practices:

- Do not carry your Social Security card.
- Carry only a photocopy of your health ID card, but *cut off* (do not just cross out) the last four numbers of your Social Security number from the photocopy.
- Give those last four numbers, your medical history, and a list of the prescription drugs you take to a trusted family member or friend.
- Carry a slip of paper in your wallet labeled "for emergency," which lists the phone numbers of that family member or friend.

Resources

The FTC ID Theft Clearinghouse Hotline

877-ID-THEFT (877-438-4338)

www.consumer.gov/idtheft

Ask for or download the FTC document:

Identity Theft: When Bad Things Happen to Your Good Name

Credit Bureaus

Equifax

www.equifax.com

To order a credit report, call: 800-685-1111

To report fraud, call: 800-525-6285

To opt out of information sharing, write to:

Equifax, Inc.

Options

PO Box 740123

Atlanta, GA 30374-0123

Experian

www.experian.com

To order a credit report or to report fraud call: 888-EXPERIAN (397-3742)

To opt out of information sharing, write to:

Experian

Consumer Opt-Out

701 Experian Parkway

Allen, TX 75013

TransUnion

www.transunion.com

To order your report, call: 800-916-8800

To report fraud, call: 800-680-7289

To opt out of information sharing, write to:

TransUnion

Marketing List Opt Out

PO Box 97328

Jackson, MS 39288-7328

More

To reduce the amount of junk mail you receive, request a form from:

>Direct Marketing Association
>
>Mail Preference Service
>
>PO Box 643
>
>Carmel, NY 10512
>
>Or go to *www.the-dma.org/consumers/offmailinglist.html*

To lessen the number of telephone solicitations you receive, request a form from:

>Direct Marketing Association
>
>Telephone Preference Service
>
>PO Box 1559
>
>Carmel, NY 10512
>
>Or go to *www.the-dma.org/consumers/offtelephonelist.html*

To lessen the number of junk emails you receive, go to:

>*www.dmaconsumers.org/offemaillist.html*

For information and victim assistance, contact:

>The Identity Theft Resource Center
>
>858-693-7935
>
>*www.idtheftcenter.org*

Privacy Rights Clearinghouse

>619-298-3396
>
>*www.privacyrights.org*

Afterword

Climb out of that cave! Get going, see the world.

Do we make it seem as if the world is populated by thieves and scoundrels who are out to get you and lurk around every corner? Of course it's not like that. But in a book of thieves, we speak of thieves. Pick up any other travel book for enthusiasm, exciting destinations, and descriptions of the pretty sights.

The thieves will continue to prowl. After all, they've been around since loincloths got pockets and sharks' teeth were wealth. And they'll prey, as they always have, on the easy marks. They'll have little interest in *you*, the savvy traveler. Opportunists will find no invitation. Strategists will fail to engage you in their plots and ploys. Con artists will not succeed in tempting you with their seductive promises of easy money, something for nothing.

This book is just one thrust of our campaign to put street thieves out of business. Our live presentations and television appearances are other "back-end" efforts that target the would-be victim. On the front lines, we work with law enforcement, sharing our knowledge base and video footage. In so many ways, though, the hands of police are tied. The cop on pickpocket detail works intense, focused shifts, fights boredom, and often has little to show at the end of the day. There's only so much he can do, only so many places he can be.

As the world becomes increasingly dangerous—and it is, sad to say—it's up to individuals to take responsibility for our own safety and security. Our hope is that travelers learn new habits. Acknowledge the threat, take appropriate precautions, then go about the business and pleasures of travel. We'd like to see smart stashing become as commonplace as safe sex and seat belts.

Theft prevention is a balancing act: trust and openness toward strangers versus doubt and caution; awareness versus relaxation; type of destination; value of what is carried; the traveler's image and the signals sent—how others perceive the traveler.

At the same time, it's important to realize when one *can* let one's guard down. In books, we can list rules and recommendations. In real life, the traveler must choose which fit his circumstance and style.

As we've tried to stress throughout this book, personal security is an art, not a science. Learn the risks peculiar to your destination, then adjust your awareness and the level of your security precautions. Thus prepared, you'll turn your travel concerns into travel confidence.

If you enjoy the study of human behavior, try a little sleuthing yourself. Next time you're on the beach in Honolulu, in the Paris Metro, or crushed in a crowd at Disneyland, tune in. Scan the group, analyze individuals, and look for inappropriate behavior. If you notice a suspicious pair, do a double take. It just might be us.

Bambi Vincent and Bob Arno's Theft First Aid

Keep the following information in your luggage or hotel room, or, better yet, keep it permanently in your e-mail inbox so you can access it from any Internet point anywhere.

If you lose your wallet:

1. Cancel your credit and debit cards ASAP. Your cards are:

Card company	Account number	Phone number from abroad
_____	_____	_____
_____	_____	_____
_____	_____	_____
_____	_____	_____
_____	_____	_____
_____	_____	_____

2. Call all three main credit-reporting agencies and report your loss.

Equifax	800-525-6285
Experian	888-397-3742
TransUnion	800-680-7289

3. If you are abroad and your passport has been lost, take the following items to your embassy or consulate:

a. Photocopy of the first pages of your passport, and

b. Your spare credit card, in order to pay for a new passport.

4. File a police report if you suffered a theft.

✂ *Cut and keep in a safe place while you are traveling, separate from your wallet, passport, and credit cards.*

Glossary

allora. "Then," in Italian. A multipurpose interjection used as "well," "so," and "you see" are used in English.

asleep. When a victim is unaware he is being, or has been, pickpocketed.

baksheesh. A tip, gratuity, donation, or bribe in India and the Middle East.

beat, beat a mark, beat a sting. To steal, steal from a victim, steal a wallet.

blocker. A pickpocket's accomplice whose function is to prevent passers-by from observing the theft. Also called "shade".

broad tosser. One who throws or manipulates the cards in a game of three-card monte.

cannon. A pickpocket.

carabinieri. Italian police officers.

catch a blow. Caught in the act of pickpocketing.

chop. Cut, or portion of proceeds.

ciao. Goodbye, in Italian.

con. From the word confidence; to trick, cheat, swindle, or defraud a victim out of money or property after first gaining his confidence.

con artist, con man, con. From the word confidence; a swindler who first gains the confidence of his or her victim.

crown. Former monetary unit of Denmark; in 2001, the monetary unit became the euro.

dead work. Illicitly obtained identity documents, including a drivers' license, Social Security card, and a credit card that has been canceled.

dip. A pickpocket, also called cannon, wire, pick, whiz player, shot player. To dip is to pick a pocket (or purse).

downstairs. Pants pockets.

drachma. Former monetary unit of Greece; in 2001, the monetary unit became the euro.

dreidel. A spinning top used in a game during Channukah.

duomo. Cathedral, in Italian.

euro. The new monetary unit of the European Union.

fan, fanning. To lightly and surreptitiously touch a person in order to determine the location of his or her valuables.

fence. One who deals in stolen goods.

fire the whiz. To pick a pocket (or purse).

front slide. Front pants pocket.

gig. A job for a performer.

grazie. Thank you, in Italian.

grift sense. The ability to recognize and/or pull off cons, swindles, and scams.

gull. A victim, a dupe.

heart. Nerve.

hide. Wallet.

kick the poke. To reposition a wallet for easier extraction.

klepsimo. Pickpocket, in Greek.

koruna. Monetary unit of the Czech Republic.

laying in the bed. Wallet that is sideways in a pocket.

leather. Wallet.

lira. Former monetary unit of Italy; in 2001, the monetary unit became the euro.

lone wolf. One who works alone, without partner or accomplice.

look-alike. Imposter who will stand in for the person whose identity cards have been stolen for the purpose of withdrawing cash from the victim's credit card or bank account. Also called "stepper" and "writer".

lush worker. One who robs sleeping drunks in public.

mark. Target; intended victim of a thief.

masala chai. Indian spiced milky tea.

mechanic. Cheater.

medina. Outdoor marketplace in North Africa and the Middle East.

M.O. Method of operation.

modus operandi. Method of operation.

mug. A victim, a dupe.

naira. Monetary unit of Nigeria.

nanny. Female target.

on fire. Awareness by law enforcement of recent pickpocket activity in a specific area.

pappy. Male target.

pastisseria. Pastry shop, in Catalan (the language of Barcelona).

peseta. Former monetary unit of Spain; in 2001, the monetary unit became the euro.

pick. A pickpocket.

pickpocket. Specifically, a *local* pickpocket; an insult within the trade.

play it, play him. To steal it, to steal from him.

poke. Wallet.

policia. Police, in Spanish.

polizia. Police, in Italian.

por favor. please, in Spanish.

portofoli. Wallet, in Greek.

punter. Gambler.

R&R. Rest and relaxation.

rand. Monetary unit of South Africa.

raw scratch. Cash.

retsina. A unique Greek wine.

rupee. Monetary unit of India.

sangria. A potent and delicious drink of fortified wine and fruit.

scippatori. Thieves on scooters, in Italian.

scusa. Excuse me, in Italian.

set of works. Illicitly obtained identity documents, including a driver's license, Social Security card, and a credit card. Also called "spread". *See* **dead work.**

shade. *See* **blocker.**

shill. A con artist's teammate whose function is to pose as a satisfied customer or an enthusiastic gambler to induce bystanders into participating.

shot player. A pickpocket.

sì. Yes, in Italian and Spanish.

SIM card. Electronic chip which gives some cell phones their identity, including their phone numbers and, in some, prepaid cash value.

spread. *See* **set of works.**

stall. A pickpocket's accomplice whose function is to prevent the mark from moving away before and during the theft. Also called "stick".

stepper. *See* **look-alike.**

stick. *See* **stall.**

sting. Wallet.

suri. Pickpocket, in Japanese.

tip. A crowd.

torte. Cake, in Italian, usually made in layers.

tosser. One who throws or manipulates the cards in a game of three-card monte.

tube. The London underground mass transit system.

tzadziki. A Greek dish of yogurt, garlic, and cucumber.

upstairs. Shirt or breast pocket.

vespa. Wasp, in Italian. Also the name of a popular Italian motor scooter.

vic. Victim.

wake up. To become aware of being, or having been, pickpocketed.

whiz, whiz player. A pickpocket; in some circles, specifically a professional pickpocket who crosses state borders to practice his trade. Also called "wire".

wire. *See* **whiz.**

writer. *See* **look-alike.**

Index

About the Authors

Bambi Vincent was born in 1955 and raised in California. She has lived in the Bahamas, South Africa, Holland, Sweden, Singapore, and Elsewhere, and spends several months each year roaming the Mediterranean countries. She writes travel documentaries and advertising campaigns during and between her sojourns.

Since marrying Bob Arno in 1985, she has spent most of her time on the road, hauling her laptop computer through 85 countries. An enthusiastic traveler, she explores the cities and towns of Elsewhere with a writer's eye for ambiance. From Antarctica to Zambia, Stockholm to Sydney, and Sitka to Santiago, Bambi and Bob savor the natural and cultural differences that make each place unique. When not scouring their surroundings for scams and cons, Bambi focuses on the traditions of street food and outdoor markets.

Bambi studied art at San Jose State University, law at Santa Clara University, and crime on the streets of the world's favorite cities. She has interviewed hundreds of practicing criminals, their victims, and their pursuers. She has received and given assistance to police forces and security agencies in America and abroad.

While Bambi treks the planet with Bob Arno, their furniture lives in Las Vegas.

Time magazine called **Bob Arno** "the world's foremost expert on the techniques of first-rank 'wires,'" the slang term for pickpockets. Years of research and Bob's fascination with real street crime have made him an authority frequently consulted by police, security experts, and television producers.

Born and raised in Stockholm, Sweden, Bob began entertaining at the age of 16 and traveling the world at age 18. As his performances took him to ever more exotic locations, he combined entertaining with freelance photography. For a series on swindles in the Southeast Asian marketplace, he observed short-change artists, pickpockets, and counterfeit gem hustlers, whose main targets were GIs on R&R leave. After adapting the street scams for his stage show in the form of exposés, he was asked to give lectures for the U.S. military.

Bob Arno, professor of pickpocketry, frequently appears on television news and magazine shows to share his expertise. As a speaker, Bob gives presentations and lectures to security and law enforcement professionals, as well as to the public, in America and abroad.